REASSESSING
PSYCHOTHERAPY RESEARCH

Reassessing Psychotherapy Research

Edited by
ROBERT L. RUSSELL

THE GUILFORD PRESS
New York London

© 1994 The Guilford Press
A Division of Guilford Publications, Inc.
72 Spring Street, New York, NY 10012

Printed in the United States of America

This book is printed on acid-free paper.

Last digit is print number: 9 8 7 6 5 4 3 2 1

Library of Congress Cataloging-in-Publication Data

Reassessing psychotherapy research / edited by Robert L. Russell.
    p. cm.
   Includes bibliographical references and index.
   ISBN 0-89862-755-9
   1. Psychotherapy—Research.   I. Russell, Robert L.
   [DNLM: 1. Psychotherapy—methods. 2. Research—methods.
   WM 420
   R2885   1994]
   RC337.R43   1994
   616.89′14′072—dc20
   DNLM/DLC
   for Library of Congress   94-8548
                                          CIP

Contributors

Cheryl Anderson, PhD, Department of Psychology, University of Toledo, Toledo, Ohio.

David Bird, MSc, The Health Unit, Wakefield and Pontefract Community Health Trust, Wakefield, England, United Kingdom

Robert Elliott, PhD, Department of Psychology, University of Toledo, Toledo, Ohio.

Leslie S. Greenberg, PhD, Department of Psychology, York University, Downsview, Ontario, Canada

Heather Harper, BA, MRC/ESRC Social and Applied Psychology Unit, Department of Psychology, University of Sheffield, Sheffield, England, United Kingdom

Clara E. Hill, PhD, Department of Psychology, University of Maryland, College Park, Maryland

David E. Orlinsky, PhD, Committee on Human Development, University of Chicago, Chicago, Illinois

Shirley Reynolds, MSc, MRC/ESRC Social and Applied Psychology Unit, Department of Psychology, University of Sheffield, Sheffield, England, United Kingdom

Robert L. Russell, PhD, Department of Psychology, Loyola University, Chicago, Illinois

David A. Shapiro, PhD, MRC/ESRC Social and Applied Psychology Unit, Department of Psychology, University of Sheffield, Sheffield, England, United Kingdom

Mike Startup, PhD, MRC/ESRC Social and Applied Psychology Unit, Department of Psychology, University of Sheffield, Sheffield, England, United Kingdom

William B. Stiles, PhD, Department of Psychology, Miami University, Oxford, Ohio

Anne Suokas, MA, Department of Clinical Psychology, Muurola Hospital, Rovaniemi, Finland

Preface

This book contains chapters that in part or in whole offer critical assessments of aspects of the psychotherapy research tradition—substantive results, research methods, theoretical and metatheoretical models, or general aspects of the conduct of inquiry. In addition, each chapter contains suggestions and/or examples of alternative investigative strategies that can augment traditional psychotherapy research at all levels of research, from choice of constructs and design to ways of analyzing and interpreting data or implicit theoretical assumptions.

Importantly, the authors of the individual chapters have often been proponents and practitioners of the research practices that are critically assessed, at least in their "early" research years; they are thus critically examining, not simply other theories and methods viewed from afar, but work and attitudes that were once their own. Moreover, the authors have provided their chapters knowing in advance that they would be situated in the wider historical context of psychotherapy research in the last chapter of the book, which is written by an experienced psychotherapy researcher and scholar in collaboration with myself. This cycle of collaborative criticism is thought to be in itself a demonstration of one of the methods of discourse that might be more widely practiced in the future of our discipline.

The organization of the chapters into an uncomplicated storyline has not been a primary goal. One should think in reading them, not of the linear categories under which we have learned to organize the subsections of our journal manuscripts (e.g., theory/rationale, methods, conclusions), but of the thematic layering and the use of counterpoint and leitmotifs that characterize "postmodernist" writing. The impact of the whole is expected to far exceed the sum of its parts.

Briefly, however, I might simply point out that Chapter 1 raises serious questions about what we can count as known about psychotherapy; it contrasts the results of a meta-analysis of the impact of techniques with a widely cited narrative review of this area. In the second chapter, questions are raised about what we take as sound models of how to discover knowledge concerning psychotherapeutic processes and outcomes and their interrelationships. Specifically, problems with correlational methodology for assessing process–outcome relationships are delineated, and a method is proposed that offers an alternative for researchers not entirely satisfied with aspects of the medical model and its recommended research strategies.

Chapter 3 picks up these critical threads from a different perspective, and confronts the phenomena of psychotherapy from the perspective of the ways in which it can, is, and ought to be methodically "simplified" or "complexified" for the purposes of research. Such simplifying and complexifying options are explicated in relation to most of the key methodological tasks involved in doing psychotherapy research. Chapters 4 and 5 take up the issue of method or orientation from slightly differing perspectives. Chapter 4 pushes the methodology of discovery as the appropriate orienting perspective for our descriptive and explanatory investigations. The author suggests what I might call "episodic contextualism" as at least a preliminary method of study to identify probable causal relationships between processes and outcomes that can later be put to more critical empirical tests. Chapter 5 also recommends exploratory methods of study as a way to begin to redress the failures of experimentalism in the study of psychotherapy research. Here the call for naturalistic but systematic research is shown to result from the need to augment the tradition of experimental analogue research.

Chapter 6 takes issue with the terminological frameworks used to "denominate" therapeutic techniques, and with taking these techniques as analogues of doses of pharmacological medications. It attempts, through an analysis of such terminological frameworks and their embodiment in current research, to model a type of critical reading that can expose conceptual weaknesses in our theories and methods. Its emphasis is on the need for meticulous analysis of constructs and the way they are (mis)used in conceptualizing techniques, as a productive way to lead to scientific progress.

Together, the chapters present some of the most central issues confronting psychotherapy researchers as conceived by a handful of its 4th generation of practicing scholars. As noted above, the seventh chapter assays the six chapters that have come before, providing a critical/historical framework for the work presented. In other words, it attempts to situate the work of previous authors within a historical understanding of the development of psychotherapy research, and to characterize the likely substantive and methodological influence of the contributing authors' perspective. This final chapter also serves as a kind of in-house invitation to readers to join in the critical dialogue—one that is intended to span generations, as well as theoretical and methodological orientations.

ROBERT L. RUSSELL

Contents

The High-Water Mark of the Drug Metaphor
A Meta-Analytic Critique of Process–Outcome Research

DAVID A. SHAPIRO   HEATHER HARPER

MIKE STARTUP   SHIRLEY REYNOLDS

DAVID BIRD   ANNE SUOKAS

After four decades of psychotherapy research, how strongly can we claim to know that psychotherapy is effective, or point to what it is that makes psychotherapy effective? Is there an established body of knowledge that informs practice? Have the mechanisms of change been revealed by researchers? Questions like these are central to a broad assessment of the achievements and directions of the field. Such questions demand an appraisal of what we claim to know, how we claim to have obtained this knowledge, and how useful this knowledge is. The wide range of answers supplied by different reviewers suggests a need for keener appreciation of the relationships between the methods used by researchers and reviewers, and the findings they obtain.

In relation to outcome research, a minority of reviewers (e.g., Prioleau, Murdock, & Brody, 1983; Rachman & Wilson, 1980) have been very pessimistic about the demonstrated effectiveness of psychotherapy. For example, Rachman and Wilson (1980) criticize current methodology as lacking requisite precision, specificity, and differentiation. The majority, however, have lent at least qualified support to the conclusion that psychotherapy has been shown to be in general effective (e.g., Lambert, Shapiro, & Bergin, 1986; Smith, Glass, & Miller, 1980; Stiles, Shapiro, & Elliott, 1986). However, even these more optimistic reviewers have noted the failure of this research to demonstrate the superior efficacy of any particular treatment method (Stiles et al., 1986).

Meanwhile, a separate but conceptually linked domain of research has been concerned with the relationships between psychotherapy process—usually defined as client and therapist activities and experiences during the course of therapy—and the outcome of treatment. This research is often conceptualized as a search for "active ingredients" of psychotherapy. It has been criticized for its reliance upon oversimplification and overextension of a drug metaphor as its conceptual and methodological basis (Stiles & Shapiro, 1989; see also Stiles, Shapiro, & Harper, Chapter 2, this volume). Similarly, Elliott and Anderson (this volume) review the perilous consequences of simplification in psychotherapy research.

Perhaps the most optimistic statement concerning this process–outcome research was made in Orlinsky and Howard's (1986) review in the third edition of the *Handbook of Psychotherapy and Behavior Change*. The title of the present chapter identifies this review as the most positive statement (or "high-water mark") of the conventional process–outcome research paradigm (the "drug metaphor"). The work to be presented here sprang from the suspicion that the conclusions reached by Orlinsky and Howard were dependent upon conceptual and methodological limitations both of the research they reviewed and the relatively uncritical approach they took to reviewing it.

We will describe a meta-analysis of 33 published studies reviewed by these authors that related therapist interventions to the outcome of treatment. To summarize the findings to be presented, the overall effect size was small at 0.26. Although some interventions appeared more effective than others, these differences were virtually abolished by statistical control for methodological features of studies, several of which were significantly related to the effect size obtained. These findings suggest that traditional methods of conducting and aggregating process–outcome studies have not yielded strong evidence for the efficacy of therapist interventions. They lead us to conclude by supporting appeals made by others (including Orlinsky and Howard) for more complex models of psychotherapy process, and by emphasizing the need for methodological diversity and pluralism in this field.

THE DRUG METAPHOR

Stiles and Shapiro (1989) describe the drug metaphor as

an investigative paradigm . . . [which] views psychotherapy as comprising active ingredients, supplied by the therapist to the client, along with a variety of fillers and scene-setting features. The supposed "active ingredients" are process components—therapeutic techniques such as interpretation, confrontation, reflection, self-disclosure, challenging assumptions, focussing on affect, efforts to give support, or (more abstractly) empathy, warmth, or genuineness. If a component is an active ingredient, then a high level of it is supposed to yield a positive outcome. If it does not, the ingredient is presumed to be inert. (p. 522)

These authors' critique of process–outcome research suggests that studies in this field typically make at least one of the following key assumptions of the drug metaphor:

(a) that process and outcome are readily distinguishable from, and bear a simple cause–effect relationship to, one another; (b) that component names refer to ingredients of consistent content and scope; (c) that the potentially active ingredients are known and measured or manipulated; (d) that the active ingredients are contained in the therapist's behavior, with the patient in a correspondingly passive role; (e) that the dose–response curve is ascending and linear in the range being examined; and (f) that the best way to demonstrate a psychotherapeutic procedure's efficacy is by controlled clinical trial. Finally . . . the common methodological assumption that a process component's efficacy is shown by its correlation with outcome. (p. 525)

THE REVIEW BY ORLINSKY AND HOWARD

As noted above, a major review of research linking psychotherapeutic process to outcome was undertaken by Orlinsky and Howard (1986). This review addressed the question "What is effective about psychotherapy?" The attempt was to go beyond the general statement, from quantitative reviews such as those of Smith et al. (1980) and Shapiro and Shapiro (1982), that psychotherapies are typically effective, to specify occurrences between and within the client and therapist during their work together that are associated with positively valued changes in the client's life and personality.

The scope of the review was broad, but limited to studies of "real" patients and therapists in "real" treatment situations. To be included, a study had to analyze process variables (i.e., everything that could be observed to occur between, and within, the patient and the therapist during their work together) in relation to outcome. Orlinsky and Howard (1986, p. 312) defined outcome as "output with respect to the life and person of the patient . . . judged in terms of some particular value standard . . . the patient's life should be demonstrably better in some way, or the patient's personality improved—from somebody's point of view." The authors attempted to search all published and accessible books, monographs, articles, and dissertations on the subject in the English language up to December 1984.

The review was organized in terms of the authors' 'generic model' (Orlinsky & Howard, 1987), and yielded the following list of treatment processes linked with favorable outcomes:

> (1) The patient's and therapist's therapeutic bond—that is, their reciprocal role-investment, empathic resonance, and mutual affirmation . . .
> (2) Certain therapeutic interventions, when done skilfully with suitable patients . . . (3) Patient's and therapist's focusing their interventions on the patient's feelings . . . (4) Preparing the patient adequately for participation in therapy and collaborative sharing of responsibility for problem solving . . . (5) Within certain limits, having more rather than less therapy. (p. 371)

Orlinsky and Howard's (1986) conclusions are significant, because they appear to vindicate the claim that empirical research following the methodological conventions of the drug metaphor can both inform practice and identify change mechanisms. Particularly important are their positive conclusions (2 and 3) concerning therapeutic interventions. These conclusions are the literature's strongest empirically based claims that treatment techniques affect outcome. They contradict the conclusions of most reviews of outcome research, which find that treatment methods, despite their diversity of technical content, yield broadly similar outcomes (Stiles et al., 1986); they also contrast markedly with reanalyses showing technique variables to account for less outcome variance than who (i.e., which therapist) is administering the treatment (Lambert, 1989).

It should be noted that the Orlinsky and Howard (1987) generic model of psychotherapeutic change does not itself adhere to the oversimplification and overextension of the drug metaphor as applied to process–outcome research. The generic model emphasizes nontechnique factors, and postulates complex interrelationships among these in their impact upon client change, that find no place in the drug metaphor. However, the studies of therapist interventions reviewed by Orlinsky and Howard (1986), and these authors' aggregation of findings across these studies, do exemplify the methodological tradition criticized by Stiles and Shapiro (1989). To the extent that Orlinsky and Howard (1986) have presented an unusually positive review of the effects of therapist interventions upon outcome, their contribution may be seen as the high-water mark of the drug metaphor.

However, Orlinsky and Howard acknowledged that the breadth of their review limited them to "a rather coarse-grained sorting of empirical findings" (p. 315), which did not amount to a detailed, critical examination of the evidence. Therefore, we felt it important to establish whether their conclusions concerning treatment interventions would stand up in the face of a more detailed, systematic, and focused examination. Simply put, it may be that their unusually positive conclusions concerning therapist interventions may have reflected this relatively uncritical approach. In addition, we felt it worthwhile to ask to what extent the studies reviewed did indeed exhibit the limitations of drug metaphor research criticized by Stiles and Shapiro (1989).

Throughout their review, Orlinsky and Howard (1986) categorized findings by conceptual distinctions among three observational perspectives on therapeutic process and among four perspectives on outcome. They produced tabulations for each process parameter, in which findings from each combination of process and outcome perspectives obtained from each study were listed as positive, null, or negative. Each table was summarized in "box scores" for each process perspective by outcome perspective cell and for row, column, and overall totals. No account was offered of the magnitude of effects obtained in any given study, and there was no methodological critique of each piece of evidence.

METHOD AND SUBSTANCE IN
PSYCHOTHERAPY RESEARCH

Traditionally, critical research reviews tended to operate on a principle of selectivity: the reviewer sought to decide whether or not a given study warranted consideration as evidence concerning the substantive issue at hand, such as the effectiveness of a given treatment (e.g., Rachman & Wilson, 1980). However, in an imperfect world, scientific knowledge of such complex, "real-life" undertakings as psychotherapy is seldom clear-cut. A rigorous classification of studies as methodologically "acceptable" and "unacceptable" is bound to lose us interpretable, albeit imperfect, evidence.

A seminal formulation of methodological weaknesses in quasi-experimental research was provided by Cook and Campbell's (1979) account of threats to validity. These authors discussed four types of validity. "Statistical conclusion validity" refers to the validity with which a study permits conclusions about covariation between the assumed independent and dependent variables. Threats to statistical conclusion validity typically arise from unsystematic error rather than systematic bias. "Internal validity" refers to the validity with which statements can be made about whether there is a causal relationship from independent to dependent variables, in the form in which they were manipulated or measured. Threats to internal validity typically involve systematic bias. "Construct validity" of putative causes and effects refers to the validity with which we can make generalizations about higher-order constructs from research operations. Finally, "external validity" refers to the validity with which conclusions can be drawn about the generalizability of a causal relationship to and across populations of persons, settings, and times.

The undoubted relevance of threats to these four types of validity to psychotherapy process–outcome research may not be immediately apparent. However, every step in the procedures undertaken to study the relations between process and outcome is liable to carry implications for the validity of the endeavor. As an example, consider the case of construct validity. A meaningful process–outcome study must permit generalizations concerning such higher-order constructs as clinical improvement, the process element or elements under study, and the method of treatment in question. The research operations undertaken must represent these constructs appropriately (e.g., outcome measures must be known to tap the psychological functions that the treatment is designed to change, the therapists must be adequately trained to deliver the treatment method competently and as specified by theory, etc.).

Armed with the Cook and Campbell (1979) formulation, we can go beyond simple acceptance or rejection of a given piece of evidence to a more differentiated view of its value in answering a specific question. For example, a study that is relatively free of threats to statistical conclusion or internal validity but weak in terms of construct and external validity, (such as a well-controlled laboratory analogue), is more helpful in identifying the causal role of an independent variable than it is in establishing the importance of that variable in treatment as practiced.

The advent of meta-analysis (Glass, McGaw, & Smith, 1981; Hedges & Olkin, 1985; Robinson, Berman, & Neimeyer, 1990; Shapiro & Shapiro, 1982, 1983; Smith et al., 1980) has permitted a further step in this more sophisticated approach to method and substance in psychotherapy research. A meta-analysis can "profile" a given literature in terms of the extent to which the four validity types are threatened (Shapiro & Shapiro, 1983). In addition, it can address empirically the impact of these validity threats upon the substantive findings obtained in research.

Meta-analysis enables us to approach the question of the relationship between methodological and substantive determinants of research results in a systematic and quantitative way. The findings of a series of studies may be considered as individual observations obtained under conditions that vary in terms of both methodological (e.g., sample size, type of outcome measure used, study design) and substantive (e.g., type of intervention investigated) factors. Methodological factors can be grouped according to the type of validity they threaten (and, hence, the type of question with respect to which they weaken the evidence of the study concerned). Quantitative methods, such as multiple regression, can be used to identify both methodological and substantive sources of variation in the effects obtained, taking account of the patterns of association among these sources of variation themselves.

This use of meta-analysis allows us to address the question of whether research findings may be a function of methodological strengths and limitations of individual studies. To the extent that variance in outcomes among studies is predictable from variations in their methodological features, then it is plausible to argue that the outcomes can be attributed to these methodological features. Multiple regression allows us to control for the effects of methodological factors in examining the effects of substantive variables, such as the treatment method or process variable that is the focus of a group of studies.

LIMITATIONS OF THE DRUG METAPHOR

In addition to evaluating the studies reviewed by Orlinsky and Howard (1986) in terms of the conventional methodological concerns identified by Cook and Campbell (1979), we were concerned in the present study with identifying limitations of the source studies attributable to their adherence to the assumptions of the drug metaphor. To put the matter more positively, we were interested in the extent to which studies addressed specific issues that Stiles and Shapiro (1989) saw as crucially neglected by process–outcome research grounded in the oversimplified and overextended drug metaphor.

We sought to determine whether studies considered (1) interactions between client variables and treatment technique in determining outcome; (2) more than just two levels of a process variable; (3) the possibility of nonlinear relationships between process and outcome; (4) the influence of variables other than therapist technique and client variables upon the process–outcome relationship; (5) the possibility that the therapist's in-session behavior is influenced by client requirements; and (6) the possibility of outcome–process effects. As with the validity criteria, we were interested both in describing the studies in these terms and in assessing the impact of these variables upon the findings obtained.

SUMMARY OF STUDY OBJECTIVES

Orlinsky and Howard (1986) reviewed findings relating seven therapist interventions (interpretation, confrontation/feedback, exploration and questioning, support and encouragement, advice, reflection, and self-disclosure) to outcome. They also reviewed studies of the content focus of interpretations and confrontations, including focus on affect, on the "here and now," and on the transference. We re-evaluated all available published studies included in these sections of the Orlinsky and Howard (1986) review. In the interests of a clear focus and a manageable task, we did not consider evidence on therapist skillfulness or on patient contributions to process. Our first concern was to evaluate, according to orthodox methodological standards, the evidence that the type of treatment intervention delivered by the therapist has a direct effect upon outcome; our second interest was in the extent to which source studies exemplified key limitations of the drug metaphor.

First, we wanted to know how substantial were the effects recorded in the Orlinsky and Howard box score tables, so we obtained quantitative indices for all these findings, expressed as Cohen's d (a difference between means divided by the within-group standard deviation). In a related question, we were concerned with how much these effects varied with the particular intervention examined in a given study.

Our second concern was with the quality of the evidence provided by these studies, according to the usual scientific conventions. Our assessment was guided by the account of the threats to validity offered by Cook and Campbell (1979; see also Shapiro & Shapiro, 1983). We were interested in the overall quality of the evidence, as revealed by this analysis, together with the impact of variations in that quality upon the findings obtained (e.g., did the more dependable evidence yield more positive findings?). This portion of our review did not question conventional process–outcome research methodology; rather, it applied traditional evaluative criteria to the data at hand.

Our third focus was upon considerations that Stiles and Shapiro (1989) have alleged to be neglected by traditional psychotherapy process–outcome research conducted within the constraints of an oversimplified and overextended drug metaphor. Again, our interest was in both the extent to which the studies addressed these concerns, and the effects of this upon the findings obtained.

METHOD

Studies Included

We included all the studies published in journals or as chapters in books that were included in the following subsections of the Orlinsky and Howard (1986) review: "Interpretation," "Confrontation,"

"Content Focus" (focus on affect, focus on here and now, focus on transference), "Exploration," "Support," "Advice," "Reflection," and "Self-Disclosure." The 33 included studies are listed in a separate bibliography. This includes 32 publications. Two of these (O'Malley, Suh, & Strupp, 1983; Suh, Strupp, & O'Malley, 1986) were reports of the same study, where two (Jacobs & Warner, 1981; Staples, Sloane, Whipple, Cristol, & Yorkston, 1976) were considered each to report two studies.

Development of Coding System

Extensive pilot and development work was undertaken for this analysis over a 2-year period. The first stage involved three of us (D. A. S., H. H., and A. S.) discussing project aims and requirements of the coding system. Some of our coding categories and criteria were familiar from previous efforts—in particular, the review of comparative outcome studies by Shapiro and Shapiro (1982), and the Orlinsky and Howard (1986) review. However, new categories were required to capture the varied designs used, the process instruments and their implementation, and the conceptual and data-analytic limitations of the drug metaphor.

In the second stage, an initial version of the coding system was constructed. At weekly meetings, the three authors mentioned above discussed their independent codings of three randomly selected studies. The third stage involved coding all studies relating confrontation and interpretation to outcome. This yielded conference presentations of narrative reviews of these studies, together with a revised version of the coding system. The fourth stage involved an effort to increase reliability via refinement of the coding system by D. B. and D. A. S. and independent coding of all studies by D. B. The fifth stage involved further, iterative refinement of the system in weekly meetings among three coders (D. A. S., H. H., and S. R.), who independently coded four studies prior to each meeting. This yielded a 20-page coding manual, including criteria and examples drawn from consensus achieved in coding and discussion.

The data analyzed in this chapter were generated in a final round of coding by H. H. and S. R., which included confidence ratings for each item. Because of the long time elapsing between successive coding efforts, we assumed the effects of memory of prior codings or of discussions concerning particular studies to be minimal.

The coding scheme fell into seven sections, concerning (1) therapists, (2) patients, (3) treatment and setting, (4) design, (5) outcome measurement, (6) process measurement, and (7) conceptual issues. The variables that yielded reliable codings are described in the "Results" section, which is organized in terms of Cook and Campbell's (1979) conceptualization of threats to validity.

Aside from the usual and expected coding errors, we found insufficient information in many studies to permit us to code on several of the criteria, especially the section on conceptual issues. The uneven reporting quality of the studies appeared inferior to that of comparative outcome research (Shapiro & Shapiro, 1983). In addition, however, discussions among coders revealed that some of the constructs we were attempting to code were problematic—a not uncommon finding (Orwin & Cordray, 1985). Several indices were eventually discarded on account of unacceptable reliability (see below).

Coding

The data presented here were supplied by two coders (H. H. and S. R.), who had taken part in development work on the coding scheme. They each coded every study, without discussion during the coding process. The coders were a graduate research student studying psychotherapy process (H. H.), and a recently qualified clinical psychologist engaged in psychotherapy research (S. R.). Where possible, interrater agreement or reliability was calculated by product–moment correlation (Pearson's r for continuous variables, phi coefficient for dichotomous nominal variables). Otherwise, weighted kappa (Cohen, 1968) was used for ordinal categorical variables, and unweighted kappa (Cohen, 1960) for nominal categorical variables.

Confidence Ratings

Orwin and Cordray (1985) have advocated the use of confidence judgments as a way of identifying well-reported information. They argue that such judgments are better indicators of deficient reporting in the literature than are measures of interrater reliability, since coding errors and idiosyncratic interpretations of the literature will lower indices of reliability even when reporting quality is high. When they calculated the mean interrater reliability across 12 variables used to code studies of psychotherapy outcome, they found that the mean reliability for cases judged with high confidence was more than double that for cases judged with low confidence.

In the present study the confidence with which each variable was coded was judged on a 3-point scale with labels as follows: 0 = "completely uncertain, a guess"; 1 = "more likely than not"; 2 = "certain or almost certain." Interrater agreement on confidence judgments was calculated as weighted kappa for all variables.

Effect Size Calculation

One author (M. S.) calculated and checked all effect sizes. In theory, effect size estimates might have been available for the pairing of every process measure with every outcome variable in each study. The majority of studies included only 1 measure of process, but some included as many as 18. Similarly, many studies employed only 1 measure of outcome, but as many as 11 were employed by some researchers. If an effect size had been available for every pairing of the these dependent and independent variables, there would have been 165; however, in 44 cases it was not possible to calculate an effect size, either because no data were reported or because the data that were reported came from a study whose design was unsuitable.

The remaining 121 effect sizes were expressed as d, which was given a positive sign when the outcome for patients receiving the given intervention was more favorable than the outcome for patients receiving a control treatment or some other intervention. It was given a negative sign when the reverse obtained. In theory, d is the difference between the group means divided by the within-group standard deviation. In fact, only 4 effect sizes could be calculated directly from published means and standard deviations. Another 21 effect sizes were calculated from an exact F or t; 3 were estimated from the sample sizes and exact probability levels associated with F or t tests; 77 were calculated from a correlation coefficient; 4 were retrieved from factorial designs; and 4 were calculated via probit transformations of proportions (Glass, et al., 1981). In the remaining 8 cases, there was no alternative to estimating effect sizes from the means and standard deviations portrayed in graphic presentations.

Agreement on Codings

Orwin and Cordray (1985) have argued persuasively against the practice of quoting overall agreement rates across variables. They observe that the variables coded for meta-analysis are not like a multi-item measure of a trait, for which a total-scale reliability would be meaningful; but rather, they constitute a list of disparate items. Some variables may have very high agreement rates while others do not. In the present study, the average agreement between the coders for the 37 variables for which agreement was calculated by kappa or weighted kappa was .54, but the range was from .05 to 1.00. The average interrater correlation coefficient (r or phi) for the remaining 16 variables was .59 but again the range, from −.03 to 1.00, was large. Orwin and Cordray (1985) obtained similar levels and ranges of reliability, with median kappas of .62 and .66 in two data sets, and kappas for individual variables ranging from −.05 to 1.00.

In general, only those variables coded with adequate interrater agreement should be retained for subsequent analyses. Where agreement was measured by a correlation coefficient, the conventional .70 level was chosen as a cutoff. Seven of the 16 variables satisfied this requirement. Choosing a cutoff for kappa is more problematic, however, since kappa is a proportionate measure whose value depends on the numbers recorded. We decided, therefore, to follow Landis and Koch (1977), who regard values between .40 and .75 as represent fair to good agreement beyond chance, and values above .75 as representing excellent agreement beyond chance. We thus adopted a criterion of .40. Twenty-six of the 37 variables satisfied this criterion. In sum, therefore, data were obtained on 53 variables, but only 33 of these were sufficiently reliable for analysis.

Agreement among Confidence Ratings

Orwin and Cordray (1985) found in their meta-analysis that confidence and interrater agreement were associated, and that agreement tended to be appreciably higher when confidence judgments were high rather than low. However, in the present study, although the mean confidence judgment across variables was high (mean = 1.49 out of a maximum of 2.00), agreement between coders on confidence ratings was low (weighted kappa = .20), and the correlations across variables between mean confidence judgments and indices of agreement were low and nonsignificant.

Following Orwin and Cordray, we hoped that some variables that had been discarded because coding agreement was inadequate might be rescued by considering confidence judgments. Taking all those variables for which the agreement was initially inadequate, we recalculated agreement three times for those studies for which the combined confidence ratings were (1) at least 2, (2) at least 3, or (3) 4 (the maximum combined confidence). As expected, agreement tended to rise and the sample size dropped as the confidence requirement increased. However, agreement rarely attained an acceptable level except when confidence was at its maximum, and in these cases the sample size was too small to be useful. Therefore, we abandoned our attempt to rescue variables in this way. We simply retained for further analysis the 33 variables meeting the above-described reliability criteria. In the case of continuous variables, we entered the mean over two coders for each coding; for categorical variables, data for a given study were selected from one coder, and the choice of coder was alternated from one study to the next, in alphabetical order of first author. In what follows, the reliability of each variable is cited when that variable is first introduced.

RESULTS

Mean Effect Size across All Studies

The studies by Greenberg and Rice (1981) and by Greenberg and Dompierre (1981) compared the effects of confrontation and reflection, two of the interventions under consideration. As a result, the same eight effect sizes appeared twice in our database, once with a positive sign (for confrontation) and once with a negative sign (for reflection). In order to avoid biasing either upward or downward, all effect sizes from these two studies were therefore removed before the mean of the effect size findings was calculated across studies.

The mean effect size across studies was calculated by first weighting each estimate by the inverse of its variance (Hedges & Olkin, 1985) and then summing across to give d_+, which took the value 0.26. In Cohen's (1977) terms, this would be a small effect, although not one to be dismissed from consideration by the behavioral scientist. The homogeneity statistic Q_T reveals whether the inconsistency in findings across studies is large enough to reject the hypothesis that they are drawn from a common population (Hedges & Olkin, 1985). It has an approximate chi-square distribution with $k - 1$ degrees of freedom, where k is the number of effect sizes. As would be expected, given that the collection of reports represented studies of diverse therapist interventions, the findings varied significantly across the sample ($Q_T = 239.17$, $df = 104$, $p < .001$).

Profile of Studies in Relation to Validity Criteria

In appraising the validity of the studies as a set, methodological features were grouped in terms of threats to the four types of validity described by Cook and Campbell (1979) and reviewed above. For all analyses involving validity criteria, the studies by Greenberg and Rice (1981) and Greenberg and Dompierre (1981) were each entered once, and considered to be studies of confrontation.

Statistical Conclusion Validity

Statistical conclusion validity is threatened by inadequate statistical power (Cohen, 1977). Given the large amount of change during psychotherapy that may be attributed to common factors (Frank, 1982), studies relating specific process elements to outcome require substantial power in order to detect the relatively modest effects that are likely to obtain, relative to the influence of these common factors. Sample size was recorded very reliably by the coders ($r = .99$). The number of treated clients included ranged from 3 to 210, with a median of 38 and a mean of 45. We consulted Cohen's (1977) power tables to evaluate these sample sizes. At the median sample size, a correlational analysis setting a .05 significance level, testing for an effect in just one direction (e.g., a positive relationship between interpretation and outcome), would have a 58% chance of detecting an effect equal to a medium-sized correlation of .30; a 33% chance of detecting a correlation of .20; or a 15% chance of detecting an effect equal to a correlation of .10. The obtained mean effect size of 0.26 would correspond to a correlation not much greater than .10. According to Cohen's (1977, p. 23) equation 2.2.6, the equivalent r would be .13.

When patients were divided into two groups, a one-tailed test of a true difference between two group means amounting to a medium-sized effect of .5 of a standard deviation (large for a process–outcome analysis), had only a 45% chance of significance at the .05 level when there were 19 subjects in each group (corresponding to the median study n of 38). Crucially, we found that, at the obtained mean effect size of 0.26, the power of this comparison was reduced to about 20%. We therefore concluded that, taken alone, the typical study in this analysis had insufficient statistical power to detect an effect of the typical magnitude observed. Thus, a null result from a single such study would be uninterpretable.

The power of these process–outcome studies was even lower than that reported by Kazdin and Bass (1989) for outcome studies comparing different active treatments. These comparisons yielded a considerably larger median effect size of 0.47, so that the typical sample size (about 16 per group) was sufficient to yield a median 74% power to detect this difference, with a two-tailed alpha of .05. However, the very low power of the present studies is quite typical of behavioral science research more generally. Sedlmeier and Gigerenzer (1989) overviewed 12 previous power studies, yielding mean power to detect a .20 correlation ranging from .10 to .55. These authors conducted their own analysis of the 1984 *Journal of Abnormal Psychology*. Setting alpha at .05, they found a mean power to detect a .20 correlation coefficient of just 21%.

The design used for process–outcome analysis was recorded with acceptable reliability (kappa = .60). Sixteen studies were correlational, of which 3 used within-subject designs; a further 13 studies used group comparison designs, and 4 studies used within-subject experimental designs.

Statistical conclusion validity is also threatened by uncontrolled variation in the delivery and measurement of process elements. We focused on measurement, and noted the duration of treatment (in hours) encompassed in process measurement; this was recorded with acceptable reliability (r = .70). The more material sampled, the more reliable the resulting estimate of process–outcome relations. The mean of 24.5 hours contrasted with the median of 3 hours of therapy sampled, reflecting the considerably skewed distribution. We dichotomized process measures into established measures with known reliability and ad hoc instruments with no such pedigree (kappa = .63). Of the 165 effect sizes, 78 (47%) were derived from established process measures, and 87 (53%) from ad hoc instruments.

In sum, the statistical conclusion validity of the typical single study was inadequate, because the sample size was insufficient to detect the magnitude of effect typically found. The modest size of that effect may be partially explained in terms of the widespread use of potentially unreliable, ad hoc process measures, and the small sample of therapy process actually measured in many studies.

Internal Validity

Internal validity is threatened by systematic bias. When relevant (i.e., for 74 of the 165 pairings of process and outcome measures in the corpus), we noted how clients were assigned to groups or conditions (kappa = .64). Here, we were concerned with the presence or absence of randomization and of matching on salient variables to prevent accidental bias. Randomization was employed for all but 2 of these 74 observations; matching on relevant variables was incorporated in the randomization procedure for only 11 observations. Thus, the predominant method of assignment (61, or 81% of 74 observations) was randomization without matching. With sample sizes as modest as is typical of these studies, unconstrained randomization would carry a substantial risk of accidental bias in assignment to groups.

We attempted to measure attrition, a potential source of bias, but were unable to do this reliably. We suspect that the reason for this was uneven reporting of this information by source study authors, reflecting numerous, nontrivial conceptual issues in the definition of attrition (Howard, Krause, & Orlinsky, 1986).

Construct Validity

Construct validity was assessed with reference to the relevance of outcome measures to the rationale of treatment (weighted kappa = .73) and to the client's presenting problem (weighted kappa = .57), each measured on 3-point scales requiring firm evidence for the coder to depart from the central, "moderate" category. Accordingly, we rated 75.2% of outcome measures as being moderately relevant to the treatment rationale and 64.2% as moderately relevant to the client's presenting problem. We rated 4.2% of outcome measures as poor in respect of relevance to treatment rationale (i.e., the measure was more clearly relevant to some other treatment rationale). We rated 20.6% of outcome measures as highly relevant to the treatment rationale (i.e., the measure related directly to aspects of functioning addressed in the treatment rationale), and 35.8% as highly relevant to the client's presenting problem (i.e., specifically appropriate to the syndrome or problem, such as the Beck Depression Inventory for depression, or relating to target complaints).

Construct validity is also served by the spread of outcome measures across a wide variety of domains (major categories included symptom, behavioral, self-concept, and attribution for changes experienced) ($r = .94$); and by long follow-up ($r = .99$). Across the 33 studies, a mean of 1.8 domains were assessed in a given study; 16 studies confined themselves to a single domain. The length of follow-up is important to the construct validity of a process–outcome study, because the clinical and theoretical importance of the outcomes predicted requires them to be of substantial duration. The mean length of follow-up was 1.9 months, but this figure was heavily influenced by a small number of long-term follow-ups, and 92.1% of measures were coded as obtained immediately after treatment.

We coded the perspective of the outcome measure, following Orlinsky and Howard (1986). Construct validity requires that measures be from theoretically appropriate perspectives. We found 45.5% of measures to be from the patient's perspective, 12.1% from the therapist's perspective, 9.7% from the rater's perspective, and 31.5% from test scores. Although specific measures might be most appropriately obtained from specific sources, in general the therapist's perspective could be seen as somewhat less appropriate than the others, since the goal of therapy would be less to improve the client's functioning in the eyes of an involved professional than to improve it as experienced by the client, as expressed by the client in completing a test, or as perceived by less involved observers.

Indirect evidence of the therapist's capacity to deliver the intervention was derived from clinical experience (kappa = .56); of the 33 studies, 16 used qualified practitioners, 9 therapists of mixed status, 4 postgraduate therapists, and 4 undergraduate trainee therapists. The finding that half the studies relied to varying degrees upon unqualified practitioners constituted a threat to construct validity, in that psychotherapies are generally considered to require substantial professional training to ensure skilled and appropriate delivery.

Also bearing on construct validity was the "best" control group included in the study (kappa = .68). Ideally, an investigation should reveal whether the process–outcome relationship under study is specific to a given treatment model. Fourteen studies included a comparison group undergoing a different treatment; whilst the remaining 19 were coded in a residual category including a no-treatment period, no control group or period, or the treatment group as its own control. No studies were coded as having a minimal treatment control group.

An index of the relationship of the process measure to the treatment rationale was not reliably codable (weighted kappa = .35). The process perspective, following Orlinsky and Howard, was coded "patient" for 12.1% of the observations, "therapist" for 23.0%, and "observer" for 64.8%. The temporal unit of process measurement (kappa = .46) ranged from the most microscopic, statements within speaking turns (just 4.2% of observations), through speaking turns (24.2%), segments or events within sessions (39.4%), and sessions (17.0%), to the most macroscopic, the entire treatment (15.2%).

In sum, the ways in which process and outcome were measured varied widely across studies in terms of their implications for construct validity. Similarly, many studies were compromised by the use of unqualified therapists and by the lack of comparison groups receiving contrasting treatments.

External Validity

External validity concerns the generalizibility of the findings to populations, treatments and settings of interest. For example, we considered the representativeness of treatment in terms of the method used (kappa = .52). Of the 33 studies, 11 concerned psychodynamic treatment; 10 concerned heterogeneous treatments; 4 concerned behavioral, cognitive, or skills training; 4 combined elements of psychodynamic and experiential treatments; 3 concerned experiential treatment alone; and one combined psychodynamic and behavioral. Another element of external validity was the duration of therapy, expressed here either as the overall mean duration ($r = .92$, mean = 20.0 hours, median = 15 hours) or as the minimum duration of therapy for cases admitted into the study ($r = .69$, mean = 9.4 hours, median = 5 hours).

Patient factors bearing upon external validity included: age group (kappa = .78), with 12 of the 33 studies concerning young adult clients; employment status (kappa = .80), with 10 studies involving full-time students; diagnosis (kappa = .53), with 10 studies of neurotic patients, 10 of patients with mixed diagnoses, 3 of psychotic patients, 2 of antisocial patients, and 8 of clients with no psychiatric diagnosis; source of clients (kappa = .68), with 20 studies of clients voluntarily seeking treatment, 5 of patients committed for treatment, 3 of clients solicited by investigators for treatment, and 5 of clients recruited in two or more of these ways.

In sum, external validity was somewhat better than for the comparative outcome studies reviewed by Shapiro and Shapiro (1983), although even these data may have somewhat overrepresented students receiving brief therapy.

Study Limitations Reflecting the Drug Metaphor

As noted above, we attempted to code studies on scales constructed to determine whether studies addressed specific issues that Stiles and Shapiro (1989) have alleged to be neglected by process–outcome research grounded in the assumptions of the oversimplified and overextended drug metaphor. Six scales were devised:

1. *Client–technique interactions*: Did the study consider the moderating effect of (outside-session) client variables upon the relationship between the therapist intervention and outcome?
2. *Nonbinary relations*: Did the process variable have more than two values on the process continuum?
3. *Nonlinear relations*: Did the study consider anything other than a linear relationship between process and outcome?
4. *Influence of other variables*: Did the study consider variables other than client variables as influencing the process–outcome relation?
5. *Technique responsivity*: Did the study consider the possibility of the therapist's in-session behavior being influenced by the state or characteristics of the client (i.e., the delivery of the techniques as responsive to the client's requirements)?
6. *Outcome–process effects*: Did the study consider the effect of client functioning (as tapped by outcome variables) upon the process variable (measuring the intervention)?

On each scale, studies were coded 0 if no attempt was made to address the relevant issue, 1 if it was considered in the text but did not figure in the data analysis, and 2 if it was addressed via analysis of data. Despite extensive training and discussion, acceptable reliability was obtained only for nonlinear relations (weighted kappa = .65), technique responsivity (weighted kappa = .60), and outcome–process effects (weighted kappa = .42). We found that 3 studies took account of nonlinear relations (all of these doing so via data analysis), 8 of technique responsivity (only 2 of these via data analysis), and 6 of outcome–process effects (1 of these via data analysis).

Given our particular interest in these variables, we considered whether useful information could be added by relaxing our reliability requirements. Client–intervention interaction attained a weighted kappa of .30, with 16 studies taking account of this, including 13 that did so via data analysis; nonbinary relations (weighted kappa = .21), were judged to be considered in the data analysis of 11 studies; the influence of other variables was judged to be considered in 16 studies, including 9 via data analysis.

The low reliability achieved with respect to these judgments may have reflected residual fuzziness in the concepts; however, these data suggest that some of the concerns advanced by Stiles and Shapiro (1989) were in fact addressed to some degree in a substantial proportion of the source studies of this meta-analysis.

Mean Effect Sizes within Intervention Categories

The effect size findings were grouped according to intervention, and the weighted estimator d_+ was calculated within each group. For this calculation, the effect sizes for both confrontation (with a positive sign) and reflection (with a negative sign) from the studies by Greenberg and Rice (1981) and by Greenberg and Dompierre (1981) were included. Table 1.1 shows the value of d_+ for each intervention, together with values of the goodness-of-fit statistic Q_T and its associated probability. It can be seen from this table that mean effect sizes varied considerably according to the intervention studied, and that there was significant variance among the effect sizes within intervention categories for five categories. It is noteworthy that the largest mean effects (for confrontation and transference focus) were among those showing least variation among effect sizes.

This obtained variation indicated that factors other than the

TABLE 1.1. Weighted Estimates of Effect Size and Goodness-of-Fit Statistics for Nine Therapist Interventions

Process	d_+	Q_T	df	p
Interpretation	0.20	59.4	13	<.001
Confrontation	1.03	14.6	9	>.1
Focus on affect	0.25	14.0	6	<.05
Focus on transference	0.60	5.2	6	>.1
Exploration	0.29	63.8	21	<.001
Support	0.31	41.4	18	<.01
Advice	0.17	8.8	9	>.1
Reflection	−0.28	48.1	23	<.01
Self-disclosure	0.30	4.1	7	>.1

Note. No effect sizes could be calculated for the intervention "Focus on here and now."

nature of the intervention influenced the effect size obtained. This suggested a multivariate approach, in which the intervention type was entered as a predictor of effect size alongside other features of the studies described in the meta-analysis. In addition, the variation among effect sizes within five categories could reflect differences among studies in the specific intervention denoted by the descriptors "interpretation," "focus on affect," "exploration," "support," and "reflection." This would have implications for the construct validity of the studies of these interventions, suggesting that the studies of each intervention could not be unquestioningly interpreted as having measured and evaluated a single construct.

Substantively, the findings of Table 1.1 suggest that confrontation and focus on transference were the most effective interventions, although each was represented by relatively few effect sizes. Reflection was apparently the least effective intervention, although there was considerable variation among effect sizes for this intervention. However, these differences may not have been independent of methodological differences among studies of the different interventions.

Multiple-Regression Analysis

To enable interpretation of F statistics (Hedges & Olkin, 1985) and the inclusion of sample size as a predictor, multiple-regression analysis was conducted using unweighted effect size as the dependent measure. Variables were grouped into sets according to the type of validity (Cook & Campbell, 1979) to which they were primarily relevant. Nominal variables (such as therapist intervention categories) were represented by sets of dummy variables. All reliably coded variables were entered, except where tolerance limits required the exclusion of variables that were too highly intercorrelated. The effects of these exclusions were examined by running additional analyses excluding the other member of each pair of such redundant variables. There were a total of 113 effect sizes in the data set, and the analysis involved some 40 predictors. The use of F statistics enabled us to interpret findings concerning this number of predictors with reference to a residual term with over 70 degrees of freedom.

The full equation yielded a highly significant multiple R of .84, $F (40, 72) = 4.33, p < .0001$. The effect of removing each set from the full equation was used to test its independent contribution to predicting effect size (Table 1.2). Additional analyses removing alternative members of pairs of redundant variables did not yield substantially different results of the tests reported here. In addition, the full equation was examined. The contribution to effect size of any single variable whose independent effects achieved at least the marginally significant probability value of .10 was considered.

TABLE 1.2. Multiple-Regression Analysis of Unweighted Effect Sizes: Tests of Specific Variable Sets

Type of variable	df	Sum of squares	R^2 change	F	Significance
Statistical conclusion	3	1.26	.028	2.29	.08
Internal	3	2.29	.051	2.60	.06
Construct	12	7.00	.157	3.20	.001
External	13	7.99	.179	3.38	.0004
Intervention	7	1.48	.03	1.16	.34
Regression[a]	40	31.52	—	4.33	.0000
Residual	72	13.10	—	—	—

[a]Includes variables not included in tests reported in this table.

Statistical Conclusion Validity

Sample size, the duration in time of therapy process assessed, and reliability (established vs. ad hoc) of measure represented statistical conclusion validity, whose independent effect attained marginal statistical significance, F (3, 72) = 2.30, p = .08, and accounted for 3% of the variance. The only one of these variables to exert a significant independent effect upon effect size was the duration of therapy process sampled (beta = 1.02, p = .04). Larger effects were obtained in studies assessing greater amounts of therapy process, zero order r (111) = .22, p < .01. This finding supports the argument of Stiles, Shapiro, and Firth-Cozens (1988) that the inherent instability of psychotherapy process requires extensive samples for adequate representativeness.

Internal Validity

Internal validity was reflected in dummy variables representing methods of assignment to groups or conditions, and attention to the effect of client on therapist behavior (technique responsivity). The independent effect of this set of variables was significant, F (4, 72) = 3.14, p = .02, and accounted for 5% of the variance. Two of these variables exerted an independent effect upon effect size. First, randomization with matching was associated with smaller effect sizes (beta = −5.42, p = .01). This suggests that studies failing to match clients may have capitalized on chance variation among clients; this variation may itself have influenced the delivery of treatment interventions and/or their effects upon the clients. Second, attention to technique responsivity was associated with larger effect sizes (beta = 1.22, p = .05). (However, most studies attending to this factor did so only in their text rather than in the data analysis.)

Although not included as a direct index of internal validity, the design of the process–outcome analysis, coded as group comparative designs (effect size = 0.20) versus all other designs (correlational and within-subject; effect size = 0.40), was found to be independently related to effect size (beta = 6.39, p = .02). This apparent insensitivity of the group comparative design can be interpreted either positively, as a reflection of its greater control over extraneous variables, or negatively, as indicative of its artificiality and lack of ecological validity for the appraisal of psychotherapeutic interventions.

Construct Validity

Construct validity was represented by the unit size of the process measure, the process and outcome perspectives, clinical experience of the therapist, relevance of outcome measure to the patient's problem and to the treatment rationale, the number of outcome domains assessed, and the presence of a comparative treatment group. These parameters were indexed by a set of 12 variables, whose combined independent effects were highly significant, $F(12, 72) = 3.20$, $p = .001$, and accounted for 16% of the variance. However, none of these variables alone exerted a significant independent effect upon effect size. Univariate analysis, on the other hand, suggested an association between number of outcome domains and effect size, $r(111) = .32$, $p < .01$. The 10 effect sizes from studies tapping the greatest number of domains (4) took a mean value of .91. Thorough outcome measurement appeared to be characteristic of studies revealing powerful effects.

External Validity

External validity was represented by a set of 13 variables, including the number of hours of treatment, client age (young adult vs. other), and client employment status (student vs. other), diagnosis, treatment setting, and treatment method. This variable set exerted highly significant independent effects, $F(13, 72) = 3.38$, $p = .0004$, accounting for 18% of the variance. Within this set of variables, single sets of dummy variables representing treatment setting, $F(3, 72) = 3.42$, $p = .02$, and treatment method, $F(4, 72) = 4.63$, $p = .002$, showed significant independent effects, and accounted for 4% and 8% of the variance, respectively.

In relation to treatment settings, smaller effects were found for outpatient (effect size = 0.18) and student health (effect size = 0.18) than for other settings, primarily coded as "mixed." With respect to treatment methods, relatively large effects were found in the context of experiential (effect size = 0.84), and behavioral (effect size = 0.79) treatments, and relatively small effects in the context of psychodynamic (effect size = 0.17) and mixed psychodynamic and experiential (effect size = 0.06) treatments.

In interpreting these treatment differences, we must emphasize that these effect sizes were not measures of the effectiveness of the treatments as a whole, but of the relation within these treatments of specific interventions to outcome. The findings suggest that the interventions studied in the context of experiential and behavioral therapies may have been better specified or more powerfully manipulated. The statistical independence of this treatment method effect, as revealed by multiple-regression analysis, argues against its being simply attributed to the prevalence of more potent intervention categories (such as confrontation [effect size = 1.03] or focus on transference [effect size = 0.60]) in experiential and behavioral treatments.

Although the set of three dummy variables representing diagnosis did not make a significant contribution to the prediction of effect size, $F (3, 72) = 1.76, p = .16$, one of these variables, representing neurotic disorders, approached significance in the full equation (beta = 0.91, $p = .10$), suggesting somewhat larger effect sizes for studies involving neurotic clients (mean effect size = 0.45) than for other diagnostic groups (mean effect size = 0.29).

Effects of Interventions Independent of Design Features

Interestingly, seven dummy variables representing the effects of eight types of therapist intervention exerted no significant independent effect upon effect size; removing these intervention variables from the full equation including the above-reported validity factors did not significantly reduce predictive power, $F (7, 72) = 1.16, p = .34$. The analysis was rerun eliminating a predictor that had caused one of the intervention variables to be removed because of tolerance problems, whereupon the eight intervention variables approached significance, $F (8, 72) = 1.71, p = .11$.

Overview of Findings

Reliability and confidence data were somewhat disappointing. Three factors probably accounted for this: First, the quality and consistency of descriptions of source study reports were quite poor; second, the source studies varied very widely in method and approach, rendering coding quite difficult; third, some of the concepts we were trying to code may have remained fuzzy, despite our efforts to refine them. However, sufficient variables survived reliability analysis to permit worthwhile description of the source studies.

The overall mean effect size of 0.26 was small, although not negligibly so (Cohen, 1977). To conceptualize this in terms of hypothetical normal distributions of individuals receiving an intervention compared with those not receiving it, the average recipient of an intervention attained outcomes at about the 60th percentile of those not receiving the intervention. This would be equivalent to a correlation of about .13, and the intervention would account for a little under 2% of the variance in outcomes. The clinical importance of an effect of this magnitude is, of course, questionable. Not surprisingly, it is very much smaller than the typical effect size approaching 1.00 found in studies comparing treated and untreated groups (Shapiro, 1985).

Methodologically, the validity of these 33 studies appears to have been moderate to fair. Inadequate sample sizes and measures of variable reliability threatened statistical conclusion validity; reliance upon unconstrained randomization threatened internal validity, and attrition was hard to assess from the reports provided. Construct validity was found to be variable, with clear room for improvement in choice of measures, length of follow-up, and experience of therapists. External validity was, in general, somewhat better than for comparative outcome research, although still leaving something to be desired.

It proved difficult to assess studies' attention to some of the factors neglected by the drug metaphor approach. However, some studies did address some of these concerns, such as client intervention interaction and the moderating influence of other variables. Nonetheless, it would appear that most of these studies made one or more of the assumptions critiqued by Stiles and Shapiro (1989).

We confirmed the impression formed by Orlinsky and Howard (1986) of variation among interventions in the extent of their relationship with outcome, with mean effect sizes ranging from −0.28 for reflection to 1.03 for confrontation. Reassuringly, the mean effect size reflected the proportion of positive findings reported for an intervention by Orlinsky and Howard (1986). However, regression analysis suggested that much of this variation could be attributable to concurrent variation across studies in methods and samples. With such a small and heterogeneous set of studies, no definitive priority could be accorded to either substantive (intervention) or methodological factors in their effects upon outcome.

All four types of validity appeared to impinge upon the obtained effect size. Noteworthy findings included the stronger effects from studies sampling therapy process more extensively and tapping a wide range of outcome domains, and the more modest effects associated with matching constraints upon randomization and with group comparative designs. In addition, smaller intervention–outcome effects were found in outpatient and student health settings, and with psychodynamic and psychodynamic/experiential methods, whereas large effects were found in the context of experiential and behavioral treatments.

DISCUSSION

What does this review add up to? In sum, we consider that it demonstrates the low yield of conventional process–outcome research seeking to identify therapist interventions yielding favorable treatment outcome. We re-evaluated 33 publications included by Orlinsky and Howard (1986) in their landmark review of process–outcome relations, and found an average effect size accounting for less than 2% of the variance in outcome. Although some interventions appear to have been more powerful than this, we cannot rule out methodological factors as an alternative explanation of these findings. Our attempts to describe the studies systematically and to relate their characteristics to outcome were hindered by variable reporting quality. But we nevertheless discerned considerable variation in sophistication and quality among these investigations, and found the overall methodological quality to be quite poor.

Our conclusion concerning interventions within treatment methods resembles Stiles et al.'s (1986) assertion of equivalent outcomes of demonstrably nonequivalent treatment methods. These results thus re-present us with the "equivalence paradox," and it is therefore worthwhile to consider their implications for each of the three main resolutions discussed by Stiles et al. (1986; see also Elliott, Stiles, & Shapiro, 1993).

The first option reviewed by Stiles et al. (1986) was to assert that true differences in effectiveness between treatments were masked by weaknesses in the research. Is there any evidence from the present analysis to suggest that therapist interventions had powerful effects that were obscured by methodological limitations of the studies reviewed? Threats to statistical conclusion and construct validity could indeed have weakened the apparent effects of interventions. Specifically, we identified problems in relation to statistical power, measurement, and therapist experience levels that might be expected to dilute any effects attributable due to interventions. Moreover, some of these factors (e.g., amount of therapy process sampled, number of outcome domains assessed) revealed relationships with the strength of the observed process–outcome relation that were consistent with this possibility. Additional weaknesses may have been hidden from view by the uneven quality of reporting that gave rise to difficulty in securing reliable codings. Furthermore, the above-noted threats to internal and external validity, although perhaps less likely to account for the modest effects of interventions revealed in our analysis, represent further weaknesses of this research. Even before we consider the drug metaphor limitations of the research reviewed, it may be justly criticized for failing to live up to the orthodox methodological standards embodied in Cook and Campbell's (1979) analysis of threats to validity.

Stiles et al. (1986) considered a second option—attributing equivalent outcomes of differing treatments to the overriding importance to outcome of factors common across treatment methods. Such factors were, of course, extensively considered in sections of the Orlinsky and Howard (1986) review that were deliberately excluded from the present analysis. Our review did not greatly emphasize common factors contributed by therapist, client, or the dyad. However, several relevant features were considered under external validity; for example, indirect evidence was obtained implicating client diagnosis in the magnitude of effects attributable to therapist interventions.

A third option considered by Stiles et al. (1986) was to take issue with the practice of comparing the contents and outcomes of entire therapies. Exemplified by the "events paradigm," this approach is further discussed in several chapters of the present volume. Similar arguments can be made in light of the modest effects of therapist interventions revealed by the present analysis (see also Stiles & Shapiro, 1989). The search for uniform, monotonic relationships between therapist interventions and outcome is predicated upon unsound simplifying assumptions about the nature of psychotherapeutic process. For example, Stiles (1988) argues that studies using process–outcome correlations to identify "active ingredients" are doomed to failure, because they depend upon the false assumption that such ingredients are delivered by therapists at random and regardless of the state or "requirements" of the client.

We had hoped to examine the deleterious effect of such limitations by coding studies' efforts to overcome them and then relating these to the magnitude of effects obtained. However, these efforts were dogged by low reliability. This may reflect a lack of clarity in the constructs we tried to measure, alongside variable quality and style of reporting of features that are not uniformly understood features of current research orthodoxy. Scant evidence is thus available on this point. However, studies paying attention to technique responsivity—albeit largely in their discussion sections rather than in the analyses per se—tended to obtain larger effects. In addition, the two "events paradigm" studies by Greenberg and Rice (1981) and Greenberg and Dompierre (1981) yielded large effects, although the clinical significance of such findings would be enhanced by embedding them within studies of long-term outcome (Shapiro et al., 1991).

The results of this meta-analysis indicate how insubstantial is our empirical knowledge of effective psychotherapeutic techniques. Our efforts to validate such basic elements as interpretation, focus on affect, and exploration by showing their relationship with treatment outcome were conspicuously unsuccessful. The apparent effect of each of these interventions varied substantially among studies of a given intervention, centering on a very modest mean value. Although some interventions appeared more powerful than others, these differences among interventions were reduced to marginal statistical reliability when the effects of methodological variation among studies were controlled via multiple-regression analysis. These findings are equally challenging, whether they are interpreted to reflect limitations of the research paradigms and methods used, or of the treatment techniques themselves.

In conclusion, this analysis indicates that therapist interventions are not shown by the available, conventional process–outcome analysis to exert strong effects upon the effectiveness of treatment. Recent findings consistent with this conclusion have been obtained by Stiles and Shapiro (in press). The present analysis lends support to calls from Orlinsky and Howard (1986, 1987), as well as from others represented in this volume, for research to adopt more complex and realistic conceptual models of the psychotherapy process. These models, in turn, require much more complex and diverse methodological approaches than these that have characterized the predominant research tradition. In its relatively optimistic conclusions concerning the demonstrated effects of therapist interventions, we have characterized the Orlinsky and Howard (1986) review as representing the high-water mark of the drug metaphor. It is conceivable, although in our view unlikely, that a comparable analysis of relevant portions of the more recent review by Orlinsky, Grawe, and Parks (in press) would yield more positive conclusions.

ACKNOWLEDGMENTS

Heather Harper was supported by a Medical Research Council Training Award, and Anne Suokas by the British Council. Portions of this chapter were presented at the meeting of the Society for Psychotherapy Research, Ulm, West Germany, in June 1987; and at the meeting of the U.K. Chapter of the Society for Psychotherapy Research, Ravenscar, England, in April 1988.

REFERENCES

Cohen, J. (1960). A coefficient of agreement for nominal tables. *Educational and Psychological Measurement, 20,* 37–46.

Cohen, J. (1968). Weighted kappa: Nominal scale agreement with provision for scaled disagreement or partial credit. *Psychological Bulletin, 70,* 213–220.

Cohen, J. (1977). *Statistical power analysis for the behavioral sciences* (2nd ed.). New York: Academic Press.

Cook, T. D., & Campbell, D. T. (1979). *Quasi-experimentation: Design and analysis for field settings.* Chicago: Rand McNally.

Elliott, R., Stiles, W. B., & Shapiro, D. A. (1993). Are some psychotherapies more equivalent than others? In T. R. Giles (Ed.), *Handbook of effective psychotherapy* (pp. 455–478). New York: Plenum.

Frank, J. D. (1982). Therapeutic components shared by all psychotherapies. In J. H. Harvey & M. M. Parks (Eds.), *Psychotherapy research and behavior change.* Washington, DC: American Psychological Association.

Glass, G. V., McGaw, B., & Smith, M. L. (1981). *Meta-analysis in social research.* Beverly Hills, CA: Sage.

Hedges, L. V., & Olkin, I. (1985). *Statistical methods for meta-analysis.* Orlando, FL: Academic Press.

Howard, K. I., Krause, M. S., & Orlinsky, D. E. (1986). The attrition dilemma: Toward a new strategy for psychotherapy research. *Journal of Consulting and Clinical Psychology, 54,* 106–110.

Kazdin, A. E., & Bass, D. (1989). Power to detect differences between alternative treatments in comparative psychotherapy outcome research. *Journal of Consulting and Clinical Psychology, 57,* 138–147.

Lambert, M. J. (1989). The individual therapist's contribution to psychotherapy process and outcome. *Clinical Psychology Review, 9,* 469–485.

Lambert, M. J., Shapiro, D. A., & Bergin, A. E. (1986). The effectiveness of psychotherapy. In S. L. Garfield & A. E. Bergin (Eds.), *Handbook of psychotherapy and behavior change* (3rd ed., pp. 157–211). New York: Wiley.

Landis, R. J., & Koch, G. G. (1977). An application of hierarchical kappa-type statistics in the assessment of majority agreement among multiple observers. *Biometrics, 33,* 363–374.

Orlinsky, D. E., Grawe, K., & Parks, B. K. (1994). Process and outcome in psychotherapy—*Noch Einmal.* In A. E. Bergin & S. L. Garfield (Eds.), *Handbook of psychotherapy and behavior change* (4th ed., 270–376). New York: Wiley.

Orlinsky, D. E., & Howard, K. I. (1986). Process and outcome in psychotherapy. In S. L. Garfield & A. E. Bergin (Eds.), *Handbook of psychotherapy and behavior change* (3rd ed., pp. 311–381). New York: Wiley.

Orlinsky, D. E., & Howard, K. I. (1987). A generic model of psychotherapy. *Journal of Integrative and Eclectic Psychotherapy, 6,* 6–27.

Orwin, R. G., & Cordray, D. S. (1985). Effects of deficient reporting on meta-analysis: A conceptual framework and reanalysis. *Psychological Bulletin, 97,* 134–147.

Prioleau, L., Murdock, M., & Brody, N. (1983). An analysis of psychotherapy versus placebo studies. *Behavioral and Brain Sciences, 6,* 275–285.

Rachman, S. J., & Wilson, G. T. (1980). *The effects of psychological therapy* (2nd ed). Elmsford, NY: Pergamon Press.

Robinson, L. A., Berman, J. S., & Neimeyer, R. A. (1990). Psychotherapy for the treatment of depresssion: A comprehensive review of controlled outcome research. *Psychological Bulletin, 108,* 30–49.

Sedlmeier, P., & Gigerenzer, G. (1989). Do studies of statistical power have an effect on the power of studies? *Psychological Bulletin, 105,* 309–316.

Shapiro, D. A. (1985). Recent applications of meta-analysis in clinical research. *Clinical Psychology Review, 5,* 13–34.

Shapiro, D. A., Barkham, M., Hardy, G. E., Morrison, L. A., Reynolds, S., Startup, M., & Harper, H. (1991). Sheffield Psychotherapy Research Program. In L. E. Beutler (Ed.), *Psychotherapy research programs* (pp. 234–242). Washington, DC: Society for Psychotherapy Research/American Psychological Association.

Shapiro, D. A., & Shapiro, D. (1982). Meta-analysis of comparative therapy outcome research: A replication and refinement. *Psychological Bulletin, 92*, 581–604.

Shapiro, D. A., & Shapiro, D. (1983). Comparative therapy outcome research: Methodological implications of meta-analysis. *Journal of Consulting and Clinical Psychology, 51*, 42–53.

Smith, M. L., Glass, G. V., & Miller, T. I. (1980). *The benefits of psychotherapy.* Baltimore: Johns Hopkins University Press.

Stiles, W. B. (1988). Psychotherapy process–outcome correlations may be misleading. *Psychotherapy, 25*, 27–35.

Stiles, W. B., & Shapiro, D. A. (1989). Abuse of the drug metaphor in psychotherapy process-outcome research. *Clinical Psychology Review, 9*, 521–543.

Stiles, W. B., & Shapiro, D. A. (in press). Disabuse of the drug metaphor: Psychotherapy process–outcome correlations. *Journal of Consulting and Clinical Psychology.*

Stiles, W. B., Shapiro, D. A., & Elliott, R. (1986). Are all psychotherapies equivalent? *American Psychologist, 41*, 165–180.

Stiles, W. B., Shapiro, D. A., & Firth-Cozens, J. (1988). Verbal response mode use in contrasting psychotherapies: A within-subjects comparison. *Journal of Consulting and Clinical Psychology, 56*, 727–733.

STUDIES INCLUDED IN META-ANALYSIS

Abramowitz, S. I., & Abramowitz, C. V. (1974). Psychological-mindedness and benefit from insight-oriented group therapy. *Archives of General Psychiatry, 30*, 610–615.

Abramowitz, S. I., & Jackson, C. (1974). Comparative effectiveness of there-and-then vs. here-and-now therapist interpretations in group psychotherapy. *Journal of Counseling Psychology, 21*, 288–293.

Alexander, J. F., Barton, C., Schiavo, R. S., & Parsons, B. V. (1976). Systems–behavioral intervention with families of delinquents: Therapist characteristics, family behavior, and outcome. *Journal of Consulting and Clinical Psychology, 44*, 656–664.

Ashby, J. D., Ford, D. H., Guerney, B. G., & Guerney, L. F. (1957). Effects on clients of a reflective and a leading type of psychotherapy. *Psychological Monographs, 71*, 24.

Baker, E. (1960). The differential effects of two psychotherapeutic approaches on client perceptions. *Journal of Counseling Psychology, 7*, 46–50.

Barrington, B. L. (1961). Prediction from counselor behavior of client perception and of case outcome. *Journal of Counseling Psychology, 8*, 37–42.

Beutler, L. E., & Mitchell, R. (1981). Differential psychotherapy outcome among depressed and impulsive patients as a function of analytic and experiential treatment procedures. *Psychiatry, 44,* 297–306.

Dreiblatt, I. S., & Weatherly, D. (1965). An evaluation of the efficacy of brief contact therapy with hospitalized psychiatric patients. *Journal of Consulting Psychology, 29,* 513–519.

Elliott, R., Barker, C. B., Caskey, N., & Pistrang, N. (1982). Differential helpfulness of counselor verbal response modes. *Journal of Counseling Psychology, 29,* 354–361.

Feifel, H., & Eells, J. (1963). Patients and therapists assess the same psychotherapy. *Journal of Consulting Psychology, 27,* 310–318.

Gomes-Schwartz, B. A. (1978). Effective ingredients in psychotherapy: Prediction of outcomes from process variables. *Journal of Consulting and Clinical Psychology, 46,* 1023–1035.

Greenberg, L. S., & Dompierre, L. M. (1981). Specific effects of Gestalt two-chair dialogue on intrapsychic conflict in counseling. *Journal of Counseling Psychology, 28,* 288–294.

Greenberg, L. S., & Rice, L. N. (1981). The specific effects of a Gestalt intervention. *Psychotherapy: Theory, Research and Practice, 18,* 31–37.

Jacobs, M. A., & Warner, B. L. (1981). Interaction of therapeutic attitudes with severity of clinical diagnosis. *Journal of Clinical Psychology, 37,* 75–82.

Kaschak, E. (1978). Therapist and client: Two views of the process and outcome of psychotherapy. *Professional Psychology,* May, 271–277.

Kernberg, O. F. (1976). Some methodological and strategic issues in psychotherapy research: Research implications of the Menninger Foundation's Psychotherapy Research Project. In R. L. Spitzer & D. F. Klein (Eds.), *Evaluation of psychological therapies* (pp. 23–38). Baltimore: Johns Hopkins University Press.

Mainord, W. A., Burk, H. W., & Collins, L. G., (1965). Confrontation vs. diversion in group therapy with chronic schizophrenics as measured by a "positive incident" criterion. *Journal of Clinical Psychology, 21,* 222–225.

Marziali, E. (1984). Prediction of outcome of brief psychotherapy from therapist interpretive interventions. *Archives of General Psychiatry, 41,* 301–304.

Mintz, J. (1981). Measuring outcome in psychodynamic psychotherapy. *Archives of General Psychiatry, 38,* 503–506.

Mintz, J., Luborsky, L., & Auerbach, A. (1971). Dimensions of psychotherapy: A factor analytic study of ratings of psychotherapy sessions. *Journal of Consulting and Clinical Psychology, 36,* 106–120.

Nichols, M. P. (1974). Outcome of brief cathartic psychotherapy. *Journal of Consulting and Clinical Psychology, 42,* 403–410.

O'Malley, S. S., Suh, C. S., & Strupp, H. H. (1983). The Vanderbilt Psychotherapy Process Scale: A report of the scale development and a process–outcome study. *Journal of Consulting and Clinical Psychology, 51*, 581–586.

Rosenbaum, M., Friedlander, J., & Kaplan, S. M. (1956). Evaluation of results of psychotherapy. *Psychosomatic Medicine, 18*, 113–132.

Rounsaville, B. J., Weissman, M. M., & Prusoff, B. A. (1981). Psychotherapy with depressed outpatients: Patient and process variables as predictors of outcome. *British Journal of Psychiatry, 138*, 67–74.

Ryan, V. L., & Gizynski, M. N. (1971). Behavior therapy in retrospect: Patients' feelings about their behavior therapies. *Journal of Consulting and Clinical Psychology, 37*, 1–9.

Semon, R. G., & Goldstein, N. (1957). The effectiveness of group psychotherapy with chronic schizophrenic patients and an evaluation of different therapeutic methods. *Journal of Consulting Psychology, 21*, 317–322.

Staples, F. R., Sloane, R. B., Whipple, K., Cristol, A. H., & Yorkston, N. (1976). Process and outcome in psychotherapy and behavior therapy. *Journal of Consulting and Clinical Psychology, 44*, 340–350.

Suh, C. S., Strupp, H. H., & O'Malley, S. S. (1986). The Vanderbilt process measures: The Psychotherapy Process Scale (VPPS) and the Negative Indicators Scale (VNIS). In L.S. Greenberg & W.M. Pinsof (Eds.), *The psychotherapeutic process: A research handbook* (pp. 285–323). New York: Guilford Press.

Truax, C. B., (1970). Therapist's evaluative statements and patient outcome in psychotherapy. *Journal of Clinical Psychology, 26*, 536–538.

Truax, C. B., & Wittmer, J. (1971). Effects of therapist's focus on patient anxiety source and the interaction with the therapist's level of accurate empathy. *Journal of Clinical Psychology, 27*, 297–299.

Truax, C. B., & Wittmer, J. (1973). The degree of the therapist's focus on defense mechanisms and the effect on therapeutic outcome with institutionalized juvenile delinquents. *Journal of Community Psychology, 1*, 201–203.

Werman, D. S., Agle, D., McDaniel, E., & Schoof, K. G. (1976). Survey of psychiatric treatment effectiveness in a medical student clinic. *American Journal of Psychotherapy, 30*, 294–302.

CHAPTER 2

Finding the Way from Process to Outcome
Blind Alleys and Unmarked Trails

WILLIAM B. STILES
DAVID A. SHAPIRO
HEATHER HARPER

Psychotherapy is widely practiced as a treatment for psychological disorders, and reviews of research indicate that it is effective in this capacity (Lambert, Shapiro, & Bergin, 1986; Smith, Glass, & Miller, 1980). However, its mechanisms of action are poorly understood and disputed among competing schools. This issue is usually cast as the relationship between process and outcome—between what happens during a psychotherapy session and the overcoming of psychological problems. The poor understanding of this issue is not a result of lack of effort; there is a sizable literature reporting attempts to identify process–outcome relationships (Orlinsky & Howard, 1986). However, the results of this research have been disappointing. Although some individual studies have claimed significant advances, there is little indication of convergence on principles or methods that reliably point to what processes are effective (Shapiro et al., Chapter 1, this volume; Stiles & Shapiro, 1989).

This chapter summarizes some of the reasons why previous research strategies may have failed; it then describes a model that recasts the process–outcome question, suggesting an alternative approach to understanding how psychotherapy works. This includes presentation of qualitative data on a case drawn from the first Sheffield Psychotherapy Project (Shapiro & Firth, 1987).

THE DRUG METAPHOR

Most process–outcome research—including ours (e.g., McDaniel, Stiles, & McGaughey, 1981; Shapiro & Firth, 1987; Stiles, Shapiro, & Firth-Cozens, 1988, 1990)—has implicitly subscribed to an investigative paradigm that we call the "drug metaphor" (Stiles & Shapiro, 1989). This paradigm views psychotherapy as comprising active ingredients, supplied by the therapist to the client, along with a variety of fillers and scene-setting features. The supposed "active ingredients" are process components—therapeutic techniques such as interpretation, confrontation, reflection, self-disclosure, challenging assumptions, focusing on affect, efforts to give support, or (more abstractly) empathy, warmth, or genuineness. If a component is an active ingredient, then a high level of it is supposed to yield a positive outcome. If it does not, the ingredient is presumed to be inert.

Insofar as process–outcome research is usually construed as a search for psychotherapy's active ingredients, it invokes the drug metaphor. Probably the metaphor also underpins most authors' and readers' understanding of attempts to match treatments with clients, as voiced in the familiar litany "*what* treatment, by *whom*, is most effective for *this* individual with *that* specific problem, and under *which* set of circumstances" (Paul, 1967, p. 111; italics in original).

Yeaton and Sechrest (1981) made the analogy to pharmacological research and treatment explicit, drawing parallels to chemotherapy for cancer and analgesic medication. They argued that judgments of a procedure's *strength*, *integrity*, and *effectiveness* should govern psychotherapeutic treatment decisions. "Strength" and "integrity" were intended as analogous to drug dosage and purity, respectively, whereas "effectiveness" referred to the methodology of assessing efficacy. "Strong treatments contain large amounts in pure form of those ingredients leading to change" (p. 156). "Integrity of treatment refers to the degree to which treatment is delivered as intended" (p. 160). "By an effect we mean the difference between measures obtained from experimental and control groups or the difference between two conditions of an experiment" (p. 162).

Orlinsky and Howard's (1986; and more recently Orlinsky, Grawe, & Parks, 1994) comprehensive overview and integration of process–outcome research, though cognizant of some of the pitfalls of the drug metaphor, nevertheless used it implicitly by drawing conclusions based on tallies of linear associations between process components and outcome measures. Their tallies led to positive conclusions concerning the therapeutic efficacy of some interventions; they thus challenged the conclusion of most outcome research reviews that treatment methods, despite their technical diversity, have broadly equivalent outcomes (Luborsky, Singer, & Luborsky, 1975; Smith, et al., 1980; Stiles, Shapiro, & Elliott, 1986). However, Shapiro et al.'s (Chapter 1, this volume) meta-analytic review of studies of therapist interventions included in the Orlinsky and Howard (1986) review takes a less sanguine view.

OBJECTIONS TO THE DRUG METAPHOR'S ASSUMPTIONS

Increasingly, authors have been re-examining the philosophical basis of the drug metaphor and the underlying medical model of psychological disorders and treatment. For example, Butler and Strupp (1986) have argued that, unlike drugs, psychotherapeutic interventions concern meaning; hence they depend on the active, conscious participation of both patient and therapist, with their idiosyncratic meaning systems. From another angle, Russell (1986) has argued that positivistic attempts to define psychotherapeutic techniques independently of specific theoretical contexts are ultimately empty. Any adequate description of an intervention must be given in terms compatible with the theory from which it derives. Such theories are not universally accepted, but are the objects of dispute and incomprehension by adherents of other systems. In contrast, the pharmacologist can define the contents of a drug much more "objectively" (i.e., consensually), without reference to some disputed biochemical theory of drug action.

The drug metaphor's failure to represent the relationship of psychotherapy process to outcome can be demonstrated by considering its implicit substantive and methodological assumptions. Among these assumptions are the following: (1) that process and outcome are readily distinguishable from, and bear a simple cause–effect relationship to, each other; (2) that component names refer to ingredients of consistent content and scope; (3) that the potentially active ingredients are known and measured or manipulated; (4) that the active ingredients are contained in the therapist's behavior, with the patient in a correspondingly passive role; (5) that the dose–response curve is ascending and linear in the range being examined; and (6) that the best way to demonstrate a psychotherapeutic procedure's efficacy is by controlled clinical trial. Of course, these assumptions do not constitute a coherent theory of process–outcome relations, nor are they internally consistent. Most psychotherapy researchers would not intentionally subscribe to all or even most of them. Nevertheless, one or more of them are present, stated or unstated, in most of the published research. We consider these assumptions and some of their deficiencies briefly in the next sections, and have done so in more detail elsewhere (Stiles & Shapiro, 1989).

Outcome Is Distinct from Process

The drug metaphor implies that psychotherapeutic effects, measured in terms of clinical improvement following treatment, are both conceptually and operationally distinct from psychotherapeutic processes measured during treatment. Drugs can be manipulated independently of clinical state (though they are not always—e.g., when dosage is adjusted to patient requirements). Psychotherapeutic process components, however, may reflect changes that have already occurred; good therapy process is more readily achievable by therapists and clients when the latter are doing well. Particularly in studies of broadly evaluative variables, process measures may be tapping early outcomes. Thus, associations between ratings of event or session qualities ("process") and long-term improvement ("outcome") may reflect early recognition of change rather than prediction of change (Stiles, Shapiro, & Firth-Cozens, 1990). To look at it another way, even if "outcome" is measured later than "process," there is no assurance that it first occurred later.

Process Component Names Signify Pure Ingredients

In drug research, the formula and dosage can be specified in a consistent manner that is portable across repeated administrations, different patients, and various treatment settings (although interactions with contextual features, such as a patient's social and emotional state, are still possible). In psychotherapy research, by contrast, "ingredients" are not so easily specified. In our view, it is absurd to suppose that psychotherapeutic interventions—in the form measured as process variables—have an "integrity" comparable to the chemical purity of drugs (cf. Yeaton & Sechrest, 1981).

Even after we allow for the unreliability of measurement and interactions with contextual elements, process categories, are less pure than chemical categories because they are far more abstract and consequently encompass a greater variety of particular events. For example, even if 31% of a psychoanalytic therapist's utterances were reliably coded as interpretations, each of these utterances may have expressed different content and used different words to do so. We cannot assume that an interpretation's content and phrasing are irrelevant to its therapeutic action. Thus, the ingredient's purity is at a level of abstraction well above that of its psychological impact (cf. Russell, 1986). Variation in definitions across studies is even more severe (Stiles, 1979).

We Are Measuring the Active Ingredients

A crucial assumption in the clinical trial of a drug is that the investigation is manipulating or at least measuring the biologically active ingredients. Therapists and clients emit an enormous variety of verbal and nonverbal behaviors within psychotherapy sessions, and researchers have no assurance that those aspects not measured in a given study are inert, analogous to fillers and flavors.

The Therapist's Behavior Contains
the Active Ingredients

Many research designs, and some theoretical writings by therapists and researchers, assume implicitly that therapeutic change is instigated by the therapist's contribution and that the level of the active ingredients is mostly under the therapist's control. A problem for this therapist-centered view is posed by the "equivalence paradox" (Stiles et al., 1986): Whereas comparative process studies confirm that therapist verbal behaviors differ sharply and systematically across theoretical approaches, comparative outcome studies show no differential efficacy. If therapists of different schools are behaving in such grossly different ways and yet are having similar results, the possibility of finding associations between specific therapist behaviors and outcomes seems remote.

The Dose–Response Curve Is Ascending and Linear in the Range We Are Examining

Users of the drug metaphor in process–outcome research often proceed on the tacit assumption that the more of a "good" process quality in a therapy, the more beneficial the effects (e.g., Gomes-Schwartz, 1978; Sloane, Staples, Cristol, Yorkston, & Whipple, 1975; Stiles et al., 1988). Drug research itself is less naive. The shape of the dose–response curve has to be investigated, not assumed. Several alternatives to the "more is better" linear model have been proposed, such as a hierarchy of process steps; a step function whereby a process variable need only be sufficiently present to achieve its effects (the "good enough" therapist); floor and ceiling effects; and the possibility of toxicity of process variables at high dosages, producing inverted-U curves. Insofar as session time is usually limited, each intervention has an opportunity cost; high levels of one component may squeeze out other components.

A Component's Therapeutic Value Is Best Demonstrated by a Controlled Clinical Trial

The drug metaphor suggests that the best way to demonstrate that therapeutic ingredients are indeed active is the controlled, comparative trial (Elkin, Parloff, Hadley & Autry, 1985; Klerman, 1986; Yeaton & Sechrest, 1981). The design of pharmacological studies typically involves experimental manipulation of the dosage of a drug, administered at random to different groups of participants, perhaps during randomly determined time periods within a study. This design is rare in psychotherapy process–outcome studies. In comparative randomized clinical trials of psychotherapies (e.g., Elkin et al., 1989; Shapiro & Firth, 1987; Sloane et al., 1975), the compared treatments have differed in many ways. It seems unrealistic to expect to conduct a full-scale clinical trial in which the only difference between groups is a single process component (e.g., percentage of therapist interpretations); however, this is what is required if each "ingredient" is to be properly evaluated via the controlled trial method. Even a factorial design in which two or three such "ingredients" are manipulated independently of one another could scarcely account for all the process differences among treatment packages.

Accommodating to this difficulty, most process–outcome research has been correlational in design, comparing outcomes with processes that vary naturally or that covary within much grosser manipulations (e.g., within treatment packages). However, the correlational approach has flaws of its own, as considered in the next section.

THE CORRELATION CRITERION PROBLEM

A standard criterion for judging the value of a psychotherapy process component (e.g., reflection of feeling) has been the degree to which it correlates with outcome measures. It has been assumed that if a particular process component is therapeutically active, then lower incidence leads to poorer outcomes, whereas higher incidence leads to better outcomes; therefore, the process and the outcome should be positively correlated across clients. Conversely, if its incidence is uncorrelated with outcome, then that component was taken to be therapeutically inert.

Broadly speaking, correlational analysis can yield either positive or null findings. A positive result is, of course, vulnerable to the traditional problems of inferring causation from correlation; investigators and reviewers have generally been sensitive to the point that they cannot infer from a significant process–outcome correlation that the process component has caused the outcome, insofar as the causation may run in the other direction or may be attributable to additional, unmeasured factors. For example, clients' pre-existing characteristics (e.g., intelligence or ability to form intense interpersonal relationships) may predispose them to have positive processes and positive outcomes, so that the two are positively correlated even though there may be no causal link between them. (In principle, such possibilities are testable; in practice, however, few studies have sufficiently comprehensive assessment or sufficiently large samples to perform the required multivariate analyses.)

Another important type of alternative explanation is represented by the "early outcome" problem described above. Process measurements taken from ongoing therapy may be the result, rather than the cause, of client improvement. In this respect, the typical ordering of process and outcome assessments may be misleading (Stiles, Shapiro, & Firth-Cozens, 1990). For example, improvement ("outcome") may enable some clients to tolerate more interpretation or to engage in deeper self-exploration ("process").

Null correlations may be equally misleading. Reviewers have interpreted the absence of a significant correlation across several studies as indicating that the process component does not contribute to the outcome. However, interpreting null correlations as suggesting a lack of efficacy is an error because (among other reasons) it overlooks wide variation in client requirements for particular process components and therapist responsiveness to those requirements. Any such responsiveness tends to attenuate (and may even reverse) the process–outcome correlation (Stiles, 1988).

We use the term "requirement" to denote any condition that facilitates a given client's benefit from therapy. The condition is considered a requirement in the abstract sense that without it, that client is less likely to benefit. Different clients require different amounts of process components (e.g., different numbers of questions, different amounts of eye contact, different degrees of emotional support). Furthermore, client requirements may change from time to time (e.g., events during an encounter may engender a need for more or fewer questions).

Responsiveness is a general feature of human verbal interaction, including psychotherapy (Goodwin, 1981; Kent, Davis, & Shapiro, 1978; Labov & Fanshel, 1977; Sacks, Schegloff, & Jefferson, 1974). Much of therapeutic training and supervision is specifically directed toward adapting to particular clients' resources and requirements. Therapists devote close attention to such issues as the choice of areas to explore, the timing and accuracy of interventions, and the depth at which an issue is confronted. Decisions about such issues turn on client requirements and resources. The effect is that clients who require more of a process component tend to get more, and those who require less tend to get less.

To the degree that therapists are responsive to client requirements, process–outcome correlations will be attenuated. Deviations from optimum will not improve outcomes. In the extreme, if therapists were perfectly responsive with respect to a process component, its expected correlation with outcome (at least the correlation attributable to the underlying causal relationship) would be zero even for components that have helped to cause those outcomes, insofar as no outcome variance would be accounted for by failure to provide an appropriate level of the process component.

As an illustration, consider therapist questions in cognitive therapy. Therapists who know what information is needed to formulate treatment will respond by asking additional questions when answers are incomplete. To the extent that they are successful, clients will be asked only as many questions as required to elicit the essential information. Statistically, then, there would be variation both in therapist questioning (responsive to client needs) and presumably in outcomes (for reasons other than lack of information about current stressors), but these would not be expected to covary, even though the questioning may be crucially and causally important to the outcomes achieved by the treatment.

Under certain conditions, the process–outcome correlations can even be reversed. Suppose that client requirements for a component vary greatly—again, take questions about current stressors in cognitive therapy as an example. Suppose further that therapists' responsiveness to this variation is substantial but imperfect: They tend to ask few questions of well-organized clients because they get the needed information quickly, whereas they tend to ask more questions of recalcitrant clients and still fail to get complete information. Then, to the extent that the information gathered via such questions contributes to positive outcomes, clients who have given incomplete information will tend to have received relatively more questions but to have relatively poorer outcomes. That is, a process component may have a negative correlation with positive outcomes that it promotes. Reviewers who see such a negative correlation may well infer that the component is inert or harmful.

WHY RELY ON THE DRUG METAPHOR?

If the drug metaphor is so inadequate, then why has the field seemed so addicted to it? Perhaps it is because, with no consensus about which theory is best, process research conducted within one framework is seen as trivial or outlandish from another viewpoint. The drug metaphor has served as a conceptual lowest common denominator—a simple model that proponents of all schools (and journal reviewers of diverse orientations) can use. More broadly, the drug metaphor represents an example of the componential thinking common in scientific research: the strategy of conceptualizing a phenomenon in terms of discriminable elements—variables or factors—that contribute to causing the phenomenon.

The drug metaphor may also have psychological appeal that is independent of its explanatory power. Its attributional bias toward the therapist as change agent may serve the profession's need to see itself as potent. Finally, the example of medicine is a socially powerful, economically compelling one for psychotherapy.

The drug metaphor has had value as a stimulus for examining process closely (in search of "active ingredients") and as a source of hope (in the extreme, the possible discovery of a "miracle process component" that will do for psychological problems what penicillin did for bacterial infections). However, as we have tried to show, the drug metaphor is seriously flawed in several respects, so that research guided by it can lead to erroneous conclusions. We suggest that it has exhausted its usefulness in psychotherapy process–outcome research (Stiles & Shapiro, 1989, in press).

AN ALTERNATIVE TO THE DRUG METAPHOR: THE ASSIMILATION MODEL

There are alternatives to the drug metaphor approach (see Stiles & Shapiro, 1989, along with other chapters in the present volume). In the remainder of this chapter, we describe one such alternative—a qualitative approach using the "assimilation model," which dissects "outcome" into changes in specific ideas, attitudes, or themes. This approach traces changes in clients' ideas across a series of psychotherapy sessions to test the hypothesis that the assimilation of problematic experiences follows a predictable path. Episodes dealing with a common theme or problem are extracted from session tape recordings and examined intensively for movement along the predicted path. By studying change in specific ideas, this new approach circumvents the vagueness and the methodological problems of assessing global long-term change, and may make it more feasible to link changes with specific in-therapy processes.

The assimilation model (Stiles, Elliott, et al., 1990) draws on conceptual and empirical work by Piaget (1962, 1970), Rogers (1959), and others to define a systematic sequence of changes in an experience (memory, feeling, idea, impulse, wish, attitude) during psychotherapy. Briefly, the model proposes that a problematic experience (an experience that is threatening to the client) is gradually assimilated into a schema (frame of reference, narrative, theory, philosophy, script, theme) that is developed during the therapist–client interaction. As the client assimilates an experience, a schema gradually changes to accommodate it and "takes it in"—integrates it, explains it, gives cognitive access to it, incorporates it into its system of associations. ("Assimilation" and "accommodation" are complementary; in using either term alone, we mean to recognize that both processes are active jointly.) After being assimilated, the formerly problematic experience is part of the schema; thus, a schema comes to consist partly of the personal insights achieved during therapy.

The model suggests that a problematic experience can be tracked through predictable stages of assimilation: from being warded off, to entering awareness as unwanted thoughts, to becoming clarified as a problem, to attracting understanding and insight, to contributing to adaptive changes, and finally to being mastered and integrated into everyday life. As the experience passes through these stages, the client is hypothesized to have a parallel sequence of emotional reactions: from being oblivious and uncaring, to experiencing the content as acutely painful, then as problematic but less distressing, then as merely puzzling, then as understood (sometimes with shock or amazement), and finally—after the understanding has been applied and worked through—as confidently mastered.

Assimilation of problematic experiences is proposed as a change process common to various forms of psychotherapy. The model is not prescriptive; that is, it does not specify the best therapeutic methods to promote the hypothesized sequence of change. However, if the sequence can be measured and verified, it can provide a reference point for evaluating the effectiveness of alternative techniques.

We review here an initial effort to track selected problematic experiences across sessions. To do this, we extracted and rated passages dealing with a common topic or theme from tape recordings of sessions. We used qualitative methods to assess the assimilation of the problematic experiences we identified, tracing the change in the content of clients' experience, as inferred from the selected passages. We also developed a rating scale to assess degree of assimilation (Stiles et al., 1991).

The Assimilation of Problematic Experiences Scale

The Assimilation of Problematic Experiences Scale (APES; Stiles et al., 1991) began with Elliott's list of "immediate therapeutic impacts," which he derived from clients' open-ended descriptions of helpful and unhelpful events within therapy sessions (Elliott, 1985; Elliott, James, Reimschuessel, Cislo, & Sack, 1985). This list has been modified and expanded, as well as ordered according to the assimilation model. The version we used in this study is an anchored 8-point rating scale. Each rating must be associated with an explicit topic; that is, the rating reflects the degree of assimilation of particular content, which is stated in making each rating.

The APES triangulates, using both cognitive and affective features to assign a rating from 0 to 7. Intermediate ratings (e.g., 0.7, 3.1, 5.5) are allowed. There is no assumption that every topic must start at level 0; the problems clients bring to therapy may represent any level. Here is a synopsis of the anchor points:

0. *Warded off.* Content is unformed; the client is unaware of the problem. An experience is considered as warded off if there is evidence of actively avoiding emotionally disturbing topics (e.g., immediately changing a subject raised by the therapist). Affect may be minimal, reflecting successful avoidance, or diffuse and negative.

1. *Unwanted thoughts.* Content reflects emergence of thoughts associated with discomfort. The client prefers not to think about the experience; topics are raised by the therapist or external circumstances. Affect (which is often more salient than the content) involves strong or overwhelming negative feelings—anxiety, fear, anger, sadness. Despite the feelings' intensity, they may be unfocused, and their connection with the content may be unclear.

2. *Vague awareness.* The client acknowledges the existence of a problematic experience, and describes uncomfortable associated thoughts, but cannot formulate the problem clearly. Affect includes acute psychological pain or panic clearly associated with the problematic thoughts and experiences.

3. *Problem statement/clarification.* Content includes a clear statement of a problem—something that could be or is being worked on. Affect is negative but manageable, not panicky.

4. *Understanding/insight.* The problematic experience is placed

into a schema, formulated, understood, with clear connective links. Affect may be mixed, with some unpleasant recognitions, but with curiosity or even pleasant surprise of the "aha" sort.

5. *Application/working through.* The understanding is used to work on a problem; there is reference to specific problem-solving efforts, though without complete success. The client may describe considering alternatives or systematically selecting courses of action. Affective tone is positive, businesslike, optimistic.

6. *Problem solution.* The client achieves a successful solution for a specific problem. Affect is positive, satisfied, proud of accomplishment.

7. *Mastery.* The client successfully uses solutions in new situations; this generalizing is largely automatic, not salient. Affect is positive when the topic is raised, but otherwise neutral (i.e., this is no longer something to get excited about).

Our purpose in introducing this scale here is to illustrate its application and then to discuss the issues raised in attempting to make quantitative ratings of an experience whose content is continually changing. That is, we offer the APES as a springboard for discussion rather than as a finished measuring instrument (cf. Field, Barkham, Shapiro, & Stiles, in press).

In this study, we applied the APES with full knowledge of both the case to be rated and the assimilation model. Consequently, the ratings are subject to biases and should be viewed as an additional, numeric language for communicating our impressions rather than as an independent measure.

Longitudinal Study of Assimilation: Method

We studied four clients who participated in the Sheffield Psychotherapy Project, a comparative study of two brief psychotherapies administered in a crossover design (Shapiro & Firth, 1987). Each client received eight sessions of a psychodynamic–interpersonal treatment (also called "exploratory therapy") and by 8 sessions of a cognitive-behavioral treatment (also called prescriptive therapy) in counterbalanced order, with the same therapist throughout.

An assessment battery was administered to each client in the Sheffield Project four times: before treatment began, after the first eight sessions, at termination, and again 3 months later. The battery included, among other measures, a structured interview that assessed psychological symptoms via the Present State Examination (PSE; Wing, Cooper, & Sartorius, 1974) and self-report questionnaires, including the Symptom Checklist—90 (SCL-90; Derogatis, Lipman, & Covi, 1973), and the Beck Depression Inventory (BDI; Beck, Ward, Mendelson, Mock, & Erbaugh, 1961). Clients' mean improvement, assessed as change on these measures from pretreatment to termination, was substantial—clinically as well as statistically significant—and the improvement was maintained at the 3-month follow-up (Shapiro & Firth, 1987).

The clients we selected for intensive study had shown relatively large changes on the assessment measures. We believed that, as these clients had shown substantial overall change, we would find evidence of change in specific problematic experiences in their sessions.

We have selected one theme from one of the four cases for presentation in this chapter. In the case of June, we have selected a process-oriented problem that began as a clearly stated (APES rating = 3) impediment to treatment and moved to problem solution (APES rating = 6), at least within the context of therapy. Themes from the other cases have been presented elsewhere (Stiles et al., 1991; Stiles, Shapiro, Harper, & Morrison, 1994).

June: Control of Expression of Feelings

June was a 33-year-old woman employed as a counselor, who was referred by her physician for treatment for depression. The problems she identified initially included lack of confidence, problems with facing colleagues at work, difficulties in communicating with her husband, and guilt regarding her mother. She received the psychodynamic–interpersonal treatment for her first eight sessions and the cognitive-behavioral treatment for her second eight sessions. Her substantial improvement during treatment is shown by changes in her scores from 31 at intake to 13 at termination on the PSE, from 26 to 2 on the BDI, and from 151 to 14 on the SCL-90.

A central theme of June's treatment was her self-containment, which had led to her feeling isolated and lonely. An important subtheme early in therapy was her difficulty in revealing and discussing her feelings. Drawing on her professional understanding of the psychotherapeutic process, June entered therapy with a fairly clear awareness of this difficulty in her relationship to the therapist. She worked systematically during the first two sessions, and by session 3 had developed a cognitive understanding of her deep reluctance to express her feelings. She then began to use this understanding to overcome the reluctance, both inside and outside of the therapeutic sessions. She became able to describe her current feelings openly and to bring them to bear on other problems.

We here trace the assimilation of June's initial problematic overcontrol of expressing feelings during her first four (psychodynamic–interpersonal) sessions. Note that this problematic experience was already partially assimilated when June began treatment.

June's anxiety about revealing her feelings was explicit from the beginning of the first session:

JUNE: I'll now know how our patients feel . . . It's quite anxious.

THERAPIST: Sort of anxious about what's going to happen to you or anxious about revealing yourself.

JUNE: . . . I suppose I'm worried about my own pain and—I'm quite private—and things I don't usually tell people . . . and how I'll go away feeling. . . .

THERAPIST: So you really feel that you can be very badly hurt.

JUNE: Um. Not . . . I don't think hurt as much as giving a lot of myself. . . . It has to be usually crises, usually, before I can do that, and I think going to the doctor [who referred me to this psychotherapy] was one of those times. I thought I just had a bug or an infection of some sort and he said, "No, it's not; I think you need to talk to someone," and I was really sort of shocked.

THERAPIST: That came as a surprise.

JUNE: Yes. Yes. I thought I was self-contained, you know, I listen to other people's problems.

Later in session 1, June described an incident in which her self-containment was breached. In this episode, she introduced the concept of "control," which was central to the schema she later used to understand the problem:

JUNE: And it's just got, I feel, out of control, the situation [at home], the whole thing. I don't know where I stand any more. . . . And so I carry on vacuuming the floor and making the beds and whatever I do, and—

THERAPIST: And pretending it isn't happening and not talking about it outside.

JUNE: Not, not at all. I told C. at work, who was very nice. . . . I was counseling for 2 or 3 hours, and . . . when I came out—I've been there for 3 years—and for the first time I sat down, and W., who works there, said . . . "Was it bad?" And I just burst into floods of tears all over them. That's the first time I've ever brought that sort of thing to work like that. . . . But I haven't said anything since. They say, "How is it at home?" and I say, "It's all right."

THERAPIST: So the shutters have gone back up.

JUNE: . . . No one's actually said, "Why don't we go out for a drink and talk about it." . . . If they'd said that, I'd have taken them up on it. But I suppose because, you know, I'm, you know, not the sort of person to do that.

THERAPIST: Right. So private. I mean, they've really got to struggle with that sense of invading your privacy.

JUNE: Mm-hm. I'll never let them do it. I wouldn't.

These passages show June's awareness of her difficulty of acknowledging feelings and personal vulnerabilities, stated clearly enough to qualify as a problem to be worked on. It is important to distinguish between June's depression (the content of her concerns, the "floods of tears," and related difficulties at home) and her explicit reluctance to acknowledge or discuss her feelings with others. What concerns us here is the latter— the anxiety and avoidance associated with any breaching of June's self-contained privacy. The combination of fairly clear awareness and strong but controllable negative affect suggests an APES rating slightly below 3, perhaps 2.8, for the problematic reluctance to reveal or discuss her feelings.

In session 2, June worked systematically on this issue. Near the beginning of the session, June reported a friend's comments about what the therapist had said in the first session. (The talk with the friend may itself be considered as work on this issue.)

JUNE: She said . . . , "You do present this package of being able to cope," and said she found it very hard to talk about anything personal with me because I'll just either change the subject or brush it off as if it's not very important. . . . I suppose, I mean, that I find it hard to take time off and look at myself. . . . Always seems to be something to do rather than sit, and I can see I've just avoided it completely.

And later, in talking about her reactions to the first session:

JUNE: Well, it was sadness at what happened, you know, things I found very difficult to cope with. . . . It was confronting my own feelings, which I'm beginning to realize I'm awful at, and won't do— but I had to and felt very sad.

The "sadness" here concerned her depression, which was also being explored in therapy. Our focus, however, is on the problematic resistance to expressing the sadness. As June worked on this issue, she began to move from her initial anxiety to a preliminary sense of progress:

JUNE: A weary sadness—well, this is it now. You know things are going to be different. There's no going back to my sort of blocking my feelings.

In the following passage, she again described her fears in terms of lack of control:

JUNE: I also realized I'm a very good skater-over of things . . . After the most horrific quarrels and I've gone into work and people have said, "Are you okay?" and I've said, "Yeah, fine," you know. Probably find the whole thing such a burden and sort of out of control a lot of the time, the home thing. And it's going back again, if I talked about it someone would confront me on something.

A few minutes later, the therapist picked up on the control concept, thus helping to elaborate the schema:

THERAPIST: . . . feeling that you're not in control, that he and I can get things out of you and maybe there's a sense of being manipulated, exploited.

JUNE: I feel that about a lot of things that go on in my life. I went to see E. T. [at the cinema], and I could have killed Steven Spielberg because I cried all the way through. I really wanted to wring his neck, you know. I thought, "You're doing this to me."

THERAPIST: "How dare you make me cry!"

JUNE: Yes, that's right, that's right. . . . If anyone would ask me, I would say I was a very emotional person—coming from my [ethnic] background, I don't see how anyone could not be. . . . It's a very stormy family. And I thought I could shout and cry and rage and scream with the best of them, which I think I can. And I thought that was what was called being emotional . . . and when I shout, I feel angry with myself for shouting . . . and I'm very angry with the person. How could this person have put me in this position that I'm behaving like some nonhuman being, shouting? . . . I've felt dreadful because it was me who was shouting and thinking, "Well, why did you provoke me in this way? Look what you've done." . . . Everyone [in my family] used to shout all the time. And I suppose I still see shouting as going to lead to other things. Once you start shouting, you know it's going to lead into other things. You're going to get absolutely out of—

THERAPIST: Out of control.

JUNE: Control. And I still get very worried when people raise their voices.

THERAPIST: You're terrified of feelings getting out of control.

JUNE: I'm not at work. I'm not in my profession. . . . You know, that doesn't worry me . . . that's safe in there. Yes—I hadn't thought about that.

I used to listen, if I heard shouting, . . . at the top of the stairs and think, "Oh, no, not again."

The insight marker "I hadn't thought about that" signals June's new understanding, connecting her current reluctance to discuss her own feelings with her childhood fear of her family getting out of control (APES rating = 4).

Near the end of session 2, with the therapist's prodding, June began to apply this new understanding to other issues, including the exploration of her depression and current relationships:

JUNE: . . . I'm going to have to stop running, aren't I?

THERAPIST: Stop running?

JUNE: Um, yeah. (*Pause for 45 seconds.*)

THERAPIST: I'm just wondering if this is like the sadness again.

JUNE: I was just thinking of the things I thought I was and I'm not. . . . I must have a hell of a system going, to allow me to do that. Why didn't it come out in my training? I probably wouldn't let it. Yeah (*sigh*).

THERAPIST: You know, you're a very effective and very powerful person.

JUNE: Um? Sorry?

THERAPIST: You're a very effective and very powerful person, and when you use that in a way that keeps things where they are, there's not many people going to get through, you know, get though the armor and sort of make contact with the other side of you.

JUNE: That's what [my husband] is always saying and I never believed him. I always thought I was, you know, just the opposite.

In session 3, this understanding—that June became personally powerful (i.e., exerted control, self-containment) as a way of avoiding the chaos of out-of-control feelings—was further elaborated. In the following passage, June was talking about how she was made to feel that she had split up the family:

THERAPIST: So you're the destructive one who breaks up families.

JUNE: It seems so. It seemed so. . . .

THERAPIST: So there's something very loaded maybe about saying you were a powerful person (*laughs*).

JUNE: That really got me, yes. . . .

THERAPIST: So in a way, people have been telling you this before, that you're powerfully destructive.

JUNE: (*sigh*) I never associated it with power. It was only when you said it last week and I thought, "And power in some ways means in control." And the things people have accused me of seemed very . . . seemed that I wasn't in control of, 'cause I wouldn't have done them if I'd known what I was doing.

June also elaborated her understanding by exploring the origins of her need to control her feelings in her past and current relationship with her mother. For example, she recalled, "I've never in my life—and it's something my mother is very proud of—that I've never answered her back. . . . That means so much to her."

June proceeded to discuss—openly—the feelings of helpless rage she often experienced, and the guilt she felt whenever she breached her self-control and expressed the rage (e.g., by throwing things at the wall). This openness contrasted with her initial anxiety about discussing any feelings.

THERAPIST: . . . I wonder if you get any sense of you whilst we're talking.

JUNE: I feel that I'm being very honest and I don't know if I am, but I don't feel as if I'm avoiding feelings. I'm not even trying, so that doesn't come into it, which doesn't happen usually.

THERAPIST: No, you're getting on with things. You're working. . . .

JUNE: . . . I have a hell of a lot of work to do before I can begin to feel and see a lot of things. I mean, that's how it makes me feel, but it doesn't make me unhappy. . . . It's confronting what has to be done and I'm not blocking the confrontation. . . . I don't know how I'm coming over, but I feel as if I'm not, as I usually do, stopping it. . . . For the first time, I've felt this is worth working at. I can feel something for the first time. I mean, of course I've felt things the last [two sessions], but this time I've felt that there's a glimmer.

These passages taken from session 3 appear to represent elaboration and then working through of the understanding achieved in session 2. They illustrate her within-therapy success in overcoming the excessive control (at least enough to discuss her rage) and her positive sense of progress (APES rating = 5), though the context makes it clear that this falls short of a problem solution.

Further working through—relaxing the tight control— was accomplished in the time that intervened between sessions 3 and 4. June came to session 4 saying, "I've had a hell of a week . . . and had a few brushes with colleagues yesterday which I've never had before." The "few brushes with colleagues" concerned an angry reaction to some uncharacteristically critical (but constructively intended) remarks June had made at a meeting. Although June reported that "half of me didn't want all the fuss that it caused [because of] this self-contained part of me," she "got totally upset" and "because I was upset, people kept coming up to me and saying, 'It's not like you, June. Why are you so upset? You can handle her.' And I said, 'Well, I can't. I honestly can't.' " She concluded:

JUNE: I'm seeming to me more vulnerable than I thought I was. That does seem to be happening. Whether that's because . . . I'm generally feeling tired and working too hard . . . or whether it's because something's happening here and is showing me something I wasn't very aware of, I don't know. I'm confused about it. I wonder if it's a stage I'm going through or whether it's something else emerging.

June's uncharacteristic expression of feeling toward her colleagues may be understood as a further working through in practice of her initial reluctance (APES rating = 5.5). In the following passage from the middle of session 4, June made use of her new ability to describe her feelings openly in order to do constructive work on other problems in therapy.

THERAPIST: So you're . . . all the time having to try and control your temper, to try and stop you doing things that are too painful.

JUNE: And accepting it here is easier than dealing with it. But then I can't live with it afterwards and in fact confront it with myself, which is just as painful really. And probably worse, because I've no one to actually say it to.

THERAPIST: . . . We should try to find a way through it. . . . Let's start with how you're feeling right now.

JUNE: I feel dizzy and worried . . . a lot of despair, I think. . . . The task seems so great that will I ever cope with it or will I be able to do the things that I would like to do? . . . It's not what I want to do or be. So therefore I'm going against my inner self. I'm sort of projecting this image which I don't want to. Okay, so I've realized that. So the despair is about what I want to do. . . .

THERAPIST: Sort of feeling that maybe it's not safe to get in touch with other bits and pieces.

JUNE: I feel that now, but I don't when I go away. . . . When I leave, I always feel a bit frightened and a bit sad. . . . But tomorrow I won't. . . . But when I'm sitting here, it does frighten me, and you just made me face up to it, with the "How do you feel here and now?" And I was still worried.

In this passage, June appeared to have solved—or nearly solved—her initial problem, anxiety over revealing feelings to her therapist (APES rating = 5.8 or 6). That is, she actively revealed her feelings in the service of productive therapeutic work. This by no means implies that she was aware of all of her feelings; it merely indicates that she could recognize and then let go of her unreasoning need to control what she disclosed to others, particularly to the therapist. This solution contributed to the optimism June expressed near the end of session 4:

JUNE: . . . I feel that the time has come and . . . being prepared for the first time in as long as I can remember to actually decide on something and go through with it, however painful, knowing what a great one I've been at avoiding pain. . . . But I have realized that, which I think is the first step. Surely. But I still feel frightened.

June's progress in relaxing her conscious control over revealing her feelings thus greatly facilitated her ability to work in therapy. It also opened her to a variety of other frightening possibilities, involving the experiencing and expression of underlying sadness and rage. That is, the problematic experience whose assimilation we have traced here, from stage 3 (problem statement) to stage 6 (problem solution) was a preliminary one; that became a process tool, permitting more productive, open use of the psychotherapeutic relationship.

Our qualitative tracking of this theme in this successful therapy revealed successive transformations of content approximating those proposed by the assimilation model and summarized in the APES. June moved from recognition of a problematic reluctance to reveal her feelings, through an understanding in terms of childhood fears of being out of control, to a relaxation of the tight control both inside and outside the therapy sessions.

DISCUSSION

Research based on the drug metaphor and the associated correlational approach to process–outcome relationships has failed to identify a clear set of active ingredients for treating psychological disorders. But while the drug metaphor leads up blind alleys, the alternative paths—including the assimilation approach—are largely untraveled and unmarked. The assimilation approach moves beyond some of the roadblocks encountered in the traditional approaches, such as those listed earlier. But it does not get by all of them, and it encounters some additional obstacles. Further exploration is needed to see how far assimilation or other qualitative approaches can take us.

The case of June illustrates how the assimilation approach overcomes the usual distinction between psychotherapy process and psychotherapy outcome. The content of ongoing client–therapist dialogue (process) indexed substantive changes in the client's way of being in the world (outcome). For example, June's progress in revealing and discussing feelings with her therapist during sessions was directly parallel to changes in her relationships with her co-workers. The cognitive and affective changes of assimilation are both process and outcome, and the approach illuminates how arbitrary the process–outcome distinction has been. Perhaps there is no need to search for a path from process to outcome because they have been inseparable all along.

The assimilation approach avoids metaphors that cast the curative factors in psychotherapy as ingredients—substances that are administered to clients to cause specific changes. It does not require the assumption that process components are pure. It does not suggest that process components should be divided into active ingredients on the one hand, and fillers and flavors. And it does not assume that the curative power of therapy resides in the therapist's correct performance of specified behaviors at the correct dosage. Instead, the focus is on the changes within the client. There is no necessity that there be any fixed relationship between particular process components and changes within clients, as the appropriateness of an intervention may vary in myriad ways with differences in clients and situations. Each change is understood in its particular context. The assimilation approach forces attention to the requirement that interventions be appropriately responsive to a client's current state of mind.

The strong focus on the client in the June example is not meant to imply that the therapist is unimportant. Rather, this is merely a first step, and further work is necessary to identify ways in which therapists facilitate the assimilation process. (See Stiles et al., 1994, for some preliminary work in this direction.) A detailed description of the process of change in the client should indicate where and how therapist interventions might be effective.

As presented here, the assimilation approach is a qualitative approach, which invokes a different epistemology than that of either the controlled experiment of the clinical trial or the correlational approach usually employed in process–outcome research. Among the differences entailed are (1) use of linguistic rather than exclusively numeric results; (2) use of empathy as a data access strategy; and (3) accommodation to the nonlinear, probably chaotic relationships among variables of interest (Stiles, 1990, 1993).

The "results" of the June case consist of the dialogue between therapist and client, not the projection of this onto dimensions specified by some coding system. The words are not reduced to numbers. The profit of this use of language as results is in its greater realism and clinical richness, in contrast to the impoverished descriptions provided by, for example, comparing percentages of therapist interpretations or ratings of empathy with change scores on symptom severity inventories. The cost is in the loss of the ease of manipulation (e.g., for inferential statistics) that quantification affords. In particular, it is far more difficult to assess the truth or falsity of linguistic than of numeric generalizations, because the former cannot be reduced to a probability that some null hypothesis is true.

Our use of the APES, a numeric scale, requires some comment in this regard. We have used the APES as an aid to precision in

constructing our interpretation, not as a source of data to be analyzed. That is, the APES ratings do not constitute an independent
measure of change; rather, they are used to convey our impression
of how much change occurred. If we thought differently, we would
change the numbers.

The assimilation approach makes direct demands on our (the
researchers') and your (the readers') ability to understand empathi-
cally the experience of psychotherapy clients. The client's words are
considered as reflecting meanings experienced by the client, and it
is the task of a researcher to interpret those words (e.g., by selectively
presenting them) in a way that conveys the meanings to readers. To
put it another way, clients are observed from the inside; empathic
understandings of the experiences they report constitute data to be
analyzed. This represents a break from the behaviorist tradition that
organisms should be observed only from the outside, and that inferences about internal processes must be based on explicit deduc-
tions from those observations (Stiles, 1993).

The assimilation approach can accommodate nonlinear, and
even chaotic, relationships between process and outcome. As discussed earlier (in the context of the failure of the correlation criterion), psychotherapy process and outcome are obviously in a nonlinear relationship to each other, insofar as outcome (i.e., the client's
psychological reaction to therapeutic procedures) continually feeds
back to affect process. In such systems, relationships between variables are likely to be chaotic—that is, deterministic but unpredictable because of sensitive dependence on initial conditions (Gleick,
1987). To illustrate, a therapist's way of phrasing a particular question may evoke an answer that sets off a particularly productive line
of inquiry. This may lead to a positive outcome that would not have
occurred if the phrasing had been slightly different. Although such
an interweaving of events can be unraveled in retrospect, there is no
practical possibility that the end product (e.g., the client's state at
some time after treatment) could be predicted, because the required
precision and density of sampling would be too great. As a start, one
would need to code for all possible phrasings of all possible topics.
The chaotic relationships ensue not because particular phrasings are
powerful determinants of outcome, but because the small effects of
any phrasing quickly feed back to influence both parties' subsequent
phrasings and experience, leading the dialogue in unpredictable
directions.

Qualitative accounts of psychotherapy process can lead beyond the particulars of one case to descriptions of general patterns (such as the assimilation model). These may be of use to practitioners in recognizing or conceptualizing what is taking place, and in suggesting paths of intervention. However, they do not lead to lawlike generalizations about the relation of process components to outcomes.

ACKNOWLEDGMENT

Portions of the research reported in this chapter were supported by a grant by the Miami University Faculty Research Committee to William B. Stiles.

REFERENCES

Beck, A. T., Ward, C. H., Mendelson, M., Mock, J., & Erbaugh, J. (1961). An inventory for measuring depression. *Archives of General Psychiatry, 4,* 561–571.

Butler, S. F., & Strupp, H. H. (1986). Specific and nonspecific factors in psychotherapy: A problematic paradigm for psychotherapy research. *Psychotherapy, 23,* 30–40.

Derogatis, L. R., Lipman, R. S., & Covi, M. D. (1973). SCL-90, an outpatient rating scale: Preliminary report. *Psychopharmacology Bulletin, 9,* 13–20.

Elliott, R. (1985). Helpful and nonhelpful events in brief counseling interviews: An empirical taxonomy. *Journal of Counseling Psychology, 32,* 307–322.

Elliott, R., James, E., Reimschuessel, C., Cislo, D., & Sack, N. (1985). Significant events and the analysis of immediate therapeutic impacts. *Psychotherapy, 22,* 620–630.

Elkin, I., Parloff, M. B., Hadley, S. W., & Autry, J. H. (1985). NIMH Treatment of Depression Collaborative Research Program: Background and research plan. *Archives of General Psychiatry, 42,* 305–316.

Elkin, I., Shea, M. T., Watkins, J. T., Imber, S. D., Sotsky, S. M., Collins, J. F., Glass, D. R., Pilkonis, P. A., Leber, W. R., Docherty, J. P., Fiester, S. J., & Parloff, M. B. (1989). National Institute of Mental Health Treatment of Depression Collaborative Research Program: General effectiveness of treatments. *Archives of General Psychiatry, 46,* 971–982.

Field, S., Barkham, M., Shapiro, D. A., & Stiles, W. B. (in press). Assessment of assimilation in psychotherapy: A quantitative case study of problematic experiences with a significant other. *Journal of counseling Psychology*.

Gleick, J. (1987). *Chaos: Making a new science*. New York: Penguin.

Gomes-Schwartz, B. (1978). Effective ingredients in psychotherapy: Prediction of outcome from process variables. *Journal of Consulting and Clinical Psychology, 46*, 1023–1035.

Goodwin, C. (1981). *Conversational organization: Interaction between speakers and hearers*. New York: Academic Press.

Kent, G. S., Davis, J. D., & Shapiro, D. A. (1978). Resources required in the construction and reconstruction of conversation. *Journal of Personality and Social Psychology, 36*, 13–22.

Klerman, G. L. (1986). Drugs and psychotherapy. In S. L. Garfield & A. E. Bergin (Eds.), *Handbook of psychotherapy and behavior change* (3rd ed., pp. 777–818). New York: Wiley.

Labov, W., & Fanshel, D. (1977). *Therapeutic discourse*. New York: Academic Press.

Lambert, M. J., Shapiro, D. A., & Bergin, A. E. (1986). The effectiveness of psychotherapy. In S. L. Garfield & A. E. Bergin (Eds.), *Handbook of psychotherapy and behavior change* (3rd ed., pp. 157–211). New York: Wiley.

Luborsky, L., Singer, B., & Luborsky, L. (1975). Comparative studies of psychotherapies: Is it true that "Everyone has won and all must have prizes"? *Archives of General Psychiatry, 32*, 995–1008.

McDaniel, S. H., Stiles, W. B., & McGaughey, K. J. (1981). Correlations of male college students' verbal response mode use in psychotherapy with measures of psychological disturbance and psychotherapy outcome. *Journal of Consulting and Clinical Psychology, 49*, 571–582.

Orlinsky, D. E., Grawe, K., & Parks, B. K. (1994). Process and outcome in psychotherapy—*Noch Einmal*. In A. E. Bergin & S. L. Garfield (Eds.), *Handbook of psychotherapy and behavior change* (4th ed., pp. 270–376). New York: Wiley.

Orlinsky, D. E., & Howard, K. I. (1986). Process and outcome in psychotherapy. In S. L. Garfield & A. E. Bergin (Eds.), *Handbook of psychotherapy and behavior change* (3rd ed., pp. 311–381). New York: Wiley.

Paul, G. L. (1967). Strategy of outcome research in psychotherapy. *Journal of Consulting Psychology, 31*, 109–118.

Piaget, J. (1962). *Play, dreams, and imitation in childhood* (C. Gattegno & F. M. Hodgson, Trans.). New York: Norton.

Piaget, J. (1970). Piaget's theory (G. Gellerier & J. Langer, Trans.). In P. H. Mussen (Ed.), *Carmichael's manual of child psychology* (3rd ed., Vol. 1, pp. 703–732). New York: Wiley.

Russell, R. L. (1986). The inadvisability of admixing psychoanalysis with other forms of psychotherapy. *Journal of Contemporary Psychotherapy, 16*, 76–85.

Rogers, C. R. (1959). A theory of therapy, personality, and interpersonal relationships, as developed by the client-centered framework. In S. Koch (Ed.), *Psychology: A study of a science. Vol. 3. Formulations of the person and the social context* (pp. 184–256). New York: McGraw-Hill.

Sacks, H., Schegloff, E. A., & Jefferson, G. A. (1974). A simplest systematics for the organization of turn-taking in dyadic conversation. *Language, 50*, 697–735.

Shapiro, D. A., & Firth, J. A. (1987). Prescriptive v. exploratory psychotherapy: Outcomes of the Sheffield Psychotherapy Project. *British Journal of Psychiatry, 151*, 790–799.

Sloane, R. B., Staples, F. R., Cristol, A. H., Yorkston, N. J., & Whipple, K. (1975). *Psychotherapy versus behavior therapy*. Cambridge, MA: Harvard University Press.

Smith, M. L., Glass, G. V., & Miller, T. I. (1980). *The benefits of psychotherapy*. Baltimore: John Hopkins University Press.

Stiles, W. B. (1979). Verbal response modes and psychotherapeutic technique. *Psychiatry, 42*, 49–62.

Stiles, W. B. (1988). Psychotherapy process-outcome correlations may be misleading. *Psychotherapy, 25*, 27–35.

Stiles, W. B. (1990). *Narrative in psychological research* (Occasional Papers in Psychology: Visiting Fellowship Series No. 1, ISSN 0110–6961). (Available from Department of Psychology, Massey University, Palmerston North, New Zealand)

Stiles, W. B. (1993). Quality control in qualitative research. *Clinical Psychology Review, 13*, 593–618

Stiles, W. B., Elliott, R., Llewelyn, S. P., Firth-Cozens, J. A., Margison, F. R., Shapiro, D. A., & Hardy, G. (1990). Assimilation of problematic experiences by clients in psychotherapy. *Psychotherapy, 27*, 411–420.

Stiles, W. B., Morrison, L. A., Haw, S. K., Harper, H., Shapiro, D. A., & Firth-Cozens, J. (1991). Longitudinal study of assimilation in exploratory psychotherapy. *Psychotherapy, 28*, 195–206.

Stiles, W. B., & Shapiro, D. A. (1989). Abuse of the drug metaphor in psychotherapy process-outcome research. *Clinical Psychology Review, 9*, 521–543.

Stiles, W. B., & Shapiro, D. A. (in press). Disabuse of the drug metaphor: Psychotherapy process–outcome correlations. *Journal of Consulting and Clinical Psychology*.

Stiles, W. B., Shapiro, D. A., & Elliott, R. (1986). Are all psychotherapies equivalent? *American Psychologist, 41*, 165–180.

Stiles, W. B., Shapiro, D. A., & Firth-Cozens, J. A. (1988). Verbal response

mode use in contrasting psychotherapies: A within-subjects comparison. *Journal of Consulting and Clinical Psychology, 56,* 727–733.
Stiles, W. B., Shapiro, D. A., & Firth-Cozens, J. A. (1990). Correlations of
session evaluations with treatment outcome. *British Journal of Clinical
Psychology, 29,* 13–21.
Stiles, W. B., Shapiro, D. A., Harper, H., & Morrison, L. A. (1994). *Therapist
contributions to psychotherapeutic assimilation: An alternative to the drug metaphor.* Manuscript submitted for publication.
Wing, J. K., Cooper, J. E., & Sartorius, N. (1974). *The measurement and
classification of psychiatric symptoms.* Cambridge, England: Cambridge
University Press.
Yeaton, W. H., & Sechrest, L. (1981). Critical dimensions in the choice and
maintenance of successful treatments: Strength, integrity, and effectiveness. *Journal of Consulting and Clinical Psychology, 49,* 156–167.

CHAPTER 3

Simplicity and Complexity in Psychotherapy Research

ROBERT ELLIOTT
CHERYL ANDERSON

> Our intuitions seem unanimous in favor of sparse
> ontologies, smooth curves, homogeneous universes,
> invariant equations, and impoverished assumptions.
> —ELLIOTT SOBER (*Simplicity*)

> Our life is frittered away by detail... simplify, simplify.
> —HENRY DAVID THOREAU (*Walden*)

> Simplicity is the most deceitful [lover] that ever betrayed
> man [or woman].
> —HENRY ADAMS (*The Education of Henry Adams*)

As therapists, we know that psychotherapy is a complex process. For example, we know that some events are more important that others, that many very different things happen in therapy, that context is absolutely crucial, that communications usually have more than one meaning, and that clients often surprise us with what they find important or helpful. We also know that we have learned far more about how to do therapy from descriptive accounts (by writers, supervisors, and clients) than from the quantitative results of psychotherapy research (Morrow-Bradley & Elliott, 1986). However, when we act as therapy researchers, we typically ignore this knowledge, following instead the simplifying assumptions we learned in graduate school as part of our positivist research tradition (cf. Lincoln & Guba, 1985; Polkinghorne, 1983).

We begin this chapter with a brief exploration of the issue of simplicity and complexity in science. We then present an analysis of

14 common simplifying assumptions found in psychotherapy research, together with opposing "complexifying" assumptions and our compromise recommendations. Next, we report an empirical examination of the assumptions inherent in a collection of 10 key therapy process–outcome studies. Finally, we offer some concluding comments and recommendations.

SIMPLICITY AND COMPLEXITY IN SCIENCE

Simplicity as a Goal

In science, simplicity is both a goal and a method. Scientists have generally seen themselves as seeking the hidden order in an apparently complex world, as bringing order out of chaos (Prigogine & Stengers, 1984). Einstein (quoted in Harré, 1983, p. 144) stated: "It is the grand object of all theory to make these irreducible elements as simple and as few as possible without having to renounce the adequate representation of any empirical content whatever." This search for simplicity in science is probably an expression of a more general human preference for simple structures, "a subjective selectivity that makes us tend to see the simple and miss the complex" (Quine, 1966, p. 243). For example, Gestalt psychologists have found that figures that are simple, symmetrical, and regular are more readily perceived than those that are not (Pollio, 1982).

On the other hand, Prigogine and Stengers (1984) argue that the particularly high value placed on simplicity in modern Western science probably has its roots in a foundational assumption of Western thought—that is, the belief that humans are distinct from their world. According to this assumption, (1) the natural world is basically passive; (2) human beings are separate from this world; and (3) humans are entitled (either by divine decree or by default) to manipulate and control the world. The search for simplicity is thus also the search for control, since what is simple is usually easier to predict and manipulate.

The Contrasting View: Complexity as a Goal

Harré (1972, p. 45) argues that "There can be no doubt that the history of science shows that the laws of nature are always more complex than we originally thought." Prigogine and Stengers (1984,

p. 48) suggest that the drive for simplicity is not universal or necessary, citing Needham: "The idea that nature was governed by simple, knowable laws appeared to [Chinese scholars of the 18th century] as a perfect example of anthropocentric foolishness." Instead, Prigogine and Stengers propose that it is time for scientists and members of the developed nations to enter into a "new dialogue" with nature, in which nature is seen as an active self-organizing partner with whom humans must cooperate in order to survive.

For Prigogine and Stengers (p. 7), the new dialogue with nature begins by recognizing that "Our universe has a pluralistic, complex character." They advocate studying complexity in order to discover its origin and structure, and are joined in this effort by proponents of the emerging sciences of "chaos" and "complexity" (Gleick, 1987; Waldrop, 1992)—sciences dedicated to the understanding of "messy" or nonlinear dynamic processes, such as the weather, the brain, social and economic systems, and even the development and evolution of life.

In fact, to state that humans generally prefer simplicity is itself an oversimplification. There is evidence that individuals differ in their preference for complexity versus simplicity, and that a preference for complexity is often found in creative scientists (Barron, 1969). If this is the case, we should see preferences for both simplicity and complexity expressed in science generally and in psychotherapy research in particular.

Psychology has more than its share of messy, chaotic phenomena to deal with, in the guise of the 80–95% of the variance left unaccounted for in the typical study. Psychotherapy researchers in search of the challenge of chaotic or complex systems need look no further than the "error variance" in their studies, including unexplained individual differences in clients' treatment outcomes, or unexpectedly strong client reactions to routine therapist interventions.

Simplicity and Complexity as Method

Simplicity not only is a goal in science, but also plays a key role as a method. Physical scientists and mathematicians prefer to work with very simple systems, hoping to "apply what they have discovered in these cases as principles when they turn to more involved cases" (Toulmin, 1960, p. 46; cf. Waldrop, 1992). Simplification is regarded as a necessary part of the process of acquiring knowledge, determining both the selection of research problems and the methods used.

However, as Bordin (1974) noted, there are good and bad simplifications. Unfortunately, as Bordin pointed out, philosophers of science provide little guidance on this critical issue (Anderson, Hughes, & Sharrock, 1986, make the same point). Instead, scientists are left with their own paradigms or research programs (Gholson & Barker, 1985) to guide their simplifications by providing them with metaphors and guiding assumptions.

Bordin (1974, p. 85) offered several guidelines for simplification in therapy research, but these put him on the side of the complexifiers: "We should start from and keep in central focus the natural phenomena which aroused our curiosity and about which we wish to know more. . . ." Indeed, the dialectic seems to be between those who like to keep their research problems neat and those who seek to go "back to the things themselves" in all their muddledness. For the most part, the simplifiers have been in ascendence in psychotherapy research, but there are signs that this is changing now.

COMMON SIMPLIFYING ASSUMPTIONS AND CONTRASTING VIEWS OF THERAPY PROCESS

Drawing on previous critiques in the psychotherapy research literature (e.g., Elliott, 1983a; Kiesler, 1973; Orlinsky & Howard, 1978; Rice & Greenberg, 1984; Stiles, 1988), we have revised an earlier list of oversimplifying assumptions (Elliott, 1989a). This list, given in Table 3.1, organizes simplifying assumptions into two major headings: "simplification by incompleteness" and "simplification by reliance on simple structure."

This overall division of simplifying assumptions derives from Harré's (1983, p. 138) distinction between two main meanings of the word "simplicity": (1) being "made up of very few parts," which he labels as "economy"; and (2) structural simplicity, which he refers to as "elegance." "Economy" is a version of Occam's Razor, commonly given as "entities must not be multiplied without necessity" (Sober, 1975, p. 41). In our discussion, we rely on a model of key elements of psychotherapeutic process for defining the "entities" that may or

TABLE 3.1. Common Simplifying Assumptions about Therapy Process

I. *Simplification by incompleteness* (fewer elements)
   (1) Single perspective for measurement (one perspective is enough)
   (2) Single variable type (one type of variable is enough)
   (3) Single level of measurement (one size unit is enough)
   (4) Stable effects across time (one point in time is enough for assessing effects)

II. *Simplification by reliance on simple structure*

   A. *Simplification of data structure*
      (5) Equal weighting of process units (all therapy events are equally important)
      (6) Independence of observations (data points are not related to one another)

   B. *Simplification of variable structure*
      1. *Simple main effects*
         (7) Simple combinations of variables (patterns, configurations are not important)
         (8) Context independence (context is not important for rating, variable selection)
         (9) Uniform relevance of variables (type of therapy/event is not important)
      2. *Simplification of causal structure*
         (10) Unidirectionality of causal influences (process always causes outcome)
         (11) Closed causal system (third variables are not important)
         (12) Direct effects (outcome is unmediated)
         (13) Linearity of cause–effect associations (process–outcome effects are consistent across a variable's range)
      3. *Simplification of measurement model*
         (14) Nominal scale measurement (only one thing happens at a time)

may not be left out in the conduct of research. We argue that, psychotherapy researchers, like the demon barber Sweeney Todd, have often overzealously applied Occam's Razor to the therapy process, destroying what they set out to study.

Structural simplicity, or "elegance," is critical in modern science but is notoriously difficult to define or measure (Harré, 1983). In order to apply this concept to psychotherapy research, we must specify the kinds of structures that may be involved in studying therapy. Fortunately, the classical distinction between data structure (the organization of observations in relation to each other) and variable structure (found in patterns of interrelationship among variables) (cf. Nunnally, 1978) provides a straightforward way of organizing structural simplifications. In our discussion of assumptions of structural simplicity, we argue that, by and large, the search for methodological elegance has resulted in impoverished clinical relevance.

In this section, then, we present our list of the simplifying assumptions to be found in research on therapeutic change processes. For each, we first lay out the simplification assumption and give examples. We then critique the assumption by putting forward examples of the inappropriate application of the assumption. Next, we counterpoise the simplifying assumption with the opposite "complexifying" assumption. Finally, we offer a moderate "compromise" position for therapy researchers.

I. Simplification by Incompleteness

One of the ways in which psychotherapy is complex lies in the many different elements that constitute it. However, in order to analyze how therapy is simplified in the service of carrying out research, we must have a model of what comprises therapy process. Elliott's (1991) five-dimensional therapy process model provides such a model; these five dimensions provide a conceptual framework or grid for analyzing therapy process. They include the perspective from which observations are taken (client, therapist, or researcher); the person who is observed (client, therapist, or dyad); the aspect of process observed (content, action, style, quality); the unit level or resolution of the observations (e.g., speaking turn, episode, session, or treatment); and the sequential phase (context, process, or effect). Elliott (1991) has presented an analysis of existing process measures in terms of this framework and described its implications for therapy research.

The first four of our simplifying assumptions involve bypassing or ignoring specific elements of therapy process, as defined within the five-dimensional model.

(1) Single Perspective for Measurement

The first simplifying assumption holds that a single point of view (client, therapist, or outside observer) is adequate for measuring therapy process. Examples of this belief are widespread in the therapy research literature and can take either positive or negative forms. In other words, the self-sufficiency or superiority of a given perspective over all other perspectives may be assumed or asserted; or the inferiority or invalidity of a perspective may be taken as fact. Positive versions of the assumption include the following:

a. Data provided by trained, objective raters are adequate to describe therapy process.

b. Data provided by clients are adequate to describe therapy process.

c. Data provided by therapists are adequate to describe therapy process.

Such assumptions are present in any study that relies exclusively on one particular perspective.

On the other hand, negative variants of the single-perspective assumption discount particular perspectives, and include the following:

d. Information provided by trained nonparticipant raters is not contextually grounded, and thus can be dispensed with in studying therapy process. This is implied by therapy research that relies exclusively on self-report (e.g., Gurman, 1977; Orlinsky & Howard, 1986).

e. Information provided by clients is hopelessly biased by response sets and defensive or self-presentational style, and thus can provide no valid information about therapy process. This was stated explicitly by Truax and Carkhuff (1967), who claimed that clients cannot recognize therapist empathy without training.

f. Information provided by therapists is invalidated by self-serving positive bias and/or self-critical negative bias, and thus can provide no valid information about therapy process. This widespread belief has been critiqued by Mintz (1977) and Orlinsky and Howard (1977).

Critique. The single-perspective assumption derives from a deeper assumption—the philosophical position known as "realism" or "objectivism" (see Hill, 1961): The therapy process exists independent of the act of perceiving it and can be known objectively.

It follows from this that either (a) the views of client, therapist, and researcher should agree as a matter of course and therefore be interchangeable; or (b) when they do not agree, one view is valid and the other views are biased and can be safely ignored.

In fact, existing research indicates clear differences in ratings of therapy process and outcome by clients, therapists, and nonparticipant observers (e.g., Caskey, Barker, & Elliott, 1984; Hill, 1974; Kaschak, 1978; Orlinsky & Howard, 1975). However, these differences are usually accompanied by small but statistically significant associations between perspectives or evidence for predictive validity (e.g., Gurman, 1977, Mintz; Luborsky, & Christoph, 1979). For example, several researchers (Elliott, 1986; Fuller & Hill, 1985) have reported that when therapist intentions are assessed from multiple perspectives, there is real but limited convergence; this suggests that observers, clients, and therapists sometimes agree but often see things differently, each capturing important but differing aspects of the phenomenon. It seems likely that in general, the three perspectives are divergent but valid.

Contrasting Assumption: Multiple Perspectives for Measurement. In light of these considerations, a contrasting "complexifying" assumption is held by a growing number of therapy process researchers (Greenberg, 1986; Elliott & Shapiro, 1992; Orlinsky & Howard, 1986). According to these researchers, all three perspectives have valuable and essential information to offer in the assessment of therapy process. Without all perspectives, our understanding of a process variable is incomplete.

A radical, "postmodernist," or "deconstructionist" extreme of this position (cf. Hare-Mustin & Marecek, 1988) holds that there are only "versions"—no "true" account is possible or even exists. Stated in methodological terms, the extreme version of the complexity assumption would hold (a) that *all* process variables should be measured from client, therapist, and observer perspectives; and (b) that it is also not fruitful to compare or attempt to combine perspectives!

Compromise Position: Complementary Measurement Perspectives. Between the two extreme positions, there is a more moderate view— namely, that each perspective has strengths and limitations which can be balanced by combining them. If the single-perspective assumption can be said to hold, it does so only for particular combinations of perspectives and variables. The idea of strengths and limitations to perspectives, recognized in the literature (e.g., Hill, 1974), suggests an interaction between perspectives and variables: Certain perspectives are better suited for measuring certain variables, often because of their "privileged access" to those variables (Elliott, 1991; Elliott & James, 1989). Conversely, this position allows for the possibility that a person observing from a particular perspective may be unable or unwilling to provide valid or useful data about certain variables (see Elliott, 1986, for a list of "validity threats" relevant to one type of self-report measure of therapy process).

This compromise position can be stated in the form of a recommendation: Wherever possible, psychotherapy researchers should use all three major perspectives, focusing data collection so as to use each to its best advantage. For example, clients can provide valuable information about recent life events and previous sessions; what they were talking about, feeling, or intending during sessions; how they perceived their therapists' intentions and attitudes; the effects of events or processes in therapy; and delayed effects and outcome.

For their part, therapists can offer useful accounts of a wide range of contextual variables, including their own treatment principles and personal characteristics, clients' styles and conflicts, and what has happened in previous sessions. They can also provide information about their own tasks, intentions, strategies, feelings, and skillfulness, as well as their perceptions of what clients meant, the clients' affective states, and how well the clients worked in the sessions. In addition, therapists can provide information about in-therapy changes and delayed effects.

Nonparticipant observers can be selected and trained to carry out detailed analyses of moment-to-moment in-session processes, including client and therapist actions, paralinguistic behaviors, and nonverbal behaviors (e.g., client vocal quality). Observers are also valuable for assessing theoretically derived process variables such as client conflict themes (Luborsky & Crits-Christoph, 1990), the quality or skillfulness of therapist and client performances, and clinical status variables (via interview measures).

Finally, differences among these perspectives should be studied in their own right for what they reveal about the interlocking realities of clients, therapists, and researchers (e.g., Elliott & Shapiro, 1992; Orlinsky & Howard, 1986).

(2) Single Variable Type

The second simplifying assumption motivated by the principle of economy holds that single variables or single types of variables are adequate for describing therapy process. In terms of the five-dimensional model, therapy researchers often choose to simplify by focusing narrowly on the effectiveness of one particular person (client or therapy), aspect (content, action, style, or quality), or sequential phase (context, process, or effect) in the therapeutic process.

The most extreme version of the single-variable-type assumption would be the belief that a single variable (e.g., interpersonal dominance) can provide meaningful or nontrivial measurement of therapy process. More common is the view that single classes of variables can provide meaningful measurement of therapy process. This would include any research that, for example, focuses only on client variables (ignoring therapist contributions), response modes (ignoring content, style, or quality), or therapeutic processes in themselves (ignoring context and effect). One example of this assumption is research that focuses exclusively on therapist actions (response modes; e.g., Elliott et al., 1987).

Critique and Contrasting Assumption: Exhaustive Measurement. The opposing complexifying view (Greenberg, 1986, Elliott, 1984; Rice & Greenberg, 1984; Schaffer, 1982) holds that sets of different types of process variables act together in therapy. Limiting investigation to any single variable produces a fundamentally incomplete account of the change process, because all are essential components of the process of change in psychotherapy, grounded in three important properties of therapy (Elliott, 1991):

a. Therapy is an interpersonal process, involving two persons actively collaborating and interacting. The therapist is not the "prime mover" (Gottman & Markman, 1978), nor is he or she "invisible." This idea may seem obvious, yet one of the two converse assumptions (therapist as prime mover or invisible) is surely implied by focusing on one person to the exclusion of the other.

b. Therapy is a multichannel communication process, in which multiple parallel communication processes operate in concert. What the client (or therapist) says (content), what he or she does by saying it (action), how it is said or done (style), and how well it is said or done (quality) are all essential to understanding therapy process.

c. Therapy is a temporally organized process, in which both context (past) and effect/outcome (future) must be examined in order to understand the significance of a particular piece of process. Rice and Greenberg's (1984) task analysis approach attempts to describe the context–process–effect maps that implicitly guide successful resolution of client tasks in therapy.

Stated in extreme form, one might argue that an account of therapy process is inadequate unless all 24 cells of a person × aspect × phase (2 × 4 × 3) matrix are filled (e.g., Elliott, 1984).

Compromise Position: Focused Investigation and Sampling of Process Dimensions. A more moderate position is that the full range of process variables should be considered, but may not be relevant in a given investigation. For example, the effect that a significant therapy event has on the therapist is usually not of great interest. Similarly, a theory-testing investigation of the accuracy of therapist interpretations (e.g., Crits-Christoph, Cooper & Luborsky, 1988) might not need to consider the style in which the interpretation was delivered. Instead, a good rule of thumb would probably be that at least two persons, phases, and aspects should be tapped in a given study, with only those person × aspect × phase cells filled that are relevant to the current research questions.

(3) Single Level of Measurement

Simplicity by economy can also be achieved by limiting measurement to units at a single level (speaking turns, "events" or episodes, sessions, or treatments). This "one size fits all" assumption holds that therapy can be simplified by staying at a particular level of analysis to the exclusion of all others. That this assumption is widespread in the research literature can be seen in the fact that there are major genres of therapy process research organized around the different levels, usually to the exclusion of others: (a) sequential analysis studies (see review by Russell & Trull, 1986) typically take as their sole focus the relationships between successive speaking turns; (b) task analysis (Rice & Greenberg, 1984) and events paradigm studies

(Elliott & Shapiro, 1988) focus on episodes within sessions; (c) "good-session" studies (e.g., Hoyt, 1980) operate at the session level; and (d) retrospective attribution studies (reviewed by Elliott & James, 1989) rely on the treatment level. To the extent that a study remains exclusively within any one of these paradigms, it implicitly endorses the single-level assumption.

Critique and Contrasting Assumption: Measurement at All Levels. Like all communication, therapy is actually a hierarchically organized process, in which units at different logical levels subordinate and constitute one another (e.g., turns make up episodes and derive their meaning from the episodes in which they are embedded) (Russell & Staszewski, 1988). Clients and therapists simultaneously maneuver themselves through speaking turns, keep track of the current task or topic (episode), form impressions about the current and previous sessions, and entertain at least a glimmering of how the treatment as a whole is progressing.

Thus, it has been argued (e.g., Elliott, 1991; Greenberg, 1986) that process and outcome should be measured at all major levels of analysis in order to provide a complete, valid, and clinically meaningful assessment of therapy process. Each of these levels is psychologically meaningful to the participants and has associated with it different variables (e.g., response modes go with turns, while outcome goes with treatment as a whole); therefore, a complete account of therapeutic change processes should at a minimum involve measurement at four unit levels (turn, episode, session, and treatment).

Compromise Position: Measurement at Selected Levels. As with the previous assumptions, a compromise is available here. Not all levels of process will be relevant for describing a particular phenomenon or answering a given research question. Nevertheless, the clinical significance of the research will be enhanced if two conditions hold: (a) if it can be tied to actual events or processes within the session; and (b) if it can show generalization of effects beyond the confines of the therapy session. Therefore, at least two levels of measurement should be used—a "subsession" level (turn or episode), and a "suprasession" level (session or treatment). Although this approach is more moderate than the extreme position, it would argue against exclusive use of either microanalytic or global (e.g., questionnaire) strategies in a given study.

(4) Stable Effects across Time

One additional assumption comes under the heading of simplification by economy, or limiting the number of things studied. This assumption holds that the effects associated with particular therapeutic processes are consistent across time and need only be assessed once.

The stable-effects assumption is closely related to the single-level assumption just described, and variants of this assumption appear in research using different unit levels. For instance, it is embedded in process–outcome studies where sampled episodes or sessions are correlated with outcome assessed only immediately after treatment (e.g., Mintz, Luborsky, & Auerbach, 1971). In fact, the treatment-level version of the stable-effects assumption has received partial support from Nicholson and Berman's (1983) meta-analysis of psychotherapy follow-up data, in which they found consistency across posttreatment follow-up periods, leading them to conclude that follow-up assessment was not as essential as it had previously been held to be.

In addition, the stable-effects assumption takes several other forms: It is typically embedded in turn-level sequential analysis studies, where the effect of a type of therapist behavior is assessed by examining only the next client speaking turn (first-order Markov chain; e.g., Benjamin, 1979; Hill, Carter, & O'Farrell, 1983), without looking at subsequent client turns or the postsession effects of the variable (cf. Russell & Czogalik, 1989; Russell & Trull, 1986). Similarly, the assumption appears in "good-session" studies (e.g., Orlinsky & Howard, 1975), in which client and therapist postsession ratings of process and session effects are correlated without examination of later sessions or treatment outcome.

Critique and Contrasting Assumption: Delayed and Evolving Effects. Most practicing therapists have encountered instances of therapy events that have delayed or evolving effects. Elliott, Cline, and Reid (1982) found that although many significant therapy events are consistent in their effects over time, a substantial number show changing effects. From a clinical point of view, it seems clear that particular therapeutic processes (e.g., therapist interpretations) interact with later events in and out of therapy to facilitate, diminish, and sometimes even reverse earlier effects.

Furthermore, although Nicholson and Berman (1983) reported consistency in outcome from posttreatment to follow-up periods, their meta-analysis of data on whether individual clients maintained their posttreatment status was limited to only five studies. In addition, their results are not consistent with those reported by Smith, Glass, and Miller (1980), who found differences in outcome across time.

Thus, the opposite or complexifying assumption holds that the effects of therapeutic processes evolve over time, with the methodological consequence that these effects need to be followed over time within treatment (where applicable), through the end of treatment, and beyond to follow-up.

This thinking can be applied to the analysis of therapeutic change episodes by taking three of the unit levels described above (episode, session, and treatment) and differentiating effects into immediate and delayed phases. This results in a model of six stages of effects, each of which might conceivably yield a somewhat different picture of the effects of a particular therapy event or change process:

1. Immediate within-session effects (episode level; speaking turns to end of current episode)
2. Delayed within-session effects (later episodes in same session)
3. Immediate postsession effects (session level)
4. Delayed postsession effects (e.g., in later sessions)
5. Immediate outcome (treatment level)
6. Delayed outcome (follow-up)

To take this still further, particularly with reference to treatment-level research, it should be noted that delayed effects themselves may change over time. That is, the clients who are doing well at a 6-month follow-up may not be the same ones who are doing well 2 years after treatment.

Compromise Position: Limited Tracking of Evolving Effects. Once again, a position between the two extremes of simplification and exhaustiveness appears reasonable. The thorough tracking of effects just described may often be neither feasible nor necessary for therapy researchers. Nevertheless, at least some tracking of evolving effects seems important. Issues of clinical significance suggest that there be some measurement of immediate effects connected with specific sessions as well as some assessment of delayed effects beyond the confines of the session. Thus, our compromise recommendation is that researchers at least assess effects at two points in time: One of these assessments should take place in or immediately following the session (times 1–3 above). The other assessment should occur at a later time, such as outcome (times 4–6).

II. Simplification by Reliance on Simple Structure

We now turn to the second form of simplification, based on the elusive criterion of "elegance" (Harré, 1983), in which simpler (more regular and symmetrical) structures are preferred by researchers, just as they are more generally in human perception (the law of *pragnanz*; Pollio, 1982). Because of the large number and variety of simplifying assumptions that can be subsumed under this heading, we subdivide them into two groups, following the standard distinction (e.g., Nunnally, 1978) between data structure (*q* methodology) and variable structure (*p* methodology).

A. Simplification of Data Structure

The data of therapy—that is, the observations drawn from within and between sessions and from within and between particular clients and therapists—have a more complex structure than is typically reflected in research studies. In order to make life easier for themselves, researchers generally prefer to treat all units of therapy, first, as equally important, and, second, as statistically independent of one another. These two assumptions ignore important clinical facts about therapy—the existence of "significant events," and the presence of large amounts of shared variance within sessions, treatments, and even therapists.

(5) Equal Weighting of Process Units

The idea that all units of therapy process are of equal weight or importance is a widespread assumption in the research literature (Russell, 1986). The equal-weighting assumption can be found in a number of guises. It is particularly clear in discussions that advocate the use of random sampling (e.g., Klein, Mathieu-Coughlan, & Kiesler, 1986). In addition, equal weighting is also implied by the use of any kind of *a priori,* standardized sampling procedure, including predetermined or stratified sampling of one or more points in a session or treatment (e.g., Elliott, Barker, Caskey, & Pistrang, 1982). Finally, the assumption of equal weighting is implicit in any aggregation or summarization of data across units (turns, segments, sessions) in which their significance or effect on clients is not taken into consideration.

Critique and Contrasting Assumption: Significant Events. Many writers have described various "uniformity myths" in psychotherapy research and the problems of aggregating therapy data (e.g., Grawe, 1989; Kiesler, 1966; Rice & Greenberg, 1984). However, the "myth of uniform process" (Elliott, 1983a; i.e., the equal-weighting assumption) is one of the most common of these myths. In contrast, it seems clear that clients and therapists perceive some events (turns, episodes, or sessions) in therapy as more important than others. This has been well established in several series of studies (e.g., Elliott, 1985; Elliott & Shapiro, 1988; Llewelyn, 1988; Mahrer, Dessaulles, Nadler, Gervaize, & Sterner, 1987; Martin & Stelmaczonek, 1988). Rice and Greenberg (1984) and others (Morrow-Bradley & Elliott, 1986) have advocated the study of significant events in order to improve the clinical usefulness of therapy research.

Although research data support the existence of events perceived as significant by clients and therapists, the idea that these events should be the major focus for investigation is based on another, deeper assumption: the idea that change in human and other systems occurs in discontinuous, discrete "quanta" or "leaps," and that the processes operating at those times are of critical importance. This view has been variously presented by religious writers (e.g., Kierkegaard, 1846/1941), psychologists (e.g., Guidano, 1987; Kelman, 1969; Sarbin & Adler, 1971), and those in the natural sciences (e.g., Prigogine & Stengers, 1984—discontinuous evolution, catastrophe theory). In fact, it is tempting to carry this assumption further and conclude that *only* significant events should be studied: "Ridiculous the waste sad time/Stretching before and after" (Eliot, 1935/1963, p. 181).

Compromise Position: Ordinary Events as "Baseline" for Significant Events. However, this extreme position would be an example of assumptions 2 (single variable type) and 8 (context independence). Fortunately, there is a position midway between weighing all units of process equally and focusing exclusively on significant events. In most treatments, most of what the client and therapist say, though not "earth-shaking," is recognized as at least slightly helpful—either in itself or as part of a process leading to something significantly helpful (Elliott, Barker, et al., 1982; Hill et al., 1988). Significant events identified by clients are significant not because they are simply helpful or important, but because they are *more* helpful or important than other events in therapy. As such, it is useful to think of them as representing change processes that are generally present in the treatment, but that appear in greater "strength" in significant events (Elliott, James, Reimscheussel, Cislo, & Sack, 1985).

Furthermore, it seems obvious that significant events emerge as "figure" for the person perceiving them (often the client), by virtue of their contrast with the "ground" of therapeutic business as usual. Thus, ordinary events often serve as preparation or follow-up to significantly helpful events, and are sometimes experienced as helpful simply because of the hope of "more to come" or the recollection of what has gone before (e.g., Elliott, 1983b). Because of these considerations, we recommend that researchers distinguish clearly between significant and ordinary events, but investigate both, with ordinary events providing the "baseline" function of "control sample" or measured context for significant events.

(6) Independence of Observations

Another common way in which therapy researchers simplify their work is to assume that their data points are statistically independent of one another, even when they are drawn in sequence or from the same session, client, or therapist. In other words, it is assumed that such observations do not share substantial amounts of common variance. Typically, in psychotherapy research, two major forms of common variance occur among observations.

First, it is assumed that observations drawn from the same larger unit (e.g., sessions, treatments, therapists) are not generally related to one another, that is, they do not show individual differences (as evidenced by differing baselines or differences in average levels among units). In other words, it is assumed that the variance within the larger units is equal to that among these units. This assumption is used for turns or episodes within sessions (e.g., Elliott, Barker, et al., 1982), for sessions within treatments (e.g., Stiles, 1980), and for clients seen by the same therapist (see review by Crits-Christoph et al., 1991).

Second, it is assumed that observations of successive units (e.g., turns, sessions) cannot be predicted from one another. In other words, trends across time, carry over effects, or correlations between successive observations are treated as either nonexistent or not important (e.g., Silberschatz, Fretter & Curtis, 1986).

The independence-of-observations assumption lies at the heart of the Fisherian statistical tradition, which includes almost all the statistical procedures used in therapy process and outcome research. Holding this assumption (or at least assuming that common variance is trivial in scale and consequences) has the major advantage of avoiding alternative statistical approaches that are difficult or underdeveloped (e.g., time series analysis, generalized least squares).

Critique. Unfortunately, individual differences and sequential relationships are common in psychotherapy research. Crits-Christoph et al. (1991) have reviewed evidence suggesting that large amounts of variance in outcome can be attributed to therapist individual differences. The situation holds equally for research on therapy sessions and episodes within sessions: Substantial amounts of variance have been found to be attributable to differences between clients (i.e., treatment level) (e.g., Howard, Orlinsky, & Perilstein, 1976). In addition, sequential analyses of sessions, repeated change measures (e.g., Elliott, 1989b), and speaking turns (see review by Russell & Trull, 1986) suggest the existence of substantial and important effects, especially between successive observations of the same measure. To ignore these effects is to ignore an important, clinically meaningful set of phenomena.

In addition, violating statistical independence has serious consequences for significance testing. The larger the nonindependence of observations, the more the degrees of freedom for significance testing are overestimated. This results in the error term's being underestimated, which in turn increases the likelihood of type I errors (i.e., finding effects that are not present) (Kazdin, 1984).

Contrasting Assumption: Focusing on Sequential Processes and Individual Differences. The alternative to assuming independence of observations is to embrace nonindependence and to make it the central focus of investigation. Several current trends in therapy research reflect this reorientation.

First, there has been a resurgence of interest in understanding consistencies within clients across the course of treatment and within therapists across clients. This amounts to an increased focus on the role of individual differences in therapy. It takes seriously the general form of nonindependence, which is held implicitly by therapists whenever they characterize a session as more "productive" or "heavy" than other sessions with the same client; when they characterize a particular client as "good" or "resistant"; or when they describe a colleague as "a good therapist." The work of Luborsky and colleagues probably best exemplifies this trend, including their research on consistencies in client core conflict themes across therapy (Luborsky & Crits-Christoph, 1990) and on therapist differences in outcome (reviewed in Crits-Christoph et al., 1991).

Second, there has been a great growth of interest in the sequential analysis of therapy process in the past 10 years (see reviews by Russell & Czogalik, 1989; Russell & Trull, 1986). In therapy, sequence is essential; for example, more experienced therapists think sequentially (Pinsof, 1986). New statistical methods for dealing with sequentially nonindependent data have been developed and are continuing to emerge, including classical time series analysis (Glass, Willson, & Gottman, 1975), pooled time series analysis (e.g., Gaston & Marmar, 1989), and logit–loglinear analysis (e.g., Wiseman & Rice, 1989). (A related approach is the analysis of interactions and contextual effects, as we discuss shortly under assumptions 7 and 8.)

Compromise Position: Living with Nonindependence. In spite of the increased interest in sequential analysis and individual differences, it seems to us that it would be inadvisable to redirect the bulk of the field's efforts into these two research fronts. For one thing, doing so would probably require relying on other simplifying assumptions, such as the single-level assumption, and would have to be traded off against the dangers discussed earlier. In addition, the statistical methods available are still at a relatively early stage of development: Some are seriously limited by their methodological requirements (e.g., for long series of observations); others are daunting in their complexity. Finally, there are controversies over the use of sequential methods for exploratory research and problems with handling delayed effects (e.g., Hill et al., 1983; Russell & Czogalik, 1989).

We recommend the following: Researchers should be aware of the dangers of assuming independence and exercise caution. Sources of possible nonindependence should be measured, and corrective action should be taken where needed, using the newer statistical approaches where these are appropriate. Because of the familiarity and ease of use of Fisherian statistics, researchers should not overlook the possibility of adopting more stringent significance levels to compensate for nonindependence.

B. Simplification of Variable Structure

In addition to assuming simplicity in data structure (q simplification), researchers have also sought to simplify by relying on simple, straightforward models of relationships among their variables (p simplification). A wide variety of assumptions about simple variable structure have been relied upon, but these fall into three groups:

1. Assumptions about simple main effects ignore various kinds of interactions.
2. Assumptions about simplification of causal structure assumptions hold that influences among variables are unidirectional, complete, linear, and direct.
3. Finally, an assumption about simplification of the measurement model involves substituting a conceptually simpler scale of measurement for a more complex one.

1. Simple Main Effects

Interaction effects are problematic for therapy researchers in several ways: They require large sample sizes in order to be detected with adequate statistical power (Cook & Campbell, 1979); they are sometimes difficult to interpret; and they remind researchers of the limits beyond which their findings may not generalize.(external validity). Thus, it is both easier and more comfortable to ignore interaction effects in therapy research, especially since the field is plagued by problems of low statistical power, interpretability, and limited generalizability to begin with. Therapy researchers have found at least three different ways of simplifying by ignoring interaction effects: restricting investigation to simple combinations of variables, ignoring context, and assuming that the same variables are relevant across a wide range of therapeutic phenomena.

(7) Simple Combinations of Variables

The general case of the simple-main-effects group of assumptions is the belief that it is possible to carry out therapy research with simple combinations of variables—that is, without reference to more complex multiplicative patterns. Many investigations limit themselves to main effects or simple correlations. When therapy researchers go beyond bivariate correlations to look for patterns of variables, they generally stop with simple linear combinations of process variables, as in multiple regression. In other words, more complex patterns, interpreted quantitatively as multiplicative (rather than additive) combinations of variables or qualitatively as configurations of features, are assumed to be either infrequent enough or small enough to ignore.

Critique and Contrasting Assumption: Interaction Effects are All. The opposing view holds that interaction effects and complex configurations are the rules rather than the exceptions in psychotherapy research. Although there is research evidence for this view (e.g., Grawe, 1989), it derives from the deeper philosophical assumption of pluralism, most clearly articulated by William James (Viney, 1989). According to the pluralistic view, the diverse processes of change operate for different therapies, therapists, clients, and even moments in therapy. Thus, the assumption that interaction effects are critical in understand therapy is an expression of a more general belief in pluralism.

For example, the time course of change and the variables that predict outcome may vary among therapies (Grawe, 1989). Clients with more dysfunctional beliefs may not fare as well in cognitive therapy, whereas clients with poor social adjustment may not do as well in interpersonal therapy (Sotsky, Glass, Shea, & Pilkonis, 1986). Beyond this, assuming interaction effects is very useful for making sense out of contradictory findings in the literatures on therapist and client predictors of outcome (Garfield, 1986; Luborsky, Crits-Christoph, Mintz, & Auerbach, 1988). To the extent that the assumption about interaction effects holds, it becomes essential to disaggregate samples in order to carry out more fine-grained analyses (Cook & Campbell, 1979).

In addition, interaction effects are also embedded in descriptive process research where complex configurations of features are used to define descriptive variables such as client vocal style (Rice & Kerr, 1986), which make explicit the way in which unique patterns of defining features apply to each category. Horowitz's (1987) "states-of-mind" measurement approach carries this still further by assuming that the process variables themselves are unique to each client. The logical extreme of this position would be the relentless pursuit of uniqueness and diversity for its own sake, going beyond case studies to the analysis of particular moments in therapy, perhaps exemplified by Elliott's (1989a) method of comprehensive process analysis.

Compromise Position: Continuing the Search for General Principles. However, pluralism has its dangers, the most important of which is the possibility that the search for useful general principles will be abandoned in favor of a fascination with unrelated but interesting detail. If psychotherapy research is to maintain its place as an applied discipline devoted to developing knowledge useful to practicing therapists, then it cannot afford to give up the search for principles that apply to fairly broad classes of therapeutic situations. Furthermore, we follow phenomenological researchers such as Wertz (1983) in arguing that the best route to understanding general human phenomena is through the detailed understanding of the individual.

(8) Context Independence

Kiesler (1973) used the phrase "contextual unit" to refer to "that portion of the interview that is considered when one assigns a score" (p. 38). Another assumption in the simple-main-effects group holds that the meaning of therapy events is largely independent of context; in other words, the meaning of a unit of therapy does not interact with its context. Like the other assumptions reviewed so far, context independence derives from a deeper assumption—in this case, that communication events have universal meanings that are not context-bound (Packer & Addison, 1989).

As Russell (1986) notes, Bergman (1951) was the first to advocate this assumption explicitly. The assumption of context independence is particularly clear in the practice of rating extracted brief randomly sampled segments in scrambled order (e.g., Gomes-Schwartz, 1978; Silberschatz et al., 1986). However, it can also be found in the distrust of the client and therapist perspectives discussed earlier (assumption 1), in that nonparticipant raters are assumed to be less biased because of their lack of involvement in the therapy context.

Critique and Contrasting Assumption: Contextualism. In spite of persistent context-free rating practices, few philosophers, communications researchers, or therapy researchers today doubt that meaning and action are strongly conditioned by context (e.g., Messer, Tishby, & Spillman, 1992). The same sentence (e.g., "It's cold in here") may, depending on its context, be heard as a disclosure, as an indirect request, or as a complaint, in either literal or metaphorical form (Stiles, 1986).

The issue, instead, is how to go about taking context seriously in therapy research. A number of different avenues for this are available: (a) use of large contextual units (e.g., entire sessions) for ratings (e.g., Horowitz, Marmar, Weiss, DeWitt, & Rosenbaum, 1984); (b) use of participants as raters (Orlinsky & Howard, 1986); (c) development of measures of context (e.g., "markers" for therapist intervention; Rice & Greenberg, 1984); (d) development of higher-order variables (e.g., accuracy of interpretation) that enfold a configuration of lower-order contextual variables (e.g., patient plan) and process variables (e.g., transference interpretation; Silberschatz et al., 1986); and (e) the development of models of context (Beutler, 1989; Elliott, 1989a; Heatherington, 1989; Orlinsky & Howard, 1987). Taken to extremes, the contextualist position holds that all ratings must utilize detailed contextual information.

Compromise Position: Limits of Contextualism. One problem with paying greater heed to context in rating therapy process is that context is potentially boundless; it is always possible to locate more information that may be relevant about previous sessions, the client's history, previous cases seen by the therapist, and so on. The advice to take context more seriously needs to be spelled out and tempered in relation to specific variables. In fact, for some variables (e.g., client vocal quality; Rice & Kerr, 1986), detailed contextual information may distract raters and interfere with their performance).

(9) Uniform Relevance of Variables

Repeated complaints about one-shot studies and the proliferation of measures in the field (e.g., Kiesler, 1973) have generated a strong push for uniformity in therapy research. A logical outgrowth was the proposal of measurement batteries, which began with Waskow and Parloff's (1975) recommended outcome battery and has subsequently been extended to the measurement of therapy process. This idea is reflected in a number of "general-purpose" instruments including the Therapy Session Reports (Orlinsky & Howard, 1986), the Vanderbilt Psychotherapy Process Scale (Suh, Strupp, & O'Malley, 1986), and the Psychotherapy Process Q-Sort (Jones, Cumming, & Horowitz, 1988). These instruments were constructed with two major criteria in mind: (a) to provide a "standard language" for describing treatments of varying orientations and with varying clients and therapists; and (b) to measure therapy in a comprehensive, thorough manner.

This assumption is a generalization of the main-effects assumption, in that it assumes that the same dimensions, variables, or categories are relevant for all therapies (or at least all individual therapies). This is not to say that all therapies, or events within therapies, will score the same—only that they will be commensurate, that their important features can be described by a common set of variables. In Kelly's (1955) terms, the assumption is that the "range of convenience" of these therapy process variables encompasses all the important features of all forms of professional individual therapy. Put another way, the uniform-relevance assumption holds that it is possible to identify a set of variables that can be generalized across the range of treatments and types of therapy event. Specifically:

   a. The same process variables can be used meaningfully to measure process in different types of therapy.
   b. The same process variables can be used meaningfully to measure process in different types of therapeutic event (e.g., insight, empathy, chair work, unfolding) in the same type of treatment.

Critique and Contrasting Assumption: Specificity of Variables. The opposing view is that the uniform, comprehensive measurement of all relevant characteristics of all types of therapy process is impractical and undesirable. Each type of therapy and each type of change process within it has certain unique elements; thus, there is an "interaction" between variables and type of treatment or event studied. Although it is conceivable that researchers might eventually accumulate a set of variables that incorporates all the relevant features of all types of therapeutic process, such a set would be too long to be practically useful and would contain a large proportion of irrelevant variables, thus obscuring the measurement task.

The opposing assumption that variables must be specifically tailored to specific types of therapy and therapy events is exemplified in Rice and Greenberg's (1984) task analysis and in Elliott's (1989a) comprehensive process analysis. In task analysis, "task-relevant molar codes" are developed through close, open observation and description to capture the different stages in the resolution of a particular therapeutic task. For example, in Rice and Sapiera's (1984) work on the resolution of puzzling or problematic reactions, two relevant variables are "vivid description of stimulus situation" and "re-examining shoulds and oughts." These variables are not assumed to be relevant to understanding the resolution of an internal conflict (cf. Greenberg, 1984), although some common variables may in fact emerge from investigation.

Compromise Position: Open Measurement of Common and Unique Features. Intensive research approaches such as task analysis and comprehensive process analysis probably underestimate the interest and value of understanding the factors that are common to different treatments and events. The common-factors question has been a central concern of therapy researchers since Fiedler's (1950) classic study purporting to show commonality between experienced therapists of widely differing orientations. It is also a central motivating interest in the psychotherapy integrationist movement (Goldfried, 1982).

Consistent with this, two compromise solutions have been proposed: First, Rice and Greenberg (1984) advocate measuring therapy outcome and process by using both a "common core" of measures and a unique set of measures tailored specifically to the treatment or event being studied. Second, variables thought to be unique can be examined within a general framework of "sensitizing concepts" (e.g., client extratherapy events), as is done in comprehensive process analysis (Elliott, 1989a).

2. Simplification of Causal Structure

Psychotherapy researchers also frequently simplify the presumed causal relationships between the variables they study. Thus, they design research based to varying degrees on the assumptions that potential causal relationships between therapy process and outcome are unidirectional, unmediated, linear, and not attributable to outside variables. Because of therapy researchers' shared grounding in positivistic philosophies of science, much of this is familiar ground (see also Stiles, Shapiro, & Harper, Chapter 2, and Greenberg, Chapter 4, this volume). In general, our recommendations will be the standard remedies for increasing internal validity—measuring or controlling for alternative causal explanations (Cook & Campbell, 1979). In addition, the discussion is used to highlight a deeper underlying assumption about the nature of explanation in psychotherapy research.

(10) Unidirectionality of Causal Influences

As therapists, we like to assume that what we do with our clients is responsible for any changes that may occur; we subscribe to a belief in the therapist as "prime mover" (Gottman & Markman, 1978). Similarly, in studying therapy, it is also common for researchers to assume that what happens in therapy is responsible for outcome, and to conclude that any statistically significant correlations between process and outcome variables reflect this simple causal model.

Critique and Contrasting Assumption: Bidirectionality. Unfortunately, the relationship between therapy process and outcome probably reflects a continuous bidirectional influence between what happens in therapy and the evolving effects of treatment. Beginning with the first session, the client's openness and investment in the therapy process reflect the effect or outcome of what has happened already (i.e., "early outcome"). For example, the Penn Helping Alliance Scales (Alexander & Luborsky, 1986) include items tapping perceived outcome to date.

If bidirectionality is taken seriously, therapy researchers must measure process and outcome at relatively low unit levels (see assumption 3)—probably at the session level or below—in order to trace the effects of early outcome or postsession effects on subsequent process and outcome. Very little research has been done on this (e.g., Foreman & Marmar, 1985) and it seems clear that much initial descriptive work needs to be done, particularly on the emergence of the therapeutic alliance (e.g., Safran, Crocker, McMain, & Murray, 1990).

Compromise Position: Acknowledging Bidirectional Influences. Short of an all-out attack on the bidirectionality problem, it seems to us that researchers can do two things. First, they can highlight possible bidirectional influences in correlational process–outcome studies, as Stiles (1988) has done. Second, they can incorporate measures of early outcome into process–outcome studies.

(11) Closed Causal System

The most common way in which psychotherapy researchers simplify causal structure is by assuming that no third variables operate strongly enough to produce correlations between process and outcome. In path-analytic terms (Cook & Campbell, 1979), they assume that the system of measured process and outcome variables is causally closed to outside influences. Within the terms of this assumption, outside factors are "nuisance" variables that contribute to error but can be safely ignored. This assumption is easiest to justify in experimental studies, but is also frequent in predictive or descriptive studies, as when type of therapist response (e.g., interpretation) is correlated with what the client does next (Frank & Sweetland, 1962) or client postsession ratings (e.g., Hill, 1974).

In psychotherapy research, the ignored third variables are generally contextual in nature and include initial client distress or resources (Stiles, 1988), therapist skillfulness, therapeutic alliance, and the outcome of previous sessions. The assumption of a closed causal system is most obvious when no contextual variables are measured (e.g., Frank & Sweetland, 1962). However, even when contextual variables such as client ego development and motivation are measured (e.g., Horowitz et al., 1984), the assumption is still made that additional, unmeasured contextual variables (e.g., client–therapist similarities) are either absent or trivial in their effects.

Critique and Contrasting Assumption: Open Causal System. On the other hand, outside influences are the rule in relating process to effect (or outcome) variables. These not only act to produce apparent associations between processes and effects; they also, as Stiles (1988) has noted, are likely to suppress genuine process–outcome relationships. Thus, the contrasting assumption is of psychotherapy as a complex, open causal system involving many potential third variables. Such an assumption is exemplified by complex systems models of psychotherapy (e.g., Orlinsky & Howard, 1987; Elliott, 1989a).

According to the open-system assumption, then, therapy researchers need to develop systematic methods for identifying and incorporating third variables into their thinking and studies. Although causal modeling approaches such as path analysis and LIS-REL (Jöreskog & Sörbom, 1979) are generally impractical in therapy research because of their large sample size requirements, they represent an appreciation for the role of third variables, and also provide a set of useful conceptual tools. Beyond these, and perhaps more appropriate for psychotherapy research, are qualitative causal modeling methods such as those developed by Miles and Huberman (1984). In addition, Orlinsky and Howard's (1987) generic model and Elliott's (1989a) comprehensive process analysis offer complex models of therapy that provide "checklists" of possible third variables.

Compromise Position: Acknowledgment of the Role of Third Variables. Most importantly, what is needed is an attitude of openness toward the complexity of the causal influences involved. In our analysis of 10 key process–outcome studies (described below), we were surprised by how seldom researchers acknowledged the possible influences of third variables, even in discussing the limitations of their studies. Although it is surely unreasonable to expect researchers to incorporate all possible contextual variables in a particular study, it does seem reasonable to expect them to consider the possible role of outside factors in their results.

(12) Direct Effects

In studying the process of change in therapy, it is generally simpler to assume that process and outcome are linked in a direct, straightforward manner, without the mediation of additional processes or events. This assumption is most apparent in research that uses observer ratings of client and therapist in-session behavior to predict outcome at the end of treatment. However, the same assumption also operates in sequential analysis studies, in which ratings of therapist behaviors (e.g., interpretations) are used to predict what clients will do next (e.g., as measured on the Experiencing Scale; Silberschatz et al., 1986), without consideration of possible covert mediating processes.

Critique and Contrasting Assumption: Covert, Mediated Effects. Research on client and therapist experiences in therapy has produced data that directly contradict the direct-effects assumption and support a covert mediational model of therapy process (Elliott, Barker, et al., 1982; Hill et al., 1988; Martin, Martin, & Slemon, 1987; Rennie, 1985; see also reviews by Elliott, 1986; Elliott & James, 1989; Gurman, 1977). This research has provided an approach to understanding the phenomenon of unexpected effects in therapy. The presence of such effects, and the empirical support for more complex mediational models of therapy process, point strongly to the need for research on the processes leading from session events to effect/outcome. These include both in-session covert processes, client extrasession experiences (Tarragona & Orlinsky, 1987), delayed effects (e.g., Elliott, Cline, & Reid, 1982), and later events both in and out of therapy.

Compromise Position: Acknowledging the Role of Mediational Processes. As before, our opinion is that researchers should at a minimum acknowledge the existence of covert, mediational processes; preferably, they should include more measures assessing important mediating variables, such as client and therapist perceptions of in-session and postsession events.

(13) Linearity of Cause–Effect Associations

Stiles and Shapiro (1989) describe another instance of simplification involving causal structure—the assumption that the relationship between process and outcome is linear. According to this assumption, the more of a "good" process, the better outcome will be; the more of a "bad" process, the worse outcome will be. This is an issue of statistical conclusion validity (cf. Cook & Campbell, 1979), implied by the use of linear correlation and multiple-regression techniques of analysis (see Stiles & Shapiro, 1989).

Critique and Contrasting Assumption: Nonlinearity. As Stiles and Shapiro (1989) have argued, the linearity assumption is a misapplication of the drug metaphor to psychotherapy. They point out that a number of nonlinear relationships between process and outcome are possible and likely, including step or S functions (which specify minimum levels of a process variable) and inverted-U functions (which specify optimal levels). The latter reflect the common-sense clinical understanding that there are optimal levels for process variables and that too much of *any* process variable will be counterproductive. Stiles and Shapiro believe that curvilinear relationships account for many of the null process–outcome findings reported in the literature.

Compromise Position: Sampling and Testing for Nonlinearity. As Cook and Campbell (1979) have noted, the way to deal with nonlinearity is to conduct parametric research, systematically varying the "dose" of a process variable. In process–outcome studies, this means deliberately sampling a wide range of values for the process variable. A practical guideline is to look for possible nonlinear associations whenever null correlations are obtained.

Underlying Assumption: Mechanistic Cause–Effect Relationships Can Best Explain Therapeutic Change Processes

Before we conclude this review of simplifying assumptions about causal structure, it is important to consider the deeper assumption that underlies them. This deeper assumption holds that context, process, and outcome in therapy can be best understood as analogous to a mechanical physical system of discrete causes and effects. The assumption is implicit in the application of the language of causal analysis articulated so clearly by Cook and Campbell (1979). The mechanistic assumption is also reflected in the language of independent and dependent variables, and in the practice of defining scientific explanation in terms of cause–effect relationships (Lincoln & Guba, 1985; Packer & Addison, 1989).

Critique and Contrasting Underlying Assumption: Relationships of Meaning Can Best Explain Therapeutic Change Processes. The mechanistic assumption has often been criticized as failing to do justice to the purposive, intentional nature of human action (e.g., Searle, 1983; Winch, 1958). That Cook and Campbell (1979) explicitly include intentions as a kind of cause does not help matters, because this makes intention into a mechanistic concept, which is inconsistent with everyday and philosophically coherent accounts of intention (Ryle, 1949; Searle, 1983).

Although Winch (1958) and others have contrasted "causes" and "intentions" as dichotomous ways of explaining events in the world, it seems more accurate to say that human beings typically draw on a range of different modes of explanation in accounting for their actions and the actions of others (Elliott, 1992). The alternative to the assumption of mechanistic explanation holds that therapy (and human action in general) is better explained in terms of a variety of relationships of meaning, illustrated by the following three:

a. *Intentional.* Typically, a person's actions are explained in terms of his or her intentions and reasons, including means–ends accounts. This includes explanations of client or therapist behavior by reference to intentions, purposes, tasks, goals, and treatment principles (e.g., therapist reflection reveals the intention to communicate understanding, which in turn is intended to contribute to therapeutic alliance).

b. *Narrative.* Narrative explanation is based on temporal sequences (often recognizable "scripts") depicting the origin or temporal unfolding of some state of being. This includes accounts of client or therapist action in terms of their origins, sources, or temporal or developmental sequences. An example is explanation in the form of task-analytic models of how clients successfully resolve particular immediate problems through a typical series of steps (Rice & Greenberg, 1984).

c. *Categorical.* Actions may also be explained by means of set inclusion relationships in which smaller units (e.g., actions) are described as instances or examples of larger or more abstract units (e.g., personality, goals). Examples include accounting for a client's response to treatment by reference to a DSM Axis II personality disorder (e.g., borderline), and showing that the therapist's session task of helping the client to explore anger at his or her spouse may be an instance of the therapist's more encompassing treatment goal of helping the client to become more aware of his or her anger.

It seems clear that in accounting for themselves and others, speakers and therapy researchers make use of these and other non-mechanistic modes of explanation, as well as relying on mechanistic causes. Although it is not commonly acknowledged, explanations of therapeutic change are actually complex webs made up of different kinds of explanation.

Compromise Position: Translating Causal Concepts. Mechanical cause–effect relationships are only one way of explaining something. At a minimum, the researcher should not fall into the trap of thinking of all of explanations as "causes." In addition, some of the causal concepts referred to earlier can be translated into noncausal terms: For example, a categorical part–whole relationship (e.g., between treatment goals and session tasks) can be thought of as "unidirectional" from general to specific; an account can be considered to be "closed" if the full range of its possible meanings (e.g., causes, intentions, narratives, categories) has been explicated; the sequence between a process and an effect variable may be considered to be "direct" if the result is a coherent "story" not requiring a linking narrative to fill in the intervening meanings; finally, a relationship can be regarded as "linear" if "good" and "better" degrees of a process are followed by "best" instead of "too much."

3. Simplification of Measurement Model

(14) Nominal Scale Measurement

The final simplifying assumption in our list has to do with choosing a simpler measurement model instead of a more complex one. Specifically, we have noticed that therapy process researchers seem consistent in their preference for mutually exclusive nominal scales over sets of related-interval scales. In other words, researchers prefer to classify therapy events as containing only one category of action, style, effect, and so on. Consistent with this, use of a nominal scale of measurement (Stevens, 1946) requires that each observation must go in one and only one category (properties known as "ex-clusivity" and "exhaustivity").

This assumption is most obvious in systems for rating response modes (e.g., Hill, 1986), but can also be found in measures of client and therapist vocal quality (Rice & Kerr, 1986) and family therapist behavior (Pinsof, 1986). In order to meet the requirements of nominal scale measurement, researchers have developed various strategies, including using "other" categories to achieve exhaustiveness, and resorting to "decision rules" and smaller scoring units to attain mutual exclusivity. The major argument in favor of nominal scale measurement appears to be its simplicity and intuitive appeal: It is easier to refer to a piece of therapy process as "an interpretation" (vs. "interpretative question") or as an instance of "focused voice" (vs. "mostly focused with some externalizing vocal quality"). Note that this approach also assumes that a piece of process either fits a given category or does not; ambiguity is not recognized as meaningful.

Critique and Contrasting Assumption: Multiplicity and Ambiguity. The opposing assumption, following Labov and Fanshel (1977) and others (e.g., Pea & Russell, 1987), is that in human communication ambiguity and multiple actions, features, and effects are the rules. Using nominal scale categories obscures this multiplicity and "fuzziness." If this is the case, then nominal scales will not describe therapy process adequately. Instead, one of two strategies is called for: First, the "open-coding" approach used by researchers in grounded theory (Rennie, Phillips, & Quartaro 1988; Strauss & Corbin, 1990) allows multiple classification but does not explicitly allow for ambiguous or unclear cases. Second, using multiple-interval scales handles both problems by allowing for multiple ratings on a set of confidence rating scales. This replaces categories with profiles; for example, the therapist response "Is your anger partly defensive?" might be rated "probably present" for interpretation, "clearly present" for question, "probably absent" for reflection, and "clearly absent" for other response modes (Elliott, 1985).

Compromise Position: Simultaneous "Presence" and "Predominance" Ratings. A compromise is also possible by rating for both "presence" (using open categories or scales) and "predominance" (using mutually exclusive categories). To continue with the example just given, interpretation might be judged to be the most important (predominant) mode, even though a question is more clearly present.

ANALYSIS OF SELECTED KEY CHANGE PROCESS STUDIES

Selection of Studies for Analysis

In order to examine the role of our simplifying assumptions in psychotherapy research, we sampled 10 representative key studies (see Table 3.2). In doing so, we used the following criteria:

1. Each study had to be a change process study; that is, it had to evaluate the effectiveness of some type of therapeutic process.
2. It had to represent the dominant or traditional approaches to change process research; that is, we excluded "new-paradigm" research (task-analytic, discovery, or events-oriented; e.g., Greenberg, 1980).
3. Each study had to represent a distinctive approach to traditional change process research. Following a scheme for classifying traditional change process studies (Elliott, Cline, & Shulman, 1983), we selected only one or two studies from each approach (see Table 3.2).
4. It had to be well known and well executed for its genre and time. In addition, one early new-paradigm change process study (Elliott, 1984) was selected for comparison.

Procedure

After selecting 10 articles, we developed definitions of the assumptions (brief versions of the descriptions given in the middle section of this chapter), along with a form for rating each article on the 14 simplifying assumptions. Following the procedure described as alternative to assumption 14, we rated assumptions on a non-mutually-exclusive basis. Each was rated separately on a 4–point confidence rating scale, with the following anchors: 0 = "assumption clearly absent in study"; 1 = "assumption probably absent in study"; 2 = "assumption probably present in study"; 3 = "assumption clearly present in study."

We then independently rated the 10 articles. After rating the

TABLE 3.2. Selected Change Process Studies

I. *Process–outcome paradigm studies*

    A. *Traditional* (noninteractional): Kanfer & Marston (1964); Mintz, Luborsky, & Auerbach (1971).

    B. *Interactional*: Crits-Christoph, Cooper, & Luborsky (1988); Horowitz, Marmar, Weiss, DeWitt, & Rosenbaum (1984).

II. *Sequential process studies*

    A. *Exploratory* ("fishing expedition"): Frank & Sweetland (1962).

    B. *Theory-focused*: Silberschatz, Fretter, & Curtis (1986); Speisman (1959).

III. *Studies of immediate perceived impact*: Barkham & Shapiro (1986); Hill, Helms, Tichenor, Speigel, O'Grady, & Perry (1988).

IV. *Study of retrospective perceived effective ingredients*: Sloane, Staples, Whipple, & Cristol (1977).

V. *Events paradigm study* (for comparison): Elliott (1984).

---

articles, we met to discuss our ratings and to resolve any disagreements. Although there were some minor disagreements involving scale points 0 and 1 (clearly vs. probably absent) and scale points 2 and 3 (probably vs. clearly present), there were no disagreements between judgments of presence or absence (0 or 1 vs. 2 or 3; kappa = 1.0).

Results

The results of this small study are presented in Table 3.3.

Analysis by Assumptions

We found that every assumption appeared in at least 1 of the 10 studies. The proportions varied from 10% (for assumptions 2 and 8) to 100% (assumption 11). The majority of assumptions (9 out of 14) appeared in at least 60% of the articles (see Table 3.3).

Analysis by Articles

As Table 3.3 indicates, Frank and Sweetland's (1962) classic sequential analysis study contained the largest proportion of simplifying assumptions (12 of 14, or 86%). The only two simplifying assump-

TABLE 3.3. Common Simplifying Assumptions in Selected Change Process Studies

1. *Single perspective for measurement:* Crits-Christoph et al. (1988); Frank & Sweetland (1962); Kanfer & Marston (1964); Mintz et al. (1971); Silberschatz et al. (1986); Sloane et al. (1977); Speisman (1959).

2. *Single variable type:* Barkham & Shapiro (1986).

3. *Single level of measurement:* Barkham & Shapiro (1986); Frank & Sweetland (1962); Horowitz et al. (1984); Mintz et al. (1971); Sloane et al. (1977); Speisman (1959).

4. *Stable effects:* Crits-Christoph et al. (1988); Frank & Sweetland (1962); Mintz et al. (1971); Silberschatz et al. (1986); Sloane et al. (1977); Speisman (1959); also Elliott (1984).

5. *Equal weighting of process units:* Crits-Christoph et al. (1988); Frank & Sweetland (1962); Hill et al. (1988); Horowitz et al. (1984); Kanfer & Marston (1964); Mintz et al. (1971); Silberschatz et al. (1986); Speisman (1959).

6. *Independence of observations:* Barkham & Shapiro (1986); Frank & Sweetland (1962); Kanfer & Marston (1964); Mintz et al. (1971); Silberschatz et al. (1986); Sloane et al. (1977); Speisman (1959).

7. *Simple conbinations of variables:* Barkham & Shapiro (1986); Frank & Sweetland (1962).

8. *Context independence:* Silberschatz et al. (1986).

9. *Uniform relevance of variables:* Barkham & Shapiro (1986); Frank & Sweetland (1962); Hill et al. (1988); Horowitz et al. (1984); Kanfer & Marston (1964); Mintz et al. (1971); Silberschatz et al. (1986); Sloane et al. (1977); Speisman (1959).

10. *Unidirectionality of causal influences:* Barkham & Shapiro (1986); Crits-Christoph et al. (1988); Frank & Sweetland (1962); Horowitz et al. (1984); Kanfer & Marston (1964); Mintz et al. (1971); Silberschatz et al. (1986); Sloane et al. (1977).

11. *Closed causal system:* Barkham & Shapiro (1986); Crits-Christoph et al.(1988); Frank & Sweetland (1962); Hill et al. (1988); Horowitz et al. (1984); Kanfer & Marston (1964); Mintz et al. (1971); Silberschatz et al. (1986); Sloane et al. (1977); Speisman (1959); Elliott (1984).

12. *Direct effects:* Crits-Christoph et al. (1988); Frank & Sweetland (1962); Mintz et al. (1971); Speisman (1959).

13. *Linearity of cause–effect associations:* Barkham & Shapiro (1986); Crits-Christoph et al. (1988); Frank & Sweetland (1962); Hill et al. (1988); Horowitz et al. (1984); Kanfer & Marston (1964); Mintz et al. (1971); Silberschatz et al. (1986); Sloane et al. (1977).

14. *Nominal scale measurements:* Barkham & Shapiro (1986); Frank & Sweetland (1962); Hill et al. (1988); Kanfer & Marston (1964); Silberschatz et al. (1986).

tions not found in this article were those regarding single variable type (assumption 2) and context independence (assumption 8). The next largest proportion of simplifying assumptions (10 out of 14, or 71%) was found in Mintz et al. (1971) and Silberschatz et al. (1986), with 8 assumptions shared by the two studies.

Only three articles held 7 (50%) or fewer simplifying assumptions: Hill et al. (1988) (5, or 36%), Horowitz et al. (1984) (6, or 43%), and Crits-Christoph et al. (1988) (7, or 50%). We rated Hill et al. (1988) as most "assumption-free," in that only 5 assumptions were utilized: equal weighting of process units (#5), uniform relevance of variables (#9), closed causal system (#11), linearity of cause–effect assiciations (#13), and nominal scale measurement (#14). Most of the assumptions made by Hill et al. occurred in the overwhelming majority (80%) of our sample of key studies.

Comparison to Elliott (1984)

As noted above, for the sake of comparison, we also sampled one events paradigm study—an analysis of four insight events by Elliott (1984). In spite of the fact that this study was chosen as an example of a new research paradigm emphasizing complexity, we still found two assumptions to be present: stable effects across time (#4) and closed causal system (#11). The presence of these assumptions reflects the fact that this study used an earlier form of comprehensive process analysis, in which effects were not tracked through time (stable effects) and inquiry was restricted to a preselected set of variables (closed causal system).

Discussion

Our analysis serves mainly to demonstrate the prevalence of simplifying assumptions in the therapy research literature. There seems to us to be a trend for the more recent studies to make fewer simplifying assumptions, even while remaining within one of the traditional research paradigms. To our thinking, this indicates the increasing influence of new-paradigm research using task analysis or significant events methods.

Some of the most prevalent assumptions were ones sharply defining differences between the new and old paradigms: equal weighting of process units (vs. significant events), uniform relevance of variables (vs. specificity), and unidirectionality of causal influences (vs. bidirectionality). However, several very common assumptions are likely to be found in new-paradigm studies as well: closed (vs. open) causal system, and linearity (vs. nonlinearity) of cause–effect associations. It may be that these assumptions represent further challenges for psychotherapy researchers and will require additional developments.

We were surprised at how easy it was to rate the studies for assumptions. It would be interesting to extend the analysis to a larger number of traditional and new paradigm studies.

CONCLUSION: SHAPES OF THINGS TO COME?

Throughout the middle section of this chapter, we have described two sets of alternatives to the simplifying tradition of psychotherapy research: one emphasizing "maximum complexity," and the other proposing compromises that would combine the values of the traditional and complexity-emphasizing approaches. Clearly, psychotherapy research as envisioned under either of these two alternative positions would be rather different from what it has been in the past and, for the most part, is now.

Maximum-Complexity Position

The maximum-complexity position is obviously an extreme one. Taking it seriously would mean a radically different form of therapy research, much more akin to qualitative sociology (e.g., Taylor & Bogdan, 1984; Whyte, 1984), formative program evaluation (Patton, 1990), action research (Whyte, 1989), or heuristic inquiry (Moustakas, 1990).

In this radical version, clients, therapists, and observers would collaborate in the process of understanding the evolving bidirectional sequences involved in the therapeutic contexts, processes, and effects associated with important moments of change. They would not use pre-existing quantitative measures, but might instead rely on a broad, comprehensive set of sensitizing headings to direct their attention to the full range of aspects and units involving each. They would seek to discover meaningful (rather than causal) relationships among views, persons, aspects, units, and phases; however, they would assume that these relationships would hold only within their unique context, and thus would not try to generalize to other important moments. Such research might be guided by one of several goals. For example, the purpose might be simply to demonstrate and illustrate the existence of nonlinearity, multiplicity, ambiguity, and evolving effects in therapy; alternatively, an action research approach (Whyte, 1989) might be taken, and these methods might be used to resolve current difficulties in particular therapy cases.

Such a vision, though presenting a clear alternative to the status quo, is probably too radical for the psychotherapy research field as a whole to contemplate seriously. Among other things, it would compromise the role of psychotherapy research as an applied field, in which researchers are attempting to develop general knowledge that is useful for training therapists and improving the practice of therapy. Using the concepts of complexity theory (Waldrop, 1992), if the traditional simplifying assumptions have imposed a stultifying "order" on the therapeutic process, the radical alternative appears to be too "chaotic" for most therapy researchers.

Recommended Compromise Position

What, then, of the proposed compromise position? Our central recommendation is that therapy researchers should continue to search for general principles, compromising the complexity of therapy no more than absolutely necessary. That is, complexity is not to be embraced for its own sake; instead, the search for underlying order (simplicity) should be balanced by an equal respect for the real complexities of therapy process. This position retains the opposing desires for simplicity and complexity in a dialectical tension with each other, which we recognize will often be less comfortable than taking a definite stand on either side.

Here is a summary of the specific compromise positions we have recommended. We do not consider them to be the last word on these issues or to eliminate the essential tension between simplicity and complexity; instead, they are offered as rough guidelines, and fall into three groups.

1. *Focused breadth*. Researchers should study a broader range of process variables, both generally and within particular studies. In particular:

a. Researchers should play to the strengths of their informants, using clients, therapists, and observers to provide the types of information they are best able to provide.

b. The full range of persons, aspects, units, and phases of therapy process should be measured; in a particular study, researchers should attempt to measure at least two persons, aspects, units, or phases, filling only the cells relevant to the particular study.

c. The elements chosen should be relevant to the focus of the study, and an attempt to sample divergent elements should be made (e.g., to include both microanalytic and macroanalytic units).

2. *Self-criticalness regarding variable structure.* Researchers should exercise greater awareness and humility in considering the complexities of interpreting or assuming particular relationships among the variables they are studying.

a. It is important to be aware of the dangers and opportunities afforded by the fact that therapy data are sequentially ordered and involve bidirectional influences (e.g., between client and therapist).

b. Researchers should be more self-critical in recognizing the role that unmeasured external variables, mediating processes, and nonlinear relationships may have played in particular studies.

c. Noncausal relationships of meaning (e.g., intentional, narrative, categorical) should be recognized as valid forms of explanation.

3. *Specific practical suggestions.* Finally, several assorted pieces of practical advice have emerged from this discussion:

a. Significant therapy events should be distinguished from ordinary therapy events, with the latter serving as context or "controls" for the former.

b. Researchers should search for both common and unique features in measuring particular therapy events.

c. Researchers may want to consider schemes that will allow them to measure process variables in terms of both presence and predominance.

These recommendations illustrate our major position throughout this chapter, which is that psychotherapy researchers can and should learn to get by on less simplification than they have in the past. That is, they can adopt fewer and less extreme simplifications. We believe that tackling the important intricacies of therapy process and outcome without giving up the search for general heuristic principles may allow psychotherapy research to join the other "emerging sciences of complexity" at the boundary between "order and chaos" (Waldrop, 1992).

REFERENCES

Alexander, L. B., & Luborsky, L. (1986). The Penn Helping Alliance Scales. In L. S. Greenberg & W. M. Pinsof (Eds.), *The psychotherapeutic process* (pp. 325–366). New York: Guilford Press.

Anderson, R. J., Hughes, J. A., & Sharrock, W. W. (1986). *Philosophy and the human sciences*. Totowa, NJ: Barnes & Noble.

Barron, F. (1969). *Creative person and creative process*. New York: Holt, Rinehart & Winston.

Barkham, M., & Shapiro, D. A. (1986). Counselor verbal response modes and experienced empathy. *Journal of Counseling Psychology, 33,* 3–10.

Benjamin, L. S. (1979). Use of Structural Analysis of Social Behavior (SASB) and markov chains to study dyadic interactions. *Journal of Abnormal Psychology, 88,* 303–319.

Bergman, D. U. (1951). Counseling method and client responses. *Journal of Consulting Psychology, 15,* 216–224.

Beutler, L. E. (1989). Differential treatment selection: The role of diagnosis in psychotherapy. *Psychotherapy, 26,* 271–281.

Bordin, E. S. (1974). *Research strategies in psychotherapy*. New York: Wiley.

Caskey, N., Barker, C., & Elliott, R. (1984). Dual perspectives: Clients' and therapists' perceptions of therapist responses. *British Journal of Clinical Psychology, 23,* 281–290.

Cook, T. D., & Campbell, D. T. (1979). *Quasi-experimentation: Design and analysis issues for field settings*. Chicago: Rand McNally.

Crits-Christoph, P., Baranackie, K., Kurcias, J. S., Beck, A. T., Carroll, K., Perry, K., Luborsky, L., McLellan, A. T., Woody, G. E., Thompson, L., Gallagher, D., & Zitrin, C. (1991). Meta-analysis of therapist effects in psychotherapy outcome studies. *Psychotherapy Research, 1,* 81–91.

Crits-Christoph, P., Cooper, A., & Luborsky, L. (1988). The accuracy of therapists' interpretations and the outcome of dynamic psychotherapy. *Journal of Consulting and Clinical Psychology, 56,* 490–495.

Eliot, T. S. (1963). Burnt Norton. In *Collected poems, 1909–1962*. New York: Harcourt, Brace & World. (Original work published 1935)

Elliott, R. (1983a). Fitting process research to the practicing psychotherapist. *Psychotherapy: Theory, Research, and Practice, 20*, 47–55.

Elliott, R. (1983b). "That in your hands. . .": A comprehensive process analysis of a significant event in psychotherapy. *Psychiatry, 46*, 113–129.

Elliott, R. (1984). A discovery-oriented approach to significant events in psychotherapy: Interpersonal process recall and comprehensive process analysis. In L. N. Rice & L. S. Greenberg (Eds.), *Patterns of change* (pp. 249–286). New York: Guilford Press.

Elliott, R. (1985). Helpful and nonhelpful events in brief counseling interviews: An empirical taxonomy. *Journal of Counseling Psychology, 32*, 307–322.

Elliott, R. (1986). Interpersonal process recall (IPR) as a psychotherapy process research method. In L. S. Greenberg & W. M. Pinsof (Eds.), *The psychotherapeutic process* (pp. 503–527). New York: Guilford Press.

Elliott, R. (1989a). Comprehensive process analysis: Understanding the change process in significant therapy events. In M. Packer & R. B. Addison (Eds.), *Entering the circle: Hermeneutic investigation in psychology* (pp. 165–184). Albany: State University of New York Press.

Elliott, R. (1989b, June). The Simplified Personal Questionnaire: Opportunities and Challenges. In M. Barkham (Chair), *Methods and approaches for understanding individual change: current research using personal questionnaires*. Symposium presented at the meeting of the Society for Psychotherapy Research, Toronto.

Elliott, R. (1991). Five dimensions of therapy process. *Psychotherapy Research, 1*, 92–103.

Elliott, R. (1992). *Modes of explanation in psychotherapy research*. Unpublished manuscript, University of Toledo.

Elliott, R., Barker, C. B., Caskey, N., & Pistrang, N. (1982). Differential helpfulness of counselor verbal response modes. *Journal of Counseling Psychology, 29*, 354–361.

Elliott, R., Cline, J., & Reid, S. (1982, June). *Tape-assisted retrospective review: A method for assessing the changing effects of therapist interventions in psychotherapy*. Paper presented at the meeting of Society for Psychotherapy Research, Smuggler's Notch, VT.

Elliott, R., Cline, J., & Shulman, R. (1983, July). *Effective processes in psychotherapy: A single case study using four evaluative paradigms*. Paper presented at the meeting of the Society for Psychotherapy Research, Sheffield, England.

Elliott, R., Hill, C. E., Stiles, W. B., Friedlander, M. L., Mahrer, A., & Margison, F. (1987). Primary therapist response modes: A comparison of six rating systems. *Journal of Consulting and Clinical Psychology, 55*, 218–223.

Elliott, R. & James, E. (1989). Varieties of client experience in psychotherapy: An analysis of the literature. *Clinical Psychology Review, 9*, 443–467.

Elliott, R., James, E., Reimschuessel, C., Cislo, D., & Sack, N. (1985). Significant events and the analysis of immediate therapeutic impacts. *Psychotherapy, 22*, 620–630.

Elliott, R., & Shapiro, D. A. (1988). Brief structured recall: A more efficient method for identifying and describing significant therapy events. *British Journal of Medical Psychology, 61*, 141–153.

Elliott, R., & Shapiro, D. A. (1992). Clients and therapists as analysts of significant events. In S. G. Toukmanian & D. L. Rennie (Eds.), *Two perspectives on psychotherapeutic change: Theory-guided and phenomenological research strategies* (pp. 163–186). Newbury Park, CA: Sage.

Fiedler, F. E. (1950). The concept of an ideal relationship. *Journal of Consulting Psychology, 14*, 239–245.

Foreman, S. A., & Marmar, C. R. (1985). Therapist actions that address initially poor therapeutic alliances in psychotherapy. *American Journal of Psychiatry, 142*, 922–926.

Frank, G. H. & Sweetland, A. A. (1962). A study of the process of psychotherapy: The verbal interaction. *Journal of Consulting Psychology, 26*, 135–138.

Fuller, F., & Hill, C. E. (1985). Counselor and helpee perceptions of counselor intentions in relation to outcome in a single counseling session. *Journal of Counseling Psychology, 32*, 329–338.

Garfield, S. L. (1986). Research on client variables in psychotherapy. In S. L. Garfield & A. E. Bergin (Eds.), *Handbook of psychotherapy and behavior change* (3rd ed., pp. 213–256). New York: Wiley.

Gaston, L., & Marmar, C. R. (1989). Quantitative and qualitative analysis for psychotherapy research: Integration through time-series designs. *Psychotherapy, 26*, 169–176.

Glass, G. V., Willson, V. L., & Gottman, J. M. (1975). *Design and analysis of time-series experiments*. Boulder: Colorado Associated University Press.

Gleick, J. (1987). *Chaos: Making a new science*. New York: Penguin.

Gholson, B., & Barker, P. (1985). Kuhn, Lakatos, and Laudan: Applications in the history of physics and psychology. *American Psychologist, 40*, 755–769.

Goldfried, M. R. (Ed.). (1982). *Converging themes in psychotherapy*. New York: Springer.

Gomes-Schwartz, B. (1978). Effective ingredients in psychotherapy: Prediction of outcome from process variables. *Journal of Consulting and Clinical Psychology, 46*, 1023–1035.

Gottman, J. M. & Markman, H. J. (1978). Experimental designs in psychotherapy research. In S. L. Garfield & A. E. Bergin (Eds.), *Handbook of psychotherapy and behavior change: An empirical analysis* (2nd ed., pp. 23–62). New York: Wiley.

Grawe, K. (1989, September). *The myth of outcome equivalence*. Paper presented at the Third European Conference on Psychotherapy Research, Bern, Switzerland.

Greenberg, L. S. (1980). An intensive analysis of recurring events from the practice of Gestalt therapy. *Psychotherapy: Theory, Research and Practice,* 17, 143–152.

Greenberg, L. S. (1984). A task analysis of intrapersonal conflict resolution. In L. N. Rice & L. S. Greenberg (Eds.), *Patterns of change* (pp. 67–123). New York: Guilford Press.

Greenberg, L. S. (1986). Research strategies. In L. S. Greenberg & W. M. Pinsof (Eds.), *The psychotherapeutic process* (pp. 707–734). New York: Guilford Press.

Guidano, V. F. (1987). *Complexity of the self*. New York: Guilford Press.

Gurman, A. S. (1977). The patient's perception of the therapeutic relationship. In A. S. Gurman & A. M. Razin (Eds.), *Effective Psychotherapy: A handbook of research* (pp. 503–543). Elmsford, NY: Pergamon Press.

Hare-Mustin, R. T., & Marecek, J. (1988). The meaning of difference: Gender theory, post-modernism, and psychology. *American Psychologist, 43,* 455–464.

Harré, R. (1972). *The philosophies of science*. New York: Oxford University Press.

Harré, R. (1983). *An introduction to the logic of the sciences*. New York: St. Martin's Press.

Heatherington, L. (1989). Toward more meaningful clinical research: Taking context into account in coding psychotherapy interaction. *Psychotherapy, 26,* 436–447.

Hill, C. E. (1974). A comparison of the perceptions of a therapy session by clients, therapists and objective judges. *JSAS Catalog of Selected Documents in Psychology, 4,* 16 (Ms. No. 564).

Hill, C. E. (1986). An overview of the Hill Counselor and Client Verbal Response Modes Category Systems. In L. S. Greenberg & W. M. Pinsof (Eds.), *The psychotherapeutic process* (pp. 131–159). New York: Guilford Press.

Hill, C. E., Carter, J. A., & O'Farrell, M. K. (1983). A case study of the process and outcome of time-limited counseling. *Journal of Counseling Psychology, 30,* 3–18.

Hill, C. E., Helms, J. E., Tichenor, V., Speigel, S. B., O'Grady, K., & Perry, E. S. (1988). Effects of therapist responses modes in brief psychotherapy. *Journal of Counseling Psychology, 35,* 222–233.

Hill, T. E. (1961). *Contemporary theories of knowledge.* New York: Ronald Press.

Horowitz, M. J. (1987). *States of mind: Analysis of change in psychotherapy* (2nd ed.). New York: Plenum.

Horowitz, M. J., Marmar, C., Weiss, D. S., DeWitt, K, & Rosenbaum, R. (1984). Brief psychotherapy of bereavement reactions. *Archives of General Psychiatry, 41,* 438–448.

Hoyt, M. F. (1980). Therapist and patient actions in "good" psychotherapy sessions. *Archives of General Psychiatry, 37,* 159–161.

Howard, K. I., Orlinsky, D. E., & Perilstein, J. (1976). Contribution of therapists to patients' experiences in psychotherapy: A components of variance model for analyzing process data. *Journal of Consulting and Clinical Psychology, 44,* 520–526.

Jones, E. E., Cumming, J. D., & Horowitz, M. J. (1988). Another look at the nonspecific hypothesis of therapeutic effectiveness. *Journal of Consulting and Clinical Psychology, 56,* 48–55.

Jöreskog, K. G., & Sörbom, D. (1979). *Advances in factor analysis and structural equation models.* Cambridge, MA: Abt Books.

Kanfer, F. H., & Marston, A. R. (1964). Characteristics of interactional behavior in a psychotherapy analogue. *Journal of Consulting Psychology, 28,* 456–467.

Kaschak, E. (1978). Therapist and client: Two views of the process and outcome of psychotherapy. *Professional Psychology, 9,* 271–277.

Kazdin, A. E. (1984). Statistical analyses for single-case experimental designs. In D. H. Barlow & M. Hersen (Eds.), *Single case experimental designs* (2nd ed., pp. 285–324). Elmsford, NY: Pergamon Press.

Kelly, G. A. (1955). *The psychology of personal constructs* (Vols. 1 & 2). New York: Norton.

Kelman, H. (1969). *Kairos:* The auspicious moment. *American Journal of Psychoanalysis, 29,* 59–83.

Kierkegaard, S. (1941). *Concluding unscientific postscript* (D. F. Swenson & W. Lowrie, Trans.). Princeton, NJ: Princeton University Press. (Original work published 1846)

Kiesler, D. J. (1966). Some myths of psychotherapy research and the search for a paradigm. *Psychological Bulletin, 65,* 110–136.

Kiesler, D. J. (1973). *The process of psychotherapy.* Chicago: Aldine.

Klein, M. H., Mathieu-Coughlan, P., & Kiesler, D. J. (1986). The Experiencing Scales. In L. S. Greenberg & W. M. Pinsof (Eds.), *The psychotherapeutic process* (pp. 21–71). New York: Guilford Press.

Labov, W., & Fanshel, D. (1977). *Therapeutic discourse.* New York: Academic Press.

Llewelyn, S. (1988). Psychological therapy as viewed by clients and therapists. *British Journal of Clinical Psychology, 27,* 223–238.

Lincoln, Y., & Guba, E. G. (1985). *Naturalistic inquiry*. Beverly Hills, CA: Sage.

Luborsky, L., & Crits-Christoph, P. (1990). *Understanding transference: The CCRT method*. New York: Basic Books.

Luborsky, L., Crits-Christoph, P., Mintz, J., & Auerbach, A. (1988). *Who will benefit from psychotherapy?: Predicting therapeutic outcomes*. New York: Basic Books.

Mahrer, A. R., Dessaulles, A., Nadler, W. P., Gervaize, P. A., & Sterner, I. (1987). Good and very good moments in psychotherapy: Content, distribution, and facilitation. *Psychotherapy, 24*, 7–14.

Martin, J., Martin, W., & Slemon, A. G. (1987). Cognitive mediation in person-centered and rational-emotive therapy. *Journal of Counseling Psychology, 34*, 251–260.

Martin, J., & Stelmaczonek, K. (1988). Participants' identification and recall of important events in counseling. *Journal of Counseling Psychology, 35*, 385–390.

Messer, S. B., Tishby, O., & Spillman, A. (1992). Taking context seriously in psychotherapy research: Relating interventions to patient progress in brief psychodynamic therapy. *Journal of Consulting and Clinical Psychology, 60*, 678–688.

Miles, M. B., & Huberman, A. M. (1984). *Qualitative data analysis: A sourcebook of new methods*. Beverly Hills, CA: Sage.

Mintz, J. (1977). The role of the therapist in assessing psychotherapy outcome. In A. S. Gurman & A. M. Razin (Eds.), *Effective psychotherapy: A handbook of research* (pp. 590–602). Elmsford, NY: Pergamon Press.

Mintz, J., Luborsky, L., & Auerbach, A. H. (1971). Dimensions of psychotherapy: A factor-analytic study of ratings of psychotherapy sessions. *Journal of Consulting and Clinical Psychology, 36*, 106–120.

Mintz, J., Luborsky, L., & Christoph, P. (1979). Measuring the outcomes of psychotherapy: Findings of the Penn Psychotherapy Project. *Journal of Consulting and Clinical Psychology, 47*, 319–334.

Morrow-Bradley, C., & Elliott, R. (1986). The utilization of psychotherapy research by practicing psychotherapists. *American Psychologist, 41*, 188–197.

Moustakas, C. (1990). *Heuristic research: Design, methodology, and applications*. Beverly Hills, CA: Sage.

Nicholson, R. A., & Berman, J. S. (1983). Is follow-up necessary in evaluating psychotherapy? *Psychological Bulletin, 93*, 261–278.

Nunnally, J. C. (1978). *Psychometric theory*. New York: McGraw-Hill.

Orlinsky, D. E., & Howard, K. I. (1975). *Varieties of psychotherapeutic experience*. New York: Teachers College Press.

Orlinsky, D. E., & Howard, K. I. (1977). The therapist's experience of psychotherapy. In A. S. Gurman & A. M. Razin (Eds.), *Effective psycho-

therapy: A handbook of research (pp. 566–589). Elmsford, NY: Pergamon Press.

Orlinsky, D. E., & Howard, K. I. (1978). The relation of process to outcome in psychotherapy. In S. L. Garfield & A. E. Bergin (Eds.), *Handbook of psychotherapy and behavior change* (2nd ed., pp. 283–330). New York: Wiley.

Orlinsky, D. E., & Howard, K. I. (1986). The psychological interior of psychotherapy: Explorations with the Therapy Session Reports. In L. S. Greenberg & W. M. Pinsof (Eds.), *The psychotherapeutic process* (pp. 477–501). New York: Guilford Press.

Orlinsky, D. E., & Howard, K. I. (1987). A generic model of psychotherapy. *Journal of Integrative and Eclectic Psychotherapy, 6,* 6–27.

Packer, M. J., & Addison, R. B. (Eds.). (1989). *Entering the circle: Hermeneutic investigation in psychology.* Albany: State University of New York Press.

Patton, M. Q. (1990). *Qualitative evaluation and research methods* (2nd ed.). Beverly Hills, CA: Sage.

Pea, R. D., & Russell, R. L. (1987). Ethnography and the vicissitudes of talk in psychotherapy. In R. L. Russell (Ed.), *Language in psychotherapy* (pp. 303–338). New York: Plenum.

Pinsof, W. M. (1986). The process of family therapy: The development of the Family Therapist Coding System. In L. S. Greenberg & W. M. Pinsof (Eds.), *The psychotherapeutic process* (pp. 201–284). New York: Guilford Press.

Polkinghorne, D. (1983). *Methodology for the human sciences: Systems of inquiry.* Albany: State University of New York Press.

Pollio, H. R. (1982). *Behavior and existence.* Monterey, CA: Brooks/Cole.

Prigogine, I., & Stengers, I. (1984). *Order out of chaos: Man's new dialogue with nature.* New York: Bantam.

Quine, W. V. O. (1966). *The ways of paradox.* New York: Random House.

Rennie, D. L. (1985, June). *Client deference in the psychotherapy relationship.* Paper presented at the meeting of the Society for Psychotherapy Research, Evanston, IL.

Rennie, D. L., Phillips, J. R., & Quartaro, G. K. (1988). Grounded theory: A promising approach to conceptualization in psychology. *Canadian Psychology, 29,* 139–150.

Rice, L. N. & Greenberg, L. S. (Eds.). (1984). *Patterns of change.* New York: Guilford Press.

Rice, L. N., & Kerr, G. P. (1986). Measures of client and therapist vocal quality. In L. S. Greenberg & W. M. Pinsof (Eds.), *The psychotherapeutic process* (pp. 73–105). New York: Guilford Press.

Rice, L. N., & Sapiera, E. P. (1984). Task analysis and the resolution of problematic reactions. In L. N. Rice & L. S. Greenberg (Eds.), *Patterns of change* (pp. 29–66). New York: Guilford Press.

Russell, R. L. (1986). The inadvisability of admixing psychoanalysis with other forms of psychotherapy. *Journal of Contemporary Psychotherapy, 16*, 76–86.

Russell, R. L., & Czogalik, D. (1989). Strategies for analyzing conversations: Frequencies, sequences, or rules. *Journal of Social Behavior and Personality, 4*, 221–236.

Russell, R. L., & Staszewski, C. (1988). The unit problem: Some systematic distinctions and critical dilemmas for psychotherapy process research. *Psychotherapy, 25*, 191–200.

Russell, R. L., & Trull, T. J. (1986). Sequential analyses of language variables in psychotherapy process research. *Journal of Consulting and Clinical Psychology, 54*, 16–21.

Ryle, G. (1949). *The concept of mind*. New York: Barnes & Noble.

Safran, J. D., Crocker, P., McMain, S., & Murray, P. (1990). Therapeutic alliance rupture as a therapy event for empirical investigation. *Psychotherapy, 27*, 154–165.

Sarbin, T. R., & Adler, N. (1971). Self-reconstitution processes: A preliminary report. *Psychoanalytic Review, 57*, 599–616.

Schaffer, N. D. (1982). Multidimensional measures of therapist behavior as predictors of outcome. *Psychological Bulletin, 3*, 670–681.

Searle, J. R. (1983). *Intentionality: An essay in the philosophy of mind*. New York: Cambridge University Press.

Silberschatz, G., Fretter, P. B., & Curtis, J. T. (1986). How do interpretations influence the process of psychotherapy? *Journal of Consulting and Clinical Psychology, 54*, 646–652.

Sloane, R. B., Staples, F. R., Whipple, K., & Cristol, A. H. (1977). Patients' attitudes toward behavior therapy and psychotherapy. *American Journal of Psychiatry, 134*, 134–137.

Smith, M. L., Glass, G. V., & Miller, T. I. (1980). *The benefits of psychotherapy*. Baltimore: Johns Hopkins University Press.

Sober, E. (1975). *Simplicity*. Oxford: Clarendon Press.

Sotsky, S., Glass, D., Shea, T., & Pilkonis, P. (1986, June). Patient predictors of treatment response. In I. Elkin (Chair), *NIMH Treatment of Depression Collaborative Research Program*. Symposium presented at the meeting of Society for Psychotherapy Research, Wellesley, MA.

Speisman, J. C. (1959). Depth of interpretation and verbal resistance in psychotherapy. *Journal of Consulting Psychology, 23*, 93–99.

Stevens, S. S. (1946). On the theory of scales of measurement. *Science, 103*, 677–680.

Stiles, W. B. (1980). Measurement of the impact of psychotherapy sessions. *Journal of Consulting and Clinical Psychology, 48*, 176–185.

Stiles, W. B. (1986). Levels of intended meaning of utterances. *British Journal of Clinical Psychology, 25*, 213–222.

Stiles, W. B. (1988). Psychotherapy process-outcome correlations may be misleading. *Psychotherapy, 25,* 27–35.

Stiles, W. B., & Shapiro, D. A. (1989). Abuse of the drug metaphor in psychotherapy process-outcome research. *Clinical Psychology Review, 9,* 521–543.

Strauss, A. L., & Corbin, J. (1990). *Basics of qualitative research: Grounded theory procedures and techniques.* Beverly Hills, CA: Sage.

Suh, C. S., Strupp, H. H., & O'Malley, S. S. (1986). The Vanderbilt Process Measures: The Psychotherapy Process Scale (VPPS) and the Negative Indicators Scale (VNIS). In L. S. Greenberg & W. M. Pinsof (Eds.), *The psychotherapeutic process* (pp. 285–323). New York: Guilford Press.

Tarragona, M., & Orlinsky, D. E. (1987, June). *Patients' experiences of therapy between sessions and their role in the therapeutic process.* Paper presented at the meeting of Society for Psychotherapy Research, Ulm, West Germany.

Taylor, S. J., & Bogdan, R. (1984). *Introduction to qualitative research methods* (2nd ed.). New York: Wiley-Interscience.

Toulmin, S. (1960). *The philosophy of science: An introduction.* New York: Harper & Row.

Truax, C. B., & Carkhuff, R. R. (1967). *Toward effective counseling and psychotherapy: Training and practice.* Chicago: Aldine.

Viney, W. (1989). The cyclops and the twelve-eyed toad: William James and the unity–disunity problem in psychology. *American Psychologist, 44,* 1261–1265.

Waldrop, M. M. (1992). *Complexity: The emerging science at the edge of order and chaos.* New York: Simon & Schuster.

Waskow, I. E., & Parloff, M. B. (Eds.). (1975). *Psychotherapy change measures.* Rockville, MD: National Institute of Mental Health.

Wertz, F. J. (1983). From everyday to psychological description: Analyzing the moments of a qualitative data analysis. *Journal of Phenomenological Psychology, 14,* 197–241.

Winch, P. (1958). *The idea of a social science and its relation to philosophy.* New York: Humanities Press.

Wiseman, H., & Rice, L. N. (1989). Sequential analyses of therapist–client interaction during change events: A task-focused approach. *Journal of Consulting and Clinical Psychology, 57,* 281–286.

Whyte, W. F. (1984). *Learning from the field: A guide from experience.* Beverly Hills, CA: Sage.

Whyte, W. F. (Ed.). (1989). Action research for the twenty-first century: Participation, reflection, and practice [Special issue]. *American Behavioral Scientist, 32.*

CHAPTER 4

The Investigation of Change
Its Measurement and Explanation

LESLIE S. GREENBERG

One of the most remarkable observations we can make about psychotherapy is that no one really knows how it leads to change. If we scratch beneath the surface of even those who confidently espouse particular theories, we find doubt and a sense of mystery and wonder. Psychotherapy is a field ripe for discovery-oriented investigation. If only we can mobilize and capture the curiosity and wonder of people who study psychotherapy, rather than deaden it within a restricting methodological strait jacket! A critical feature of psychotherapy research is that it involves the investigation of a domain in which a vast amount of practice already occurs, guided by theoretical knowledge and beliefs but not by scientifically based understanding. The researcher's task is both complicated and enhanced by this state of affairs. There is no need to start from scratch and begin to build a knowledge domain based on research or controlled experiments alone; a rich and complex domain of practice already exists, and the researcher's task is to make sense of it. This aspect of psychotherapy research is more like the task of the detective attempting to unravel what has already occurred, rather than that of the experimenter setting up a controlled experiment to study the effect of specific variables. A discovery orientation thus has special relevance to the study of psychotherapy.

The general conclusions of the outcome evaluation literature—(1) that psychotherapy is effective, and (2) that different types of psychotherapy have not been shown by existing methodology to produce significantly different degrees of benefit—are finally forcing us to re-examine the psychotherapeutic process in an attempt to understand what accounts for change in the therapeutic process.

A number of process-oriented researchers have been predicting the situation we are in and stressing the need for research on *understanding the change process*, rather than just evaluating outcome in the form of differential effects or studying process in the form of simple associations between variables (Rice & Greenberg, 1974, 1984; Elliott, 1983). This new focus on understanding the change process has led to the investigation of change episodes in therapy and to the development of "micro theory," which explains how change takes place. The focus of these efforts is on providing causal explanations of therapeutic change and on making explanation rather than prediction the primary goal of psychotherapy research.

THE CHANGE PROCESS

The "applied science" of psychotherapy outcome evaluation has now satisfied most of the critics by demonstrating that psychotherapy is on the whole more effective than no treatment. (Glass, McGaw, Smith, 1981, Bergin & Lambert, 1978). Through comparative treatment studies, meta-analyses, and at least 30 years of hard work, we are finally convinced that "Everyone has won and all must have prizes" (Luborsky, Singer, & Luborsky, 1975, p. 995). The field is now mature enough to develop a more "basic science" approach to the study of psychotherapy by systematically attending to the process of psychotherapy to discover how therapeutic change takes place. We need to investigate and discover what accounts for change in diverse treatments. We need to specify the active therapeutic ingredients or curative elements in different treatments. In doing this, however, we should not be in too much of a hurry to rush to our theories for answers to the question of what carries the therapeutic action, as our predecessors have been; rather, we should turn to the therapeutic process itself in order to discover what actually changes and how this occurs.

Two major hypotheses about the change process have logically emerged from the findings of no difference among treatments. The first is that a set of common ingredients across all treatments accounts for change; the other is that different specific processes account for about the same amount of change in each treatment, and that we need to specify more closely the processes that mediate change in different therapies.

In response to the first, "shared-ingredients" hypothesis, the research task has been to specify and measure the factors common to all therapies that account for the benefits we find across treatments. This common-factor approach, of course, is becoming one of the new clarion calls of many (and hinges on Jerome Frank's [1979] original view that a set of common factors accounts for the effectiveness of all methods of persuasion and healing). The latest and most promising candidate in the common-factors domain is the notion of the "therapeutic working alliance." The idea that the degree of collaboration between the participants in therapy predicts outcome is an intuitively sensible idea. The conceptualization of the alliance by Bordin (1979) as an agreement between client and therapist on the goals and tasks of therapy, as well as the provision of an appropriate bond to facilitate the therapeutic tasks, has proved to be an important theoretical framework for understanding how the alliance is created and maintained. Although more studies need to be done comparing different measures of the alliance to see whether they are measuring the same construct, there is a promising consistency across studies relating the working alliance to outcome (Greenberg & Pinsof, 1986).

In summary, the common-elements approach thus arises from the view that since the search for differential treatment effects has proven rather unproductive, there is a strong possibility that the preponderant weight of psychotherapeutic changes is borne by psychological forces that are shared by the various therapeutic approaches, despite the fact that different languages are used to explain the approaches.

Although I believe that the identification of shared elements is useful I think we must not overlook the second hypothesis—namely, that different approaches also rely on specific processes in specific contexts. Therapy is a complex, multivariate process including (but not limited to) factors such as reliance on the expectation of change, the provision of hope and support, and collaboration between the participants. Different processes involved in different approaches also account for change. In addition, different processes are important at different times, and all the processes combine to produce the final effects. It is this complex integration of processes that we need to investigate and understand. In fact, Bordin's (1979) notion of the alliance explicitly integrates common and specific factors by including specific technical aspects (i.e., the tasks) in the overall alliance. Orlinsky and Howard's (1987) generic model of psychotherapy also integrates common and specific factors. To support this view of the importance of specific technical processes, I would suggest that we look briefly at some aspects of the alliance research and at the recent National Institute of Mental Health (NIMH) Treatment of Depression Collaborative Research Program.

First, the findings of the alliance research suggest that a good alliance predicts at most 36% of the outcome variance, but more generally 25% (Greenberg & Pinsof, 1986; Luborsky, Crits-Christoph, Mintz, & Auerbach, 1988). This leaves a whopping 75% still to be accounted for. Moreover, as already mentioned, the alliance itself is an overarching construct that subsumes the effects of specific tasks in therapy. In fact, in our research with the Working Alliance Inventory (Horvath & Greenberg, 1986, 1989), we have found that perceived "task relevance" is the element that often correlates most highly with outcome. Thus, if clients perceive the therapeutic tasks to be relevant to the mutually agreed-on goals of therapy, treatment is more likely to be successful. This is best exemplified in one of our studies, in which a portion of the outcome variance (approximately 36%) was accounted for by clients who perceived the task (which involved having a dialogue between the opposing aspects of a conflict) as relevant to their goals of resolving decisional conflict. However, a similar proportion of the variance was also accounted for by the presence of specific processes, including expressions of feelings and wants and the softening of a previously harsh critic (Greenberg & Webster, 1982). The alliance is thus not independent of technique; rather, a good alliance is characterized by the use of appropriate technical methods, and prediction will probably be enhanced by the addition of specific processes to the alliance (Luborsky et al., 1988). If psychotherapy is to be understood in all its complexity, it will be necessary to understand the interaction of different aspects of the conditions facilitating therapeutic change and the specific "work" that goes on in therapy.

The second indication of the existence of specific process comes from an analysis of the NIMH research program (Elkin et al., 1989), in which depressed patients were given four treatments: imipramine and clinical management, cognitive therapy, interpersonal therapy, and placebo plus clinical management. There was no evidence for greater effectiveness of one of the psychotherapies as compared to the other, and no evidence that either of the psychotherapies was significantly less effective than the drug treatment. All four treatments, including the placebo, also evidenced significant change from pre- to posttreatment. We could conclude that the overall provision of a helpful relationship and the general expectation of help accounted for all change, but more intensive inspection of differences in treatment course and effects shows that the same process did not occur across groups. First, the imipramine group responded more quickly; second, the comparison of each therapy with the placebo indicated some limited evidence for the superior effectiveness of interpersonal therapy; third, and most important, when the patient group was divided accoradig to severity of depression, some treatment differences did emerge. The more functionally impaired fared best on imipramine treatment, and it and interpersonal trerapy were consistently superior to the placebo.

As I see it, claiming that all treatments work because of the same shared ingredients would be a serious mistake. Clearly, many different things are happening, and it is our job to understand the different processes involved. Imipramine and the two psychotherapies (cognitive and interpersonal therapy) do not work by the same mechanisms. A placebo is less powerful for the more distressed; it is helpful overall, but not as helpful. Even if tahe placebo were as helpful as imipramine, it is known that imipramine is not neurochemically inert, as is the placebo treatment. Imipramine and the placebo clearly do not work by the same mechanism. I believe that we need to agree that "there are more things in heaven and earth than are dreamt of in the common-ingredients philosophy" (with apologies to Shakespeare), and that we need to develop methods for studying the different change processes in therapy.

PSYCHOTHERAPY RESEARCH BASED ON INTENSIVE ANALYSIS

Science proceeds by observation, measurement, explanation, and prediction (Hempel, 1966). In psychotherapy research to date, however, limited attention has been paid to the initial three steps, especially to observation and explanation. In fact, intensive and rigorous observation of how change takes place has probably been the most sorely neglected. We need to observe the process of change in order to identify patterns that will lead to the kind of explanation that involves new understanding of what actually occurs, instead of automatic theoretical explanations from our favorite (often too strongly held) theory.

In order to satisy all of these steps a colleague and I have suggested an eight-step rational–empirical research strategy, which includes an intensive discovery-oriented phase as well as a verification-oriented phase. We have elaborated upon this research strategy more fully elsewhere (Rice & Greenberg, 1984). The approach involves having expert clinicians select change phenomena from their practice for study. The experts' implicit map is then explicated as fully as possible, providing an initial framework for studying the phenomena. Change episodes are then selected for study, and rational and empirical models of the change processes involved in the change episode are constructed. These models are constructed in an iterative manner. First, a rational model is constructed according to the investigators' current best guess of how change occurs, drawing on the experts' explicated map and current theory. Then actual episodes are intensively analyzed to see what actually occurs and to suggest ways of measuring the hypothesized change processes. The empirical findings are then used to correct and modify the rational model. Progressive rational and empirical models are developed on further cases until the researchers have developed sufficiently refined rational-empirical models of the processes and a means of rigorously measuring these processes. The research program then enters a verification stage, in which the validity of the model is tested and the change processes are related to outcome.

This approach has heightened our appreciation of how observation of what actually occurs, although it is a crucial step in science, is too often bypassed in traditional psychotherapy research. As clinicians, we are participant–observers of the change process; as scientists, we need to become objective observers of the process. It is ludicrous that currently we measure the beginning and end points of a complex process, and then, if there is no difference at the end, we claim that what went on in between these points is the same. We need to engage in process research to observe and understand change, but a new style of process research is needed. Features of this new style and some of its characteristics are outlined in Table 4.1 and discussed below.

Studying the Change Process

Again, psychotherapy research needs to focus primarily on the change process itself. In this attempt, process measures and client

TABLE 4.1. A New Style of Process Research

Features	Characteristics
1. Studying the change process	Studying the patient/client or the interactional process
2. Studying process in context	Defining therapeutic episodes
3. Discovery-oriented research	Identifying patterns of regularity and constructing measures of phenomena
4. Causal explanation	Building a mini-theoretical model with causal laws, processes, and interactions

and therapist reports should be used not only to describe *what* occurs in therapy, but to help us understand *how* change comes about. The study of change shifts the focus away from specifying or manualising therapist interventions as a primary research endeavor, and shifts it toward specifying the processes between client and therapist and within the client that carry the change process. This focus involves studying such variables as interactional stances; the content and manner of clients' verbalizations; nonverbal aspects of communication, such as vocal quality; and shifts in emotional, cognitive, and interpersonal states.

Highly specific measures of therapeutically relevant variables are greatly needed. Such variables would include the following: the degree of resolution of specific problems, such as conflicts or problematic reactions (Rice & Greenberg, 1984); the degree of resolution of unfinished business (Greenberg, Rice, & Elliott, 1993) or attainment of self-assertion or responsibility (causal self-attribution); the extent of awareness of, or change in, core conflictual relationship themes (Luborsky et al., 1988), interpersonal cycles (Strupp & Binder, 1984), or pathogenic beliefs (Weiss, Sampson, & the Mount Zion Psychotherapy Research Group, 1986); the degree of change in depth of experiencing (Klein, Mathieu-Coughlin, & Kiesler, 1986), in automatic thoughts (Beck, Rush, Shaw, & Emery, 1979), or in the clients' linguistic contrual of self or of self–other relationships (Russell, 1987); the passing of a therapeutic test (Weiss et al., 1986); or the healing of alliance ruptures.

The types of change studied and measured will depend on the hypothesized change process believed to operate in the particular therapy, in the particular disorder, or in the particular therapeutic context. A study of change will result in the specification of a variety of therapeutic change processes, and these processes will be the fundamental building blocks for the science of psychotherapy. We could delineate major types of change processes based on the basic hypotheses in the field and begin to rigorously investigate different aspects of these. One way we might proceed is to categorize change processes as follows: changes in (1) relationships, (2) insight, (3) awareness/experience, and (4) learning/experience.

With this focus on the process of change, we should attend to at least four levels of change: change in the in-session process, in session outcome, in intermediate (postsession or phase) outcome, and in final outcome (measured as change at both posttreatment and follow-up) (Greenberg, 1986a, 1986b). In addition to studying each of these separately, studying the relationships between them will become crucial, as will studying of the process of outcome. For example, cases with linear and curvilinear trends in postsession outcome are clearly engaged in different types of change processes, and these processes require independent study.

The development of intermediate-level measures of the specific types of changes that are posited to occur in a particular therapy is a high priority. Thus measures of change in core conflictual themes, in self-acceptance, in tolerance toward others and in negative views of self and the future all need to be developed. Our field is full of hypothesized changes and multiple techniques for producing these changes. A major problem is that we do not have many instruments available for measuring the intermediate-level changes brought about by specific interventions. These intermediate outcomes are not necessarily changes in symptomatology or in a specified disorder; rather, they are changes that *mediate* changes in the disorder. Measuring changes at this level would provide an important missing link in understanding and measuring complex therapeutic change and in relating processes to outcome. This would allow us to relate process to outcome in smaller steps.

Studying Process in Context

One of the most neglected variables in psychotherapy research is that of context. Both researchers and clinicians struggle to understand what is occurring in therapy—both within the client and the therapist, and between the client and therapist. The participants, however, have the advantage of having being in the situation, and thus have the whole range of context information available to inform their understanding of what is occurring. A researcher, of necessity, has to abstract information about the situation and symbolize it in order to study the situation. Unfortunately, the predominant manner in which process research has been done has stripped the behavior of its context. Observational coding systems abstract the information about certain features of behavior, independently of the context in which they occur; although this highlights certain aspects, it reduces our potential understanding of the situation by eliminating others. Failure to take context into account affects the meaningfulness of our results. Context is critical in understanding human behavior, yet in observational coding and scientific study it is not treated as the resource it is for understanding in our everyday lives (Heatherington, 1989).

In studying context, though, we are faced with complexity. Context is not unidimensional. It can usefully be described as existing at different levels, however, and I have suggested that at least four levels of context can be specified in psychotherapy change process research (Greenberg, 1986a, 1986b). Specification of the relationship level, the episode level, the level of the immediate communicative context or speech act, and the verbal content level would embed process codings in appropriate contexts. The choice of only these four levels does not mean to imply that higher-level, (situational, social, and cultural) variables are not important to the conduct of therapy; it simply implies that a study of change processes in individual therapy should at least take measures of the four suggested levels into account, and should account for other higher levels when this is necessary to a particular study.

Clearly, the meaning of particular acts in the therapeutic process depends on the relational context in which they occur. The same act—say, a confrontation—may have a vastly different meaning and impact, depending on the relational context in which it occurs. For example, within the context of a good working alliance a confrontation may be regarded as helpful and will be heard; in the context of a poor alliance, it may well be felt as an attack and be discounted or defended against.

The episode level is crucial in specifying the building blocks of the therapeutic situation, just as social episodes are in defining social situations. Thus a dinner party consists of a number of social episodes (arrival, before-dinner drink, dinner, dessert, departure). Each episode is a sequence of interaction about which there is some consensus concerning the boundaries, rules, and expectations. These are recognizable, repeated interaction sequences. Similarly, episodes in therapy can be specified and studied. They provide important contexts for understanding what is occurring.

The meaning of a speech act or message is dependent not only on episode and relationship contexts, but also on the immediate speech acts surrounding it. Thus a client's statement to the therapist, such as "I find it difficult to tell you what I feel when you look at me like that," has a different meaning in response to a question about what will help the client feel more comfortable (in which case it is an information-giving response) than in response to a confrontation or interpretation (in which case it may be a hostile, withholding response).

Finally meaning is dependent on verbal content. Although much work was initially done on specifying content by means of content coding schemes, this level of coding did not prove to be that promising mainly because content is so dependent on context and manner for its meaning. Recent attempts at identifying the narrative content or themes of therapy from thranscripts represent a promising new approach to working with content over the course of treatment (Angus & Hardtke, 1993).

Of the levels described above, the episode level seems to be of particular importance in promoting a study of change in therapy; paradoxically, however, it is the least studied of the levels (Russell, 1987). Different methods can be used for specifying episodes. Participants' views of the situation can be obtained to define episodes (Elliott, 1986), or rationally guided, inductive searches of the process can be undertaken to identify meaningful episodes. In this latter approach (Rice & Greenberg, 1984), the investigators identify different change events, each consisting of a client marker of an opportunity for change, a relevant therapist set of interventions at this marker, and the ensuing client performance. In this approach, the change events are selected on the grounds that they are recurrent, seemingly potent events; their actual potency requires empirical validation once they have been sufficiently defined.

Various other methods of identifying episodes or events can be used, such as marking an event by a shift in a particularly relevant

variable or by the occurrence of a particular performance relevant
to a clinical or theoretical formulation. At least five means of isolating
episodes have been used:

1. In-session events are identified by client markers and therapist interventions (Rice & Greenberg, 1984; Greenberg, 1986a,
1986b).

2. Clients identify events based on in-session impacts (Elliott,
1986)

3. Shifts in a variable are used to identify an event (Luborsky,
Singer, Harte, Crits-Christoph, & Cohen, 1984; Marmar, Wilner, &
Horowitz, 1984).

4. A clinical formulation of such variables as the core issue, the
problem, or interpersonal or characterological issues is used to track
certain episodes relevant to the theme (Luborsky, et al., 1988).

5. A theoretical formulation is used to derive the occurrence of
certain phenomena which are identified and investigated (Weiss et
al., 1986).

Whatever the method for locating key episodes, the procedure
involves collecting of recurrent episodes of change from tapes and
transcripts and inspecting them for regularities. Every therapy is not
a new and unique process, with little or no similarity to other therapies. There is complexity, but there is also regularity. Instead of
building theory based on clinically perceived regularities, we need to
collect samples of the phenomena, and then employ regorous, reliable observation, studying them closely to determine the presence
of regularities and patterns.

In two studies in which my colleagues and I are now engaged,
looking at the resolution of unfinished business and at therapeutic
weeping, we are collecting episodes of the phenomena we wish to
study. I cannot tell you the excitement we feel when we finally collect
12 examples of a phenomenon and see the regularities in the performances. We hold in our hands the transcripts that provide proof
of the observable, recurrent regularities in the phenomena. For
example, the mobilization of an unmet need and its expression are
necessary components of the resolution of unfinished business with
a significant other, whereas accessing and transforming a dysfunctional belief seem crucial in resolving a weeping episode related to
hopelessness. The concrete in-session episodes provide compelling

evidence that there are observable phenomena such as these in psychotherapy.

Thus, basic procedure I am suggesting here is first to locate change episodes within sessions and then to study intensively the process of change in the episodes. The result of this approach should be the development of an open-ended taxonomy of change episodes or events that have been found to occur in therapy. This would be an open scheme, in that new episodes could be added as they are discovered or invented, and episode structures could be refined with ongoing investigation.

Discovery-Oriented Research

A discovery orientation is relevant on two different fronts. On the one hand, a discovery-oriented approach can be contrasted with a verification-oriented approach; this is a contrast between investigative searching for patterns and hypothesis testing. I will not go into detail about this here, because I have discussed it elsewhere (Greenberg, 1986b). In this section, I focus instead on an aspect of discovery orientation that is particularly relevant to process research—namely, discovery in the measurement construction process. Discovery in the context of measurement involves the construction of new measures by inductive procedures, in which the investigator closely observes phenomena in order to describe them more accurately. In this approach, the investigator devises coding categories based on observation, rather than applying existing, predetermined coding schemes in which the coding categories have been rationally devised and represent the operationalization of a particular view of reality. In a discovery orientation, process measures and the categories within them should be based predominantly on observation rather than theory, and should be geared toward detailed understanding rather than abstract classification. We need measures that differentiate clinically relevant features that distinguish change in specified contexts. We need to observe these phenomena and develop coding schemes that will describe and define different features of the phenomena. It is only through the description and study of what is consensually agreed on as actually occurring in therapy that we will advance our understanding of how change takes place.

I would like to discuss below at some length certain issues relevant to discovery-oriented measurement construction that will, in my view, be important to a "new-look" style of research.

Discovery-Oriented Measurement Construction: Basic Issues

A methodological problem that is basic to the analysis of psychotherapy is the construction of systems of classification. A first requirement for process research is to devise tools that will permit the investigator to measure relevant aspects of the therapeutic interchange. In devising measures, the selection of what to measure is always dictated by theoretical as well as practical considerations. In fact, a coding system respresents a prior judgment as to what is important to measure.

Butler, Rice, and Wagstaff (1963) in their book *Quantitative Naturalistic Research,* note that a basic problem posed by naturalistic observation is moving from the act of observation to the recording of data. To achieve this, they suggest that an observer needs a definition of what constitutes a response, and a classification scheme or system into which responses are placed as they occur.

With a reliable classification scheme, an objective record of behavior can be obtained. The subjective element of this procedure is, however, the actual construction of such a scheme. It appears, therefore, that some scope for creativity exists at this stage, and thus that this is the stage at which a discovery might originate. Rather than leaving this creative endeavor to the subjective genius of a Freud or Darwin, it might be possible to throw open this part of the discovery process to a more systematic and public procedure. What I am suggesting is that we need to devise procedures utilizing disciplined observation, not to classify behavior into pre-existing schemes, but to develop classification systems.

There has been little explicit theorizing on the construction of process systems. Although there is an extensive literature on the validity and reliability of measurement instruments, the process of devising the items or categories of a system is left to the intuitive, creative capacities of system originators. Existing systems of process measurement stand as testimony to the creativity with which systems have been devised. Systems have been developed that have categories as different as the following: patient statements' being classified as "affirming as is" or "whining and defending" on the Structural

Analysis of Social Behavior (SASB; Benjamin, Foster, Roberto, & Estroff, 1986); voice qualities' being rated as being "focused" or "external" (Rice & Kerr, 1986); or a therapist response's being rated as having a "present focus" and a "linking intent" (Pinsof, 1986). How do originators come up with their codes and is there a methodology to help in this process?

Two major approaches seem to be used. In one, a strong theoretical framework already exists (as in athe case of the SASB, and the measurement system attempts to operationalize this framework. This is done by generating codes or items to capture features that are deemed measurable and that reflect concrete manifestations of the construct to be measured. Here researchers can generate a pool of items representing the domain and have a number of experts in the area select the most representative items, or they can just generate the items themselves and refine these over time with the help of validity studies. The items are usually generated by sifting through the theoretical framework for suggestions, guidelines, and concrete examples of the constructs. This method of generating item pools works well also for the construction of self-report measures— whether these are instruments that are theoretically grounded in a conceptual framework, such as the Relationship Inventory (Barrett-Lennard, 1986) or the Working Alliance Inventory (Horvath & Greenberg, 1986); more empirically constructed measures, such as the Therapeutic Alliance Rating System (Marmar, Marziali, Horowitz, & Weiss, 1986); or measures that are a cross between the conceptual and empirical, such as the Therapy Session Report (Orlinsky & Howard, 1986) or the Vanderbilt Psychotherapy Process Scale (Suh, Strupp, & O'Malley, 1986). Essentially, in this approach investigators generate a pool of items to cover the domain and refine this pool in a variety of ways.

In regard to observable in-therapy behaviors, a different type of measurement construction problem exists. When a strong theoretical framework does not exist, as in the Family Therapy Coding System (Pinsof, 1986) or Vocal Quality System (Rice & Kerr, 1986) and one wishes to study the actual in-therapy behaviors of the participants, categories representing different patterns of behavior have to be drawn from the performances themselves and from the investigators' implicit cognitive map of what is occurring. In the "harder" sciences, what is usually measured is some change in quantity, often on a single dependent variable. This has been attempted in a coding system such as the Experiencing Scale (Klein et al., 1986), but even though this system uses ordinal scale, it requires judgments about change in form rather than change in quantity. In studying complex human performance, we do not wish to know about changes in quantity as much as about changes in form. A change in the manner or style of what is being done or said is often far more important than a change in quantity. Thus the structure and organization of elements, rather than simple content or frequency of content, are the important aspects. The different arrangements or ordering of the numerous components of a performance convey more meaning about the nature of the performance than does a mere tally of those elements. How does an investigator then determine that the form of the performance has changed? This problem of measurement has kept investigators away from studying complex human performance until recently.

John von Neuman (1966), the pioneer of game theory, pointed out that in the past science has dealt with concepts related to material substance, such as "force," "energy," and "motion." However, he predicted that in the future science would be more concerned with problems of form and would make use of concepts such as "system," "information processing," and "organization." When investigators shift, as von Neuman suggested, from the domain of energy to the domain of information, measurement becomes an issue of recognizing *difference* rather than one of measuring *dimensional quantity* (Bateson, 1972). Measuring change in the form of performance, therefore, is a task of recognizing differences in form or organization from one instance to the next. Measurement becomes a type of pattern analysis. Utilizing dimensionless coding systems or category-based systems such as the measure of client vocal quality (Rice & Kerr, 1986) to recognize differences in patterns of features helps us to "see" changes in complex phenomena, much as the difference in a substance's color can actually be "seen" by a chemical or medical investigator. To facilitate this type of measurement of difference, system constructers need to select examples that represent the types of behaviors they wish to describe; they must then continually refer back to these to help explicate their maps of differences in performance, as well as to inform and enrich these implicit maps. System construction is inherently a circular process of moving from a territory to a map, back to the territory and back to the map, and so on.

This circular process, in which the terrain and the implicit map of the constructer is explicated by selecting and referring back to concrete examples of the phenomena in order to elaborate, enrich, and confirm or disconfirm the cognitive map, is the basic process that system constructers go through in developing a performance measurement system. One thing is definite: Any system worth using does not jump full-blown from the head of the system constructer, but represents a long and sometimes arduous process of explication—of checking and rechecking against concrete examples. Without a prior clear concept of what is being measured, inductively derived systems depend for the formation of different categories on the capturing of different concrete features from actual samples of the phenomena to be measured.

In this approach to measurement construction, investigators ground their categories in the behaviors studied. They collect behavior segments or specimens, and attempt by inspecting these to reduce as much as possible the distance between their preconceptions and what exists in the data. They then attempt to reproduce, in as rich and detailed a fashion as possible, the nature of those behaviors studied, and resist too great an oversimplification of the complexity of the material. This approach begins by identifying a class of behaviors—say, conflictual relationship themes or internal conflict. This is followed by disciplined observations of behavior specimens, which result in descriptions of the regularities and invariances that characterize these specimens. This is similar to the approach adopted by botanists in developing the original classification schemes for plants. Below, I describe a number of procedures that are designed to make the *carefully* imaginative construction of a classification system the central task of the research endeavor, rather than an aspect that is credited to creativity, imagination, or luck. This represents taking the inductive procedure in research one step backward—into the construction of classification schemes.

One approach to aid in the process of the construction of classification schemes is "distinctive-feature analysis," drawn from linguistics. Another promising new approach to the construction of process measurement categories is "prototype methodology." A third approach is called the "conjoint-measurement approach." These three approaches are discussed below.

Distinctive-Feature Analysis and the Testers' Training Method

Distinctive-feature analysis is a method involving the binary opposition of behaviors and the discernment of distinctive features within a domain. It originated in the work of structural linguistics (de Saussure, 1966; Jakobson & Halle, 1956). As Jakobson and Halle (1956, pp. 3–4) explained, "distinctive features involve a choice between two terms of an opposition that display a specific differential property, one diverging from the properties of all other oppositions." It involves in essence constrasting two behavior specimens (say, speech samples) in order to describe the vocal features that differentiate the specimens, and constructing a rule of category definition to describe the differences.

Using this method, I (Greenberg, 1975) developed a category scheme for measuring in-session statements of conflict, called "splits." In this approach, raters are given taped excerpts from therapy sessions, which have been selected by an expert as examples of the types of behaviors to be classified. The raters listen in a group to the taped excerpts, according to the investigators' instructions, in order to induce the rule that governs the structure of the behaviors of interest (namely, splits). This is done in the following manner. The raters are presented with examples of the behavior under study, splits (category A), juxtaposed with examples of other behaviors (category B) that, according to the expert, are not splits. Category B is therefore seen to be the category of non-A behaviors. The raters are then asked to construct a rule that describes the set of distinctive features of the behaviors in category A (splits) and shows how these features are related to one another. Three of the distinctive features for splits are (1) one part of the self (2) in opposition to (3) another part of the self. The testers are then presented with a number of successive pairs of client statements. Each pair contains one statement in category A (splits) and one in category B (nonsplits), randomly ordered. The trainees have to decide which statement of each pair belongs to category A; that is, they have to apply their rule. The expert's evaluation of class membership is given after each pair. The raters, under the direction of the leader, then describe what features they attended to in making their decisions on class membership for the pair. Using this procedure, the raters progressively modify their rule. At the end of this stage, the trainees' rules are made public.

Having induced the rule (say, for splits), the raters are then asked to rate additional taped excerpts from therapy on a four-category scale ("definite," "yes," "not sure," "no") as to the presence or absence of the set of distinctive features. They are, in addition, instructed to note the features of each excerpt that they use to make their decision. All the false positives and false negatives (i.e., cases where there is disagreement with the expert) are inspected, to enable modification and elaboration of the definition of the behavior under study, and to prevent future errors. Attention is also paid to those features used in the correct choices. In addition, the raters are encouraged to refine the rule by defining subcategories. Sufficient items are used to satisfy the investigator that his or her intuitions have been explicated and that the raters are achieving high success rates.

Constructing a classification scheme in this fashion from samples of the types of behaviors to be measured leads to categories that are truly grounded in the data. This should produce improved coding systems with greater fidelity to the phenomena under study, and therefore with higher validity and consensual relaibility. This method can thus be used to construct classification schemes that explicate implicit rules, and to develop these inductively to provide more veridical descriptive categories.

Prototype Methodology

Another interesting new approach to measurement is based upon the notion of the prototype. The concept of "prototype" refers to a kind of theoretical ideal, a theoretical standard against which what is being observed can be evaluated. No one specimen or event matches the theoretical standard perfectly, but different concrete instances approximate it to different degrees. The more closely the instance approximates the ideals, the more it typlifies the concept.

Prototype methodology, as implemented by Horowitz, Weckler & Doren (1983), uses a large number of raters (20) to describe a phenomenon and then defines the prototype on the probability of occurrence of features, based on the frequency of the raters' description of this feature. This approach could lend itself to the construction of classification system categories for rating in-therapy behviors. For example, a few behavior specimens of different types of emotional expressions in therapy (sadness or grief at loss, hostility outward, fear of abandonment, etc.) could be collected, and observers could be asked to describe the features of these. This would result in descriptions of prototypes. For example, sadness or grief might be described as follows: "Crying (1.00) with detailed descriptions of (.9) and yearning (.8) for lost object. Pleasant memories recalled (.75)." The figures in parentheses would represent the frequency noted by observers of these features.

This approach to construction of categories could be most helpful for describing clinical phenomena and developing category descriptions and feature weightings. The prototype notion could also be used in the process of coding as an alternative method of identifying or rating specimens. In certain research designs, it is more important to identify prototypic examples of a phenomenon than to rate all the material. In this type of endeavor, pure samples of the category under investigation can be identified by selecting those process segments that are rated as containing the core features by all or a high proportion of a large number of raters (say, 20). In this manner rather than concerning themselves with rater reliability, the investigators are concerned with identifying those segments in which all raters can agree on the occurrence of the phenomenon of interest. This provides an assurance that the investigation has obtained a pure sample of a phenomenon, which can then be studied further in a variety of ways.

Modern category formation theory provides some guidelines for formulating prototypic categories. Cantor and Mischel (1979) and Rosch (1978) have made useful distinctions regarding the level of abstraction used in category formation. Recognizing that objects can be categorized at varying levels of inclusiveness, Rosch (1978) identified a "basic" or "middle" category level as the optimal one for most categorization tasks. Categories at a middle level of abstraction are both rich in details, yet well differentiated from one another. At the most abstract inclusive level, termed "superordinate," categories are well differentiated from one another, but richness of detail is lost. On the other hand, categoires at the least inclusive level, termed "subordinate," require many fine discriminations to be made in order to distinguish one from another.

As mentioned, for Rosch (1978), the optimum level of categorization for an effective categorization of data is the basic or middle level. The type of methodology associated with establishing prototypes is therefore probably best for constructing categories at a middle level of abstraction, whereas the method associated with distinctive-feature analysis, discussed above, is best used where richness and detail of category description are needed. Both approaches, however, provide disciplined heuristic aids for the *construction* of categories and classification systems.

The Conjoint-Measurement Approach

Having described two approaches for constructing categories, I would like to suggest here a basic approach to measurement that I believe should be used to guide discovery-oriented measurement construction. This has been called a "conjoint-measurement approach" (Krantz & Tversky, 1971).

I have used this method in my own psychotherapy research (Greenberg, 1975) to guide in the construction of measures of a number of related phenomena. In order to ensure that such measures capture a desired relationship among the variables, definitions of variables (such as therapeutic operations, client processes, and client states that appear in reality to be related) are constructed to capture the proposed relationship. The proposed method leads through observation to the construction of definitions of the active ingredients. Applying this method, the investigator progressviely refines the notions of what is occurring in selected situations, in such a way that the active elements of the event are being defined so that they are related to one another.

This progressive refinement and distillation of the active ingredients work in the following way. Given the group of elements we are interested in—say, a client state A (a split), a therapist operation B (two-chair dialogue), and a client performance pattern C (conflict resolution), we wish, in effect, to construct a measure of a therapist operation (B) that when applied at particular client state (A) will lead to a process and outcome (C) regarded as desirable. The problem is that at the start A, B, and C are not clearly known or defined so that we must simultaneously construct the descriptions of A, B, and C and the relationship among them. What we have as given at the start are the behavior segments that exist as phenomena. The existence of the segments testifies to the fact of the relationship among the elements. The relationship of the elements can be represented as follows:

$$A \cdot B = C \qquad \text{(B in conjunction with A implies C)}$$

What is taken as given is that when B is applied at A it tends to lead to C; that is, there is a functional relationship among A, B, and C. *What A, B, and C are, however, is not entirely clear in the beginning, nor is the functional relationship among them.* It is these that must be constructed. This is done by refining the description of each element in the data one at a time (first A, then B or C, etc.) in such a way that the relationship A · B = C is always maintained. The process of building the descriptions of the ingredients is an iterative process in which the end result is a clear description of the different elements of the group, these descriptions having been constructed so as to ensure the maintenance of the functional relationship among the elements.

The contention, therefore, is that if this group (A, B, C) is studied as a group of related elements, a process of clarification of the nature of the elements and their relationships will arise. This will occur because the procedure of construction is always bound to empirical reality; that which is being constructed is that which exists. In this way, a definition of B (a therapist operation), will be constructed that, when applied at A (a client marker), has a high probability in the data sample of yielding C (a client performance pattern that is a desired process and outcome). What is, in fact, being done is that a therapist operation and a client performance pattern are being constructed to confirm the hypothesis that this therapist operation will lead to this client process when applied at a particular client state.

The conjoint-measurement approach (Krantz & Tversky, 1971) is thus a procedure of constructing measurement scales while simultaneously confirming a proposed lawful relationship. As these authors argue, conjoint measurement uses the invariance defined by a functional relationship among the elements of a group to set up a measurement structure for the group. This leads to the construction of a new measurement scale. The result of the procedure is the establishment of measurement scales for all the variables, which allows a law to be written relating the variables.

In this approach, we find the seeds for a constructive procedure—not only for measurement, but also for an induction of invariances that occur in nature. The inductive procedure proposed here for the construction of psychotherapy process measures, rather than resulting in measurement scales that satisfy the functional relationship, leads to the construction of category *definitions* of variables *so that* they satisfy the functional relationship. The final categories consist of the set of those discriminated features that are found to be related to one another, in such a way as to suggest that they combine according to the functional relationship of conjunction. For example, definitions of particular aspects of the therapist intervention and the particular types of client performance that all co-occurred could be constructed from therapy samples. The repeated co-occurrence of these features, in samples of in-therapy behaviors taken from different individuals, would suggest that this conjunction represents a lawful relationshp.

The procedure that is being suggested for measurement procedure can be summarized as follows:

1. A relationship of the elements in the event is postulated: A followed by B implies C.

2. Samples of the conjunction of these behaviors are collected.

3. A description of each variable is in turn constructed by specifying features to satisfy the conjunctive relationship.

4. Step 3 is repeated until the experimenter is satisfied that there is no more significant yield (inductive spiraling).

5. If desired, *levels* of each variable are constructed by specifying the features belonging to different levels of each variable in such a way as to satisfy an ordinal relationship among the different variables.

It is believed that this procedure is an explication of the type of thinking that goes on in clinical theorizing. These steps therefore represent an attempt to formalize an aspect of clinical theorizing into a research method. This method, with its step of inductive spiraling, allows construction to take place while at the same time ensuring a rigor that is often missing in clinical theorizing.

Causal Explanation and Model Building

In addition to describing and observing change, attending to context, and using discovery-oriented methods, we need to attempt to actually explain how change occurs in psychotherapy. The characteristics of different views of explanation are discussed below, in order to illuminate the goals of explanation and ways of engaging in explanation-oriented research.

Empiricist and Realist Views

In an empiricist view of explanation, there is a definite symmetry between explanation and prediction; in addition, in this view the goal is one of predicting regularities (Hempel, 1966). In a realist view (Salmon, 1984), explanation differs from prediction; the goal of explanation is to understand the workings of the phenomenon under study or to lay bare the underlying processes governing the functioning of a "black box."

The empiricist view holds that explanation consists of showing that what appears initially to be haphazard does actually exhibit some regularity. Although recognition of regularities is a step in the right direction—that of trying to understand a phenomenon—it does not provide us with a complete picture. Although some regularities have explanatory power, others simply cry out to be explained. Genuine scientific understanding requires that regularities or statistical relations be explained in terms of causal relations. In therapy research, just correlating process to outcome, or even experimentally manipulating variables to produce effects reliably, does not explain the causal processes involved in change. The empiricist conception of explanation thus looks at the world as exhibiting discoverable regularity; when these are known, the world can be seen as dependable. We count, for example, on regularities such as the seasons. This perspective leads to the view that there is a symmetry between explanation and prediction, that we just need to know regularities, and that it does not matter what underlying processes give rise to these regularities.

The realist view of explanation, rather than looking for regularities, would view psychotherapy as a "black box" whose workings we want to understand. Explanation would involve laying bare the underlying processes that connect observable inputs to outputs. We can explain events by showing how they fit into a causal nexus. Explanation thus involves making what appears strange understandable.

In order to explore the meaning of explanation, let us look further at the differences between these views. Empiricists claim to have explained an event when they give an antecedent from which it follows. In addition, in scientific empiricism, explanation of necessity includes rigor and specificity to make it scientific. The antecedent often may be a connection between a specific value of the antecedent for a specific outcome and a variety of other variables of specific value; it may involve statements attributing certain values to key variables that, if they had other values, would give other predictable outcomes.

A simple empirical explanation of, for example, the collapse of a bridge collapsing is given by saying that the support was too weak and that a stronger support would have kept it up. A scientific explanation in this tradition goes beyond this by also producing scientifically exact statements, which allow an exact definition of the antecedent strength of the supports and the prediction of a number of outcomes as a function of this antecedent. In psychotherapy, a simple empirical correlation is that depression is alleviated by psychotherapy. A more scientific explanation in this tradition specifically defines the treatment by a manual, and predicts and specifies more clearly particular outcomes. In science in general and in psychotherapy more specifically, we need scientific explanation at a greater depth than this empirical correlation. We need scientific explanation that sheds light on the underlying determinants of the phenomenon—in the case of the collapsed bridge, an explanation that not only adds exactness by giving measure of strength, but also gives the determinants of strength. We need, for example, to explain why the original criteria of strength (such as type of material—say, iron) are criteria of strength, and to show how these would account for the correlation between strength and the load on the bridge that lead to the collapse. True explanation would reveal why one material (say, steel) is stronger than another (say, iron) and will not collapse. Once we come to *understand* such things as the molecular strength of materials, then we can *explain* the correlations by which we previously operated, which related materials and strength. This type of deeper scientific explanation, in addition, will show connections between what we are explaining and a host of other things (not only correlations between materials and strength, but between, say, molecular structure and melting points). We will then know not only that material M has a certain structure and a certain degree of strength, but also more exactly what modifications in it would alter its strength, as well as how it differs in other ways from other material whose strength is different.

In order to provide true scientific explanation in psychotherapy, therefore, we need to associate not just two variables (the antecedent and the consequent—this treatment leads to this outcome), but to explain at a deeper level the determinants of the change process. Even though a detailed knowledge of the mechanisms of change may not be required for successful prediction of outcome, this knowledge is indispensable to the attainment of genuine scientific understanding. To understand why certain things happen, we need to see how they are produced by underlying mechanisms or processes.

Etiological versus Constitutive Explanation

It is clear from the discussion above that different forms of explanation exist. Use of a further example will help illuminate how our aims influence the type of explanation our require. The fact that an ice buildup on the wing caused a plane to crash is important to those involved in air safety as an eplanation of the crash. It is not, however, a true scientific explanation of the causal laws that govern the causal processes involved, or of the interactions among those processes. Causal laws, processes, and interactions explicate the mechanisms by which the world works (Salmon, 1984). Thus an explanation of loss of lift in terms of the shape of the wing (changed by ice buildup), the forward velocity of the plane, and the resultant loss of upward air pressure that should have lifted the plane provides the causal mechanisms that constitute a true scientific explanation of the plane crash.

To understand why certain things happen, we need to see how they are produced by underlying mechanisms. We have to elucidate the mechanisms at work. We do not want only *etiological* explanations, such as explaining why the plane crashed or the bridge collapsed in terms of antecedents, or explaining a therapeutic outcome in terms of the administration of a treatment. We want *constitutive* explanations, wh;ich consist of an exhibition of the internal causal structure of the phenomena to be explained (Salmon, 1986). Although etiological explanation may increase our predictive and controlling abilities, constitutive explanation increases our understanding of natural phenomena and our ability to create new end states. We need to move to research that provides more of the latter type of explanation. To this end we need to construct models of the processes and interactions underlying the manifest performances and attempt to establish causal laws of change.

In summary, a scientific explanation possesses two important properties: (1) It gives antecedent conditions of the explanation in terms of a set of factors which make evident its connection with others; for example, the bridge collapsed because of the weakness of one of its supports or the plane crashed because of ice on its wings. Science, however, not only needs to explain the particular situation but also a variety of other situations yielding the second property. (2) Science sheds light on underlying determinants: It provides not only exactness of prediction but also explains the correlations in (1) by providing a constitutive explanation.

Explanation is built in tiers. Correlations that explain at one level can be explained at another level, and the ability to explain a higher-level correlation constitutes scientific progress. Just as one notices when a bridge support collapses that steel supports are stronger than iron, science provides an understanding of the determinants of the strength of the materials. When we understand molecular strength then we explain the previous correlation by which we operated.

In psychotherapy we first have correlations between events, such as antecedent event (A), the problem, worked on in this way (B), the treatment manual, obtains result (C), in-session process, which in turn leads to (D), extratherapy change. We need a science to reveal the processes that will explain the relationship between A, B, C, and D.

To provide this type of explanation, we need first to identify regularities to be explained, and then to attempt to reveal the underlying processes and interactions that produce the regularities. For example, I selected a change episode in which I identified a correlation between conflict resolution and the use of a dialogue between the two opposing parts to resolve the conflict. Having identified this initial regularity, I then identified further patterned regularities, such as a shift over time from negative self-criticism through a series of identifiable interactive steps to a more affilative stance toward the self (Greenberg, 1984). These steps could all be reliably identified by raters, and thus began to give the feeling of an explanation of what was occurring to produce the correlation. The findings may be summarized as follows: In people who felt torn by a self-evaluative conflict, (1) self-criticism produced reactive loss of hope. When (2) such a person experienced this hopelessness and woundedness in a supportive therapeutic environment in which the client was guided to focus on feelings, (3) a new emotional response and a statement of needs or wants emerged. This in turn provided (4) a greater sense of power with which to combat the negative self-views. When (5) this process was followed by a spontaneous softening in the critical stance toward the self, the result was (6) either a shift to a more affiliative relation between the previously opposed aspects by negotiation, or an automatic integration of the previously opposing views. This process then led to (7) postsession reports of greater self-acceptance and inner harmony. The sequence of interactions provides a deep and detailed explanation of a change process.

There are many of these processes in psychotherapy. It is our job to discover them, to describe them, to develop measures to capture them reliably, to model the processes, and to confirm that they lead to long-term change. Then we will truly understand how change takes place.

CONCLUSION

Investigative discovery-oriented research of this nature, which focuses on describing change processes in their in-session contexts in order to build explanatory models of change, should allow us eventually to specify the determinants of different disorders that need to be changed, as well as to define the processes involved in changing them in psychotherapy. The occurrence of the appropriate change processes for the specified determinants of a disorder could then be related to specific outcomes that measured changes in the determinants. In this manner, it may be possible to establish a viable science of psychotherapy.

REFERENCES

Angus, L., & Hardtke, K. (1993). *A rating manual for the Narrative Coding Processing System*. Unpublished manuscript, York University, North York, Ontario, Canada.

Barrett-Lennard, G. T. (1986). The Relationship Inventory now: Issues and advances in theory, method, and use. In L. S. Greenberg & W. M. Pinsof (Eds.), *The psychotherapeutic process: A research handbook* (pp. 439–476). New York: Guilford Press.

Bateson, G. (1972). *Steps to an ecology of mind*. New York: Ballantine Books.

Beck, A. T., Rush, A. J., Shaw, B. F., & Emery, G. (1979). *Cognitive therapy of depression*. New York: Guilford Press.

Benjamin, L. S., Foster, S. W., Roberto, L. G., & Estnoff, S. E. (1986). Breaking the family code: Analysis of videotapes of family interactions by Structural Analysis of Social Behavior (SASB). In L. S. Greenberg & W. M. Pinsof (Eds.), *The psychotherapeutic process: A research handbook* (pp. 391–438). New York: Guilford Press.

Bergin, A., & Lambert, M. (1978). The evaluation of therapeutic outcomes. In S. Garfield & A. Bergin (Eds.), *Handbook of psychotherapy and behavior change* (2nd ed., pp. 139–184). New York: Wiley.

Bordin, E. S. (1979). The generalizability of the psychoanalytic concept of the working alliance. *Psychotherapy: Theory, Research, and Practice, 16*, 252–260.

Butler, J., Rice, L., & Wagstaff, A. (1963). *Quantitative naturalistic research*. Englewood Cliffs, NJ: Prentice Hall.

Cantor, N., & Mischel, W. (1979). Prototypicality and personality: Effects of free recall and personality impressions. *Journal of Research in Personality, 13*, 187–205.

de Saussure, F. (1966). *Course in general linguistics*. New York: Philosophical Library.

Elkin, I., Shea, T., Watkins, J. T., Imber, S. D., Sotsky, S. M., Collins, J. F., Glass, D. R., Pilkonis, D. A., Leber, W. R., Docherty, J. P., Fiester, S. J., & Parloff, M. B. (1989). National Institute of Mental Health Treatment of Depression Collaborative Research Program: General effectiveness of treatments. *Archives of General Psychiatry, 46*, 971–983.

Elliott, R. (1983). Fitting process research to the practicing psychotherapist. *Psychotherapy: Theory, Research, and Practice, 20*, 47–55.

Elliott, R. (1986). Interpersonal process recall (IPR) as a psychotherapy process research method. In L. S. Greenberg & W. M. Pinsof (Eds.). *The psychotherapeutic process: A research handbook* (pp. 503–528). New York: Guilford Press.

Frank, J. (1979). The present status of outcome studies. *Journal of Consulting and Clinical Psychology, 47*, 310–317.

Glass, G. V., McGaw, B., & Smith, M. L. (1981). *Meta-analysis in social research*. Beverly Hills, CA: Sage.

Greenberg, L. S. (1975). *Task analysis of psychotherapeutic events*. Unpublished doctoral dissertation, York University.

Greenberg, L. S. (1984). A task analysis of intrapersonal conflict resolution. In L. N. Rice & L. S. Greenberg (Eds.), *Patterns of change: Intensive analysis of psychotherapy process* (pp. 67–123). New York: Guilford Press.

Greenberg, L. S. (1986a). Change process research. *Journal of Consulting and Clinical Psychology, 54*, 4–9.

Greenberg, L. S. (1986b). Research strategies. In L. S. Greenberg & W. M. Pinsof (Eds.), *The psychotherapeutic process: A research handbook* (pp. 707–734). New York: Guilford Press.

Greenberg, L. S. & Pinsof, W. M. (Eds.). (1986). *The Psychotherapeutic process: A research handbook.* New York: Guilford Press.

Greenberg, L. S., Rice, L. N., & Elliott, R. (1993). *Facilitating emotional change: The moment-by-moment process.* New York: Guilford Press.

Greenberg, L. S. & Webster, M. (1982). Resolving decisional conflict by means of two-chair dialogue: Relating process to outcome. *Journal of Counseling Psychology, 29,* 468–477.

Heatherington, L. (1989). Toward meaningful clinical research: Taking context into account in coding psychotherapy interaction. *Psychotherapy: Theory, Research, and Practice, 26,* 436–447.

Hempel, C. (1966). *Philosophy of natural science.* Englewood Cliffs, NJ: Prentice-Hall.

Horvath, A., & Greenberg, L. S. (1986). Development of the Working Alliance Inventory. In L. S. Greenberg & W. M. Pinsof (Eds.), *The psychotherapeutic process: A research handbook* (pp. 529–556). New York: Guilford Press.

Horvath, A. & Greenberg, L. S. (1989). Development and validation of the Working Alliance Inventory. *Journal of Counseling Psychology, 36,* 223–233.

Horowitz, L., Weckler, D., & Doren, R. (1983). Interpersonal problems and symptoms. In P. C. Kendall (Ed.), *Advances in cognitive-behavioral research and therapy* (pp. 82–127). New York: Academic Press.

Jakobson, R. & Halle, L. (1956). *Fundamentals of language.* The Hague: Mouton.

Klein, M., Mathieu-Coughlin, P., & Kiesler, D. (1986). The Experiencing Scales. In L. S. Greenberg & W. M. Pinsof (Eds.), *The psychotherapeutic process: A research handbook* (pp. 21–71). New York. Guilford Press.

Krantz, D., & Tversky, A. (1971). Conjoint measurement analysis of composition rules in psychology. *Psychological Review, 78,* 151–169.

Luborsky, L., Crits-Christoph, P., Mintz, J., & Auerbach, A. (1988). *Who will benefit from psychotherapy: Predicting therapeutic outcomes.* New York: Basic Books.

Luborsky, L., Singer, B., Harte, J., Crits-Christoph, P., & Cohen, M. (1984). Shifts in depressive state during psychotherapy: Which concepts of depression fit the context of Mr. Q's shifts? In L. N. Rice & L. S. Greenberg (Eds.), *Patterns of change: Intensive analysis of psychotherapeutic process* (pp. 157–193). New York: Guilford Press.

Luborsky, L., Singer, B., & Luborsky, L. (1975). Comparative studies of psychotherapies: Is it true that "Everyone has won and all must have prizes"? *Archives of General Psychiatry, 32,* 995–1008.

Marmar, C. R., Marziali, E., Horowitz, M., & Weiss, D. S. (1986). The development of the Therapeutic Alliance Rating System. In L. S. Greenberg & W. M. Pinsof (Eds.), *The psychotherapeutic process: A research handbook* (pp. 367–390). New York: Guilford Press.

Marmar, C., Wilner, N. & Horowitz, M. (1984). Recurrent client states in psychotherapy: A quantification. In L. N. Rice & L. S. Greenberg (Eds.), *Patterns of change: Intensive analysis of psychotherapeutic process* (pp. 194–212). New York: Guilford Press.

Orlinsky, D. E., & Howard, K. I. (1986). Process and outcome in psychotherapy. In S. Garfield & A. Bergin (Eds.), *Handbook of psychotherapy and behavior change* (3rd ed., pp. 311–381). New York: Wiley.

Orlinsky, D. E., & Howard, K. I. (1987). A generic model of psychotherapy. *Journal of Integrative and Eclectic Psycotherapy, 6,* 6–27.

Pinsof, W. M. (1986). The process of family therapy: The development of the Family Therapy Coding System. In L. S. Greenberg & W. M. Pinsof (Eds.), *The psychotherapeutic process: A research handbook* (pp. 201–284). New York: Guilford Press.

Rice, L. N., & Greenberg, L. S. (1974). *A method for studying the active ingredients in psychotherapy: Application to client-centered and Gestalt therapy.* Paper presented at the meeting of the Society for Psychotherapy Research, Denver, CO.

Rice, L. N. & Greenberg, L. S. (1984). *Patterns of change: Intensive analysis of psychotherapeutic process.* New York: Guilford Press.

Rice, L. N., & Kerr, J. (1986). Measures of client and therapist vocal quality. In L. S. Greenberg & W. M. Pinsof (Eds.), *The psychotherapeutic process: A research handbook* (pp. 73–106). New York: Guilford Press.

Rosch, E. (1978). Principles of categorization. In E. Rosch & B. B. Lloyd (Eds.), *Cognition and categorization* (pp. 27–48). Hillsdale, NJ: Erlbaum.

Russell, R. L. (Ed.). (1987). *Language in Psychotherapy.* New York: Plenum.

Salmon, W. C. (1984). *Scientific explanation and the causal structure of the world.* Princeton, NJ: Princeton University Press.

Strupp, H. H., & Binder, J. (1984). *Psychotherapy in a new key.* New York: Basic Books.

Suh, C. S., Strupp, H. H., & O'Malley, S. (1986). The Vanderbilt process measures: The Psychotherapy Process Scale. In L. S. Greenberg & W. M. Pinsof (Eds.), *The psychotherapeutic process: A research handbook* (pp. 285–323). New York: Guilford Press.

von Neuman, J. (1966). *Collected works* (A. Traub, Ed.). Elmsford, NY: Pergamon Press.

Weiss, J., Sampson, H., & the Mount Zion Psychotherapy Research Group. (1986). *The psychoanalytic process.* New York: Guilford Press.

CHAPTER 5

From an Experimental to an Exploratory Naturalistic Approach to Studying Psychotherapy Process

CLARA E. HILL

In this chapter, I contrast my experiences with using analogue and exploratory naturalistic designs to study psychotherapy process. To keep the focus clear, I do not discuss other methods I have also tried for studying process.

EXPERIMENTAL ANALOGUE DESIGNS

One of the traditional methods of studying therapy process in counseling psychology is the use of experimental analogue designs, which simulate the therapy process with manipulations of the independent variable and control of other extraneous variables (Hill, 1982). Analogue designs should allow a researcher to determine the effects of each separate component, unconfounded by everything else that occurs. They also permit rigor, control, and the ability to test cause-and-effect relationships, thus yielding good internal validity. In addition, with analogue designs, researchers can study events that happen infrequently in therapy (e.g., touch—Stockwell & Dye, 1980) or that cannot be manipulated unintrusively in the therapy process (e.g., nonverbal behavior—Haase & Tepper, 1972; therapist attractiveness—Carter, 1978).

The analogue model derives from an experimental and social

psychology tradition, which in turn derives from the physical sciences. A colleague and I (Hill & Gronsky, 1984) suggested that this tradition is based on several underlying assumptions: (1) Behavior is governed by universal laws or truths; (2) science will ultimately be able to discover these truths and create a better world; and (3) the best way to seek truth is through the scientific method, generally characterized by inductive logic, linear causality, experimental research designs, complex inferential statistics, use of large samples, and measuring change as a function of an entire treatment package.

There are many types of analogue research, varying in how much they resemble the actual psychotherapy situation. In the most distant variety, volunteers read transcripts or watch videotapes of therapy sessions. For example, Tepper and Haase (1978) manipulated one verbal and five nonverbal cues on a videotape. Judges watched the videotaped segments and rated counselor empathy, respect, and genuineness. On the basis of their results, Tepper and Haase indicated that nonverbal behaviors accounted for much more of the variance in ratings of facilitative conditions than did verbal cues.

A study that another colleague and I did (Hill & Gormally, 1977) illustrates a type of analogue research more closely related to actual therapy sessions. In this study, we examined the effects of three different therapist techniques (reflection, restatement, and probe) and two different nonverbal conditions (presence or absence of nodding and smiling) on client expression of feeling. The design followed a ABAB verbal conditioning paradigm, with a baseline (minimal verbal stimuli and no nonverbal behavior) followed by the intervention (manipulation of the verbal and nonverbal stimuli), a return to baseline, and then a return to the intervention. During the intervention, therapists delivered a specific number of either reflections, restatements, or probes on a predetermined variable-interval schedule when a light flashed. Therapists were not informed ahead of time which condition they would be in, but had to wait until they saw a particular type of light to know which condition they were in. In devising the interventions, however, therapists used material that they heard from the clients. For example, rather than delivering standard reflections, therapists based their reflections on what clients had said.

In a slightly different variant of the analogue methodology, several researchers have used a standardized interview format. For example, in a study by Hoffman and Spencer (1977), clients were recruited because of their desire to discuss problems with procrastination. Counselors followed a standardized interview protocol up to a specific point, where different types of counselor self-disclosures were introduced. This format allowed for greater control than did the conditioning paradigm, because clients talked about a specific problem and all the counselor responses were standardized.

Despite the advantages of increased rigor and control, there are a number of methodological problems with analogue research (see also Hill, 1982). First, controlling all of the extraneous variables to ensure that the independent variable is the causal agent is virtually impossible. For example, therapists may compensate for strict controls on their verbal behavior by being more empathic nonverbally.

Another important problem regards external validity. Although such analogue designs might be used to demonstrate the effects of particular behaviors in isolation from other behaviors, this is not the way therapy operates. In therapy, there is a complex interaction of many variables operating simultaneously. The therapeutic relationship, client dynamics and beliefs, therapist orientation and skills, and external forces such as support systems all moderate the effects of therapist interventions (Hill, 1989). Thus, few analogue designs can approximate the therapy situation, and as a result offer little in the way of information about the process of actual psychotherapy.

We (Spiegel & Hill, 1989) noted that in several analogue studies of interpretation (e.g., Adams, Butler, & Noblin, 1962; Kanfer & Marston, 1964), the persons making the interpretations did not know the subjects, the subjects had volunteered to be in an experiment rather than in treatment, the interpretations were not appropriate to what the subjects were talking about, and the task did not resemble interactions in real therapy. Even in analogue studies that were similar to counseling (e.g., Claiborn, Ward, & Strong, 1981; Strong, Wambach, Lopez, & Cooper, 1979), the parameters of the interpretation (such as when, where, why, and how they were used) were determined by the research protocol rather than by client needs or responses in the session. Spiegel and I suggested that the effectiveness of interpretation is moderated by the relationship. Therefore, analogue studies are particularly inappropriate for studying therapist interpretation (and probably other complex therapeutic issues), because forming an adequate relationship in a brief analogue is difficult. Furthermore, because most interpretations in real therapy are delivered in the context of other interventions that are dependent on the needs of clients (e.g., Hill, 1989), it is difficult to simulate the manner in which interpretations are delivered in therapy.

In sum, experimental analogue designs may be useful for gaining rigor and studying the causal influence of selected variables, particularly of initial impression formation in therapy. Because relationship factors appear to interact so strongly with other process events in later phases of therapy, however, analogue designs seem to be of less value. Because many of the interesting process phenomena do not occur in the first few moments of therapy, alternative methods seem to be needed.

FACTORS GUIDING MY CHOICE OF METHODOLOGY

Several assumptions have guided my choice of a new methodology. First, *therapy should be studied as it naturally occurs.* This assumption derives logically from my dissatisfaction with experimental manipulations. I think that we need to step back to the observation stage of research design (Kerlinger, 1973) and learn more about the phenomena of therapy they unfold in current practice. We need to become like anthropologists who are participant–observers of the therapy process. Of course, as participant–observers, we need to be aware that our biases, or what we might think of as expectations or psychological filters, will influence everything that we observe about therapy process.

Second, although I advocate giving up the analogue designs and using a naturalistic approach, I do not advocate giving up rigor in approaching research questions. In research using the naturalistic approach, *it is important to be rigorous and to keep as many controls as possible* over therapist experience level and theoretical orientation, client diagnosis and personality characteristics, the therapy setting, and the research protocol. Furthermore, using structured process measures (e.g., the Therapist Intentions List—Hill & O'Grady, 1985), rather than just open-ended inquiries, can provide some standardization of the research protocol. Too often, open-ended inquiries can be biased by researcher beliefs and expectations. Using standardized measures that have been developed from inquiries with therapy participants allows researchers the best of both worlds—relevance to the therapy situation and standardization.

A third major factor that underlies my thinking about research methodology is an *awareness of covert processes*. Much of the earlier work in counseling and psychotherapy relied solely on external observers to judge what occurred in the process (e.g., client level of experiencing—Klein, Mathieu-Coughlan, & Kiesler, 1986). Such observer-rated measures capture overt client behavior, which is important because that is what therapists respond to, but it misses the clients' experience of the therapy process. Clients may experience something different covertly from what they convey outwardly. For example, clients may have negative reactions to therapist interventions, but feel reluctant to say anything to their therapists (Hill, Thompson, Cogar, & Denman, 1993; Hill, Thompson, & Corbett, 1992; Regan & Hill, 1992; Rennie, in press; Thompson & Hill, 1991). Thus, to get a complete picture of the therapeutic process, we must examine both overt and covert levels.

A fourth issue is that *there are different perspectives in psychotherapy, all of which are valid*. We (Hill & Gronsky, 1984) noted that there is no ultimate truth; rather, there are multiple realities, which are dependent on vantage points and psychological filters. Thus, even though they are involved in the same interaction, therapists and clients often have very different experiences of these interactions. In fact, there are often minimal correlations among therapists', clients', and outside observers' perspectives on the same events (Caskey, Barker, & Elliott, 1984; Fuller & Hill, 1985; Hill, Helms, Tichenor, et al., 1988; Orlinsky & Howard, 1975; Tichenor & Hill, 1989). The lack of correlations among perspectives suggests that more than one perspective needs to be studied to provide an adequate description of the process.

A fifth factor is an *appreciation for individual differences in psychotherapy*. Too often we have assumed a uniformity myth (Kiesler, 1966)—that is, that given processes affect everyone the same way. My examination of eight cases of brief psychotherapy with experienced therapists and anxious/depressed clients (Hill, 1989; Hill, Helms, Tichenor, et al., 1988) showed that although some therapist techniques were helpful in all eight cases (e.g., interpretation, approval), others were helpful in some cases but not in others (e.g., direct guidance, confrontation). Furthermore, context made a difference even within cases. Thus, when clients were at low levels of experiencing, there were differences between which therapist techniques were helpful (e.g., paraphrase and open questions were helpful). When clients were at moderate levels of experiencing, however, almost all therapist interventions were equally helpful.

MODEL OF PROCESS

Also influencing the approach I take to studying therapy process is the model of process that my colleagues and I have conceptualized (Hill, 1992; Hill & O'Grady, 1985). This model describes how preexisting and contextual variables affect the moment-to-moment process, which in turn leads to change. We have postulated that at any given moment, therapists draw from pre-existing variables (theory, experience, diagnostic formulations), and contextual variables in therapy (observations about the time in treatment and the quality of the relationship, and observations of client readiness) to develop intentions for the impact they want to have on clients. To implement their intentions, therapists choose specific response modes. In response to the therapist intervention, clients have both overt and covert reactions. On the basis of their reactions to therapist interventions and what they want to happen in the session, clients exhibit certain experiencing levels and overt behaviors. Therapists then devise their next intervention according to their altered perceptions of the clients' present reactions, responses, and needs, yielding a continually evolving process. This moment-to-moment process leads to client change or treatment outcome. Martin (1984) has developed a similar cognitive-mediational model, which relates client change to a continual cycle of counselor intention, counselor behavior, client perception, client cognitive processing, and client behavior.

DESCRIPTION OF METHODOLOGY

These assumptions and our process model have led me to develop an exploratory methodology for studying psychotherapy process. In an exploratory (or discovery-oriented) method (cf. Elliott, 1984; Hill, 1990; Mahrer, 1988), a researcher approaches the data with as few preconceived ideas as possible about what the phenomenon is like and tries to learn what the data reveal about the phenomenon. Exploratory process research describes what occurs within psychotherapy sessions from a nontheoretical stance. Researchers develop scales or categories to code occurrences in the session (e.g., therapist behavior) or to describe the experiences of the participants. Researchers maintain an attitude of openness to learning about process from their observations.

In the exploratory method, my colleagues and I allow therapy to evolve naturally; therapists use their clinical judgment about what interventions to employ, according to their perceptions of clients' needs. It is not completely naturalistic, however, because we recruit therapists and clients, videotape sessions, and do structured videotape-assisted recalls immediately after sessions (e.g., Hill, Helms, Tichenor, et al., 1988; Hill, Thompson, & Corbett, et al., 1992). The structured recall undoubtedly has an effect on the process of therapy, although this effect has not received enough research attention (see Hill et al., 1994).

Development of theory, based on the accumulation of replicated findings, is the ultimate goal of exploratory process research. Exploratory research thus follows the spirit of the scientific method, in which observation of clinical phenomena leads to hypothesis formulation and testing, which in turn lead to refinement of the hypotheses, replication of the results, and finally development of theory (Kerlinger, 1973). Given the few replicated results in process research, I believe that our research is presently in the observation and hypothesis-building stages, rather than at the theory development stage (Hill, 1982).

The method that I have developed involves a combination of use of outside judges to rate overt behavior and a structured review to have participants describe their covert experiences. The variables that I study (overt and covert behaviors) are directly tied to the process model described earlier.

OVERT BEHAVIORS

Therapist Response Modes

For therapists, we study response modes, which measure the grammatical structure of therapist verbal speech (independent of topic or content of speech). There are over 30 systems for therapist response modes currently available (e.g., Snyder, 1945; Stiles, 1979). I use a system that I devised some years ago (Hill, 1978) and have since revised (the Revised Hill Counselor Verbal Response Category System; Hill, 1985, 1986; 1992). This system includes nine pantheoretical, nominal, mutually exclusive therapist verbal response modes: approval, information, direct guidance, closed question, open question, paraphrase, interpretation, confrontation, and self-disclosure.

I developed this response modes system to test the common components of therapist verbal behavior across all theoretical orientations and to fit with definitions of therapist techniques in pantheoretical therapist training programs (e.g., Benjamin, 1981; Carkhuff, 1969; Ivey & Authier, 1978). Content validity was based on expert judgments (Hill, 1978); construct validity was established by determining that therapists of different theoretical orientations differed in predictable ways in their use of response modes (Hill, Thames, & Rardin, 1979; Elliott et al., 1987), concurrent validity was established by comparing the system with other response mode systems (Elliott et al., 1987); and predictive validity was established by finding that different response modes were viewed by clients and therapists as differentially helpful (Hill, Helms, Tichenor, et al., 1988).

Client Behavior

In the past (Hill, Carter, & O'Farrell, 1983), we have measured overt client behavior using the Hill Client Verbal Response Mode Category System, which consists of nine nominal, mutually exclusive categories for judging client verbal behavior: simple responses, requests, description, experiencing, insight, discussion of plans, discussion of client–counselor relationship, silence, and other. We were rather dissatisfied with this measure, however, because many (54%) of the responses ended up in the description category, which did not allow for much discrimination among client behaviors.

Therefore, in the case studies described below (Hill, 1989; Hill, Helms, Tichenor, et al., 1988), we used the Experiencing Scale (Klein, Mathieu, Gendlin, & Kiesler, 1970; Klein et al., 1986). This measure is a 7-point scale used to describe a client's level of involvement in the therapy. At a low level, discourse is impersonal or superficial; at higher levels, feelings are explored, and experiencing serves as the basic referent for problem resolution and self-understanding. Klein et al. (1986) reported high interrater reliability for 15 previous studies, and cited evidence that experiencing is related to self-exploration, insight, working through, absence of resistances, and high-quality free association. Klein et al. (1986) also reported that experiencing level, either averaged over all of therapy or at the end of therapy, has consistently been related to various measures of client outcome. Unfortunately, in our study with non-client-centered therapists (Hill, Helms, Tichenor, et al., 1988), the experiencing levels were mainly at the lower levels (scale points 2 and 3), so we again had minimal variability.

Because of our dissatisfaction with these two client measures, we revised our earlier system into the Client Behavior System, which includes eight nominal, mutually exclusive categories: resistance, agreement, appropriate request, recounting, cognitive-behavioral exploration, affective exploration, insight, and therapeutic changes. We (Hill, Corbett, et al., 1992) have provided evidence of validity and interjudge reliability. Experts indicated that clients were generally more productively involved when engaged in cognitive-behavioral exploration, affective exploration, insight, and changes than when engaged in resistance, agreement, appropriate request, and recounting.

Measuring Overt Behaviors

Overt behaviors are generally measured by having judges go through transcripts and indicate their presence or absence. In recent chapters (Hill, 1991; Lambert & Hill, 1994), my colleagues and I have outlined the steps that need to be taken in developing these types of measures and training judges to do such ratings.

COVERT BEHAVIORS

Therapist Intentions

The cognitive revolution has hit psychotherapy process research because of an awareness that more is happening in people's minds than appears in their overt behavior. Kagan (1975) introduced the notion that disparate events occur on different levels for therapy participants, and that greater awareness of these covert events enhances the therapeutic enterprise. Researchers have since incorporated these ideas into researchable measures, using various forms of stimulated recall from tapes. For therapists, the interest has centered around their intentions, which can be defined as covert reasons and goals for their interventions. Several measures have been developed for therapist intentions (Elliott & Feldstein, 1978; Hill & O'Grady, 1985; Martin, Martin, Meyer, & Slemon, 1986).

We use the Therapist Intentions List (Hill & O'Grady, 1985), which has 19 pantheoretical, not mutually exclusive intentions in eight clusters: "set limits," "assess" (get information, focus, and clarify), "support" (support, instill hope, and reinforce change), "educate" (give information), "explore" (identify and intensify cognitions, behaviors, and feelings), "restructure" (insight, resistance, challenge), "change," and ""miscellaneous" (relationship, catharsis, self-control, therapist needs). Intentions are a therapist's rationale for selecting a particular intervention to use with a client at any given moment within a session. We developed the Therapist Intentions List through numerous postsession videotape-assisted inquiries with therapists about their goals and rationales for each intervention.

We (Hill, 1992; Hill & O'Grady, 1985) reported content and construct validity for the measure. We also reported that psychoanalytic therapists used more "feelings" and "insight," whereas behavioral therapists used more "change," "set limits," and "reinforce change." Furthermore, there were decreases in "assess" intentions and increases in "restructur" intentions both within and across sessions. Therapist intentions were predictably connected with therapist response modes, although some intentions can be achieved through more than one response mode, and some response modes are used for more than one intention (Hill, Helms, Tichenor, et al., 1988). We (Hill et al., 1994) reported stability across approximately 2 weeks for intentions when therapists reviewed the videotape of the same session on both occasions.

Client Reactions

We have measured client covert behavior through the Client Reactions System (Hill, Helms, Spiegel, & Tichenor, 1988), which consists of 21 nominal, not mutually exclusive reactions organized into five clusters: "supported" (understood, supported, hopeful, relief), "therapeutic work" (negative thoughts and behaviors, better self-understanding, clear, feelings, responsibility, unstuck, new perspective, educated, new ways to behave), "challenged," "negative reactions" (scared, worse, stuck, lacking direction, confused, or misunderstood), and "no reaction." We developed the Client Reactions System by doing numerous postsession videotape-assisted inquiries with clients about their reactions to therapist interventions.

We (Hill, Helms, Spiegel, & Tichenor, 1988) reported that therapist intentions were more closely related to client reactions for successful cases than for unsuccessful cases; that pretreatment symptomatology was highly predictive of which reactions the clients reported; that there were some predictable changes in reactions across time in treatment; and that within-case correlations of reactions with session outcome indicated some similarities across cases. We (Hill et al., in press) reported stability across approximately 2 weeks for reactions when clients reviewed the videotape of the same session on both occasions.

Elliott (1985) has developed a similar measure of client impacts. His system was developed from examining events that clients indicated were most and least helpful in therapy sessions.

Assessing Covert Behaviors

In assessing covert behaviors, we chose to use a structured recall method rather than an open-ended format, such as that described by Elliott (1986). In an open-ended format, participants are allowed to stop the tape whenever they want and are asked about their experiences by means of open-ended questions. The responses of participants are then coded by outside judges into established category systems. In contrast, in our structured format, participants use established category systems to describe their experiences at moments when we stop the tapes of sessions (usually after each therapist speaking turn, which is everything between two client speeches). The advantage of this approach, from my perspective, is that participants can most precisely place their experiences within the appropriate categories of established systems. Outside judges may not put the description of the experience in the same category that participants would have. The disadvantage of this approach is that some of the richness that accrues from the open-ended descriptions of experiences is lost.

We have tested the comparability of videotape-assisted reviews to data from sessions (Hill et al., in press). In this study, therapists reported their intentions and clients reported their reactions during interruptions in sessions, and then again in videotape-assisted reviews immediately after the session. We found evidence that the data from reviews were comparable to those recorded during sessions; our findings suggest that videotaped sessions are valid for assessing feelings and reactions that occurred during sessions.

EXAMPLES OF METHODOLOGY

To illustrate our methodology, I first describe the methods we used to study the effects of therapist techniques (response modes) in eight cases of brief individual psychotherapy (12–20 sessions). These cases were conducted by experienced psychodynamic therapists with anxious/depressed clients (Hill, 1989; Hill, Helms, Tichenor, et al., 1988). Then I describe the methods we used to study therapist ability to detect client reactions (Thompson & Hill, 1991; Hill, Thompson, & Corbett, 1992; Hill et al., 1993).

Methodology for Examining Therapist Response Modes

We first carefully selected clients and therapists according to predefined criteria, so that we knew the populations to whom we could generalize. After extensive pretesting, clients were ready to begin therapy. We informed participants about all the research procedures prior to the start of therapy, using this as a means to begin establishing a working alliance between us as researchers and them as participants. We told them that we wanted to know about their experiences in therapy, and asked them to be as honest as possible about their reactions. Of course, we also assured them of full confidentiality.

Each therapy session was videotaped and monitored from another room. After each session, each client and therapist completed measures asking about the quality of the session, the working alliance, and the most and least helpful events within the session. Therapists were also interviewed about their rationales for what they did in sessions. These data provided us with global evaluations of the session, yielding a context within which to evaluate the moment-to-moment process variables.

Immediately following the therapist interview, the therapist and client were taken to another room to view the videotape. Both persons had to watch the videotape together, to ensure that they were responding to the same portion of the videotape. Therefore, they were separated by a partition so that both could see the videotape and the researcher, but neither could see the other.

A researcher stopped the videotape after each therapist speaking turn (or thought unit, if there was more than one distinct thought unit within the speaking turn). The client and therapist were instructed to review the tape and try to recall what they felt during the session, rather than what they were feeling at the time of the review. Clients rated the helpfulness of each therapist intervention (Elliott, 1985, 1986), and wrote down the numbers of up to five reactions (Hill, Helms, Spiegel, & Tichenor, 1988) that described their feelings about the therapist intervention. Therapists also rated the helpfulness of each intervention and wrote down the numbers of up to five intentions (Hill & O'Grady, 1985) that described their rationales for offering that intervention. These data provided us with the moment-to-moment process data.

After treatment, not only did participants complete the standard outcome measures, but we also conducted extensive individual interviews with them about their experiences of the entire therapy. This interviewing allowed us the opportunity to gain a qualitative perspective about the helpful and hindering aspects of the treatment. We also followed up on the clients at 6-month, 1-year, and 3–year intervals following treatments.

Verbatim transcripts were obtained for each therapy session and interview. The transcript was then unitized, according to guidelines (Hill, 1985) for making grammatical sentences out of free-flowing speech. Trained judges were used to judge therapist response modes (Hill, 1985, 1986) and client experiencing levels (Klein et al., 1970, 1986), providing indices of the overt behavior presented in our process model.

In the first major analysis of these data, we (Hill, Helms, Tichenor, et al., 1988) examined the effects of therapist response modes on immediate outcome (client and therapist helpfulness ratings, client reactions, client experiencing levels) across the eight cases. Results indicated that therapist response modes had a significant, albeit small, effect on immediate outcome. Self-disclosure, interpretation, approval, and paraphrase were the most helpful response modes. Therapist intentions (goals or rationales for their interventions) and client experiencing levels in the turn prior to the therapist intervention both added significantly more to the variance in explaining immediate outcome than did therapist response modes. Even more variance was accounted for by interactions between variables, suggesting the importance of considering all the variables in combination. In regard to client experiencing, the most helpful therapist interventions at low levels of client experiencing were therapist exploration of feelings, efforts at change, education, open questions, and giving information through direct guidance. At moderate levels of experiencing, almost all types of therapist interventions were equally effective, such that clients could use most therapist interventions productively. Unfortunately, not enough instances of high experiencing levels occurred for us to analyze.

To follow up on the Hill, Helms, Tichenor, et al. (1988) results regarding individual differences between clients, the eight cases were analyzed separately (Hill, 1989). These analyses included the data on immediate outcome mentioned above, as well as information from questionnaires and interviews regarding the most and least helpful events within each session of the therapies. These two sources of information (quantitative data on immediate outcome and qualitative data from interviews) were combined with information about the moderating effects of client pretreatment variables, therapist variables, the therapeutic relationship, and external factors to make some inferences about what variables were effective in each case.

In all eight cases, therapist approval and interpretation were effective interventions. Other techniques were effective for some clients but not for others. For example, clients who seemed dependent liked therapists to give direct guidance and information but did not like therapist confrontation; clients who seemed vulnerable and fearful found open questions and confrontation helpful but threatening; and clients who seemed insight-oriented liked interpretation. Therapist orientation also seemed to determine which techniques were used; psychodynamic therapists used more interpretation and less self-disclosure than more behaviorally oriented therapists. Therapists who appeared to be flexible and able to negotiate the treatment approach with the clients seemed to be more effective with their clients. Furthermore, a minimally acceptable relationship seemed to be necessary for therapist techniques to be heard and used by clients. Finally, hindering external influences on a client during therapy (e.g., lack of extratherapy involvement, such as not thinking about the therapy or not acting on issues brought up in therapy; lack of a support network; and negative external events) made it difficult for clients to incorporate changes from therapy.

Methodology for Examining Therapist Ability to Detect Client Reactions

In interviews with our eight clients following brief therapy, we found that several clients reported concealing negative feelings from their therapists (Hill, 1989). For example, one client did not like her therapist's focus on how she could improve her marriage. The client had already decided that the marriage was not worth saving and did not want to hear about how she could make the marriage better. Being somewhat passive, however, she did not tell the therapist that she did not want her to focus on improving her marriage. A post-therapy interview indicated that the therapist was not aware that the client was displeased with the focus on the marriage.

The idea that therapists might not be aware of what clients were feeling was intriguing, and we thought our methodology could be altered to explore this question. So we (Thompson & Hill, 1991), studied 32 single sessions of therapy with a slightly different methodology than we used in the eight cases described above. The videotape-assisted review was used immediately after sessions, with a researcher stopping the tape after each therapist speaking turn. Clients rated the helpfulness of each therapist intervention and wrote down the numbers of up to three reactions they had to that intervention. In the meantime, therapists rated the helpfulness of each of their own interventions and wrote down the numbers of up to three reactions they perceived their client to have had to that intervention. When a therapist indicated the same reaction cluster to a therapist intervention as did the client, we considered this to be a match.

We found that, overall, therapists matched on half of the client reactions, which was better than what would be expected by chance. The match rate varied according to the reaction cluster, however. Therapists were able to match at a level greater than that expected by chance for the "supported," "therapeutic work," and "no reaction" clusters, but were not able to match at a level greater than chance for the "negative reactions" and "challenged" clusters. We did not know, however, whether therapists were less able to identify these negative client reactions because clients were hiding these reactions or because therapists were less skilled in decoding negative reactions. We designed another study (Hill, Thompson, & Corbett, 1992) to determine why therapists could not identify negative reactions.

In this study, the methodology was similar to that described in the two studies above. The same videotape-assisted review technique was used immediately after sessions, with researchers stopping tapes after each therapist speaking turn. Clients rated the helpfulness of each therapist intervention and then wrote down the numbers of up to three reactions they had to that intervention, *circling* the numbers of reactions that they hid from therapists. Therapists rated the helpfulness of each intervention and then wrote down the numbers of up to three reactions they thought their client was displaying, up to two reactions they thought their client was hiding, and up to two reactions they thought were out of client awareness. We allowed the therapists more range of opportunity to report displayed, hidden, and out-of-awareness reactions, so that they could be as complete as possible about their observations. When a therapist indicated the same reaction cluster to a therapist intervention as did the client, we considered this to be a match.

Results indicated that therapists were able to match at a level better than would be expected by chance on the "supported" reaction cluster, but were no better than chance at matching on the "challenged" and "no reaction" clusters, and were worse than chance at matching on the "therapeutic work" and "negative reaction" clusters. Furthermore, we found that clients hid more negative reactions than any other type of reactions. Therapists were aware that clients were hiding and unaware of reactions, particularly negative reactions, but were not accurate at identifying *when* clients were hiding reactions.

Finally, when therapists matched on the "negative reactions" cluster, they were less helpful in subsequent interventions. According to our process model (Hill & O'Grady, 1985), if therapists are not aware of client reactions, they cannot plan effective interventions. Our data suggested, however, that when therapists were aware of negative reactions, they were actually *less* helpful. We designed yet another study (Hill et al., 1993) to determine whether long-term therapists would also be less helpful when responding to negative reactions.

In this study, therapists and clients in long-term therapy reported on their own, and their perceptions of each other's, covert processes. We found that clients did hide negative reactions, thoughts, and feelings during sessions. We also found that therapists were seldom aware of how clients were reacting or what clients were not saying. Unlike our earlier findings for brief therapy, however, therapist awareness of negative client reactions was not detrimental to the therapy process, probably because of the therapists' experience level and the long-term nature of the treatment. Furthermore, many clients had secrets (often sexual) that they did not share with their therapists, primarily because of shame or insecurity. Client match on therapist intentions was either neutrally or negatively related to immediate and session-level outcome.

This area of hidden reactions has implications for the practice of therapy. It suggests that a great deal may be occurring in therapy sessions that therapists are unaware of. We may need to teach therapists better methods of attending to clients so that they can be more aware of covert client thoughts. We may also need to train therapists about when to push clients to reveal their thoughts and when to allow them to hide these.

Advantages of the Exploratory Methodology

These descriptions of our research using an exploratory methodology demonstrate how we were able to learn things that we had not anticipated before (e.g., that therapist self-disclosure was so effective and that therapists were not aware of negative client reactions). By allowing the therapy process to evolve in a naturalistic manner and then going back over the sessions with videotape-assisted reviews, we were able to capture the experiences of participants. It would have been difficult to manipulate these variables in an analogue setting and retain the richness of the therapeutic relationship within which these events occurred.

FUTURE RESEARCH

There are several directions for future research. First, we need to examine the therapeutic process with different client populations.

Our studies thus far have focused on unspecified client populations or anxious/depressed populations. Given the findings that I reported from my case studies (Hill, 1989) regarding different reactions to therapist techniques by different types of clients, different therapist techniques are probably effective for different client populations. Thus, we need to be specific about what therapist techniques are effective with what particular types of clients.

Similarly, we need to learn more about the context in which the therapeutic process occurs. Thus, the question is not only what therapist techniques are effective with what particular types of clients, but—we need to add—in what circumstances in therapy. Therapists do not just randomly use techniques; rather, they choose which specific techniques they think will be effective at given moments in therapy based on their perceptions of client needs. Thus, they may offer support at one moment when a client is discouraged, but may offer direct guidance at another moment when a client needs to know what to do next. In our process model, we have postulated contextual variables that may alter the process: client readiness, stage of treatment, and the quality of the therapeutic alliance.

We also need to learn more about the relationship of process to outcome, using methods other than the traditional correlational approach (Gottman & Markman, 1978; Hill, 1982; Hill, Helms, Tichenor et al, 1988; Russell & Trull, 1986). We may need to go beyond exploratory methodologies and use task analyses (e.g., Greenberg, 1986) or qualitative methodologies (e.g., Hoshmand, 1989) to help us understand the conceptual pathways in which process leads to outcome for individual cases.

In our evolution from experimental to exploratory process research and perhaps on to qualitative methods, we are coming closer to being able to describe the phenomena of what occurs in therapy. The future is wide open for the exploration of new methodologies for studying psychotherapy process.

REFERENCES

Adams, H. E., Butler, J. R., & Noblin, C. D. (1962). Effects of psychoanalytically derived interpretations: A verbal conditioning paradigm. *Psychological Reports*, *10*, 691–694.

Benjamin, A. (1981). *The helping interview* (3rd ed.). Boston: Houghton Mifflin.

Carkhuff, R. R. (1969). *Human and helping relations* (2 vols.). New York: Holt, Rinehart & Winston.

Carter, J. A. (1978). Impressions of counselors as a function of counselor physical attractiveness. *Journal of Counseling Psychology, 25,* 28–34.

Caskey, N., Barker, C., & Elliott, R. (1984). Dual perspectives: Clients' and therapists' perceptions of therapist responses. *British Journal of Clinical Psychology, 23,* 30–40.

Claiborn, C. D., Ward, S. R., & Strong, S. (1981). Effects of congruence between counselor interpretations and client beliefs. *Journal of Counseling Psychology, 28,* 101–109.

Elliott, R. (1984). A discovery-oriented approach to significant events in psychotherapy: Interpersonal process recall and comprehensive process analysis. In L. N. Rice & L. S. Greenberg (Eds.), *Patterns of change* (pp. 249–286). New York: Guilford Press.

Elliott, R. (1985). Helpful and nonhelpful events in brief counseling interviews: An empirical taxonomy. *Journal of Counseling Psychology, 32,* 307–322.

Elliott, R. (1986). Interpersonal process recall (IPR) as a psychotherapy process research method. In L. S. Greenberg & W. M. Pinsof (Eds.), *The psychotherapeutic process: A research handbook* (pp. 503–527). New York: Guilford Press.

Elliott, R., & Feldstein, L. (1978). *Helping Intention Rating Procedure.* Unpublished manuscript, University of Toledo.

Elliott, R., Hill, C. E., Stiles, W. B., Friedlander, M. L., Mahrer, A. R., & Margison, F. R. (1987). Primary response modes: A comparison of six rating systems. *Journal of Consulting and Clinical Psychology, 55,* 218–223.

Fuller, F., & Hill, C. E. (1985). Counselor and client perceptions of counselor intentions in relationship to outcome in a single counseling session. *Journal of Counseling Psychology, 32,* 329–338.

Gottman, J. M., & Markman, H. J. (1978). Experimental designs in psychotherapy research. In S. L. Garfield & A. E. Bergin (Eds.), *Handbook of psychotherapy and behavior change* (2nd ed., pp. 23–62). New York: Wiley.

Greenberg, L. S. (1986). Change process research. *Journal of Consulting and Clinical Psychology, 54,* 4–9.

Haase, R. F., & Tepper, D. T. (1972). Nonverbal components of empathic communication. *Journal of Counseling Psychology, 19,* 417–426.

Hill, C. E. (1978). Development of a counselor verbal response category system. *Journal of Counseling Psychology, 25,* 461–468.

Hill, C. E. (1982). Counseling process research: Philosophical and methodological dilemmas. *The Counseling Psychologist, 10*(4), 7–19.

Hill, C. E. (1985). *Manual for the Hill Counselor Verbal Response Modes Category System* (rev. ed.). Unpublished manuscript, University of Maryland.

Hill, C. E. (1986). An overview of the Hill Counselor and Client Verbal Response Modes Category Systems. In L. S. Greenberg & W. M. Pinsof (Eds.), *The psychotherapeutic process: A research handbook* (pp. 131–160). New York: Guilford Press.

Hill, C. E. (1989). *Therapist techniques and client outcomes: Eight cases of brief psychotherapy.* Newbury Park, CA: Sage.

Hill, C. E. (1990). A review of exploratory in-session process research. *Journal of Consulting and Clinical Psychology, 58*, 288–294.

Hill, C. E. (1991). Almost everything you ever wanted to know about how to do process research on counseling and psychotherapy but didn't know who to ask. In C. E. Watkins & L. J. Schneider (Eds.), *Research in counseling* (pp. 85–118). Hillsdale, NJ: Erlbaum.

Hill, C. E. (1992). An overview of four measures developed to test the Hill process model: Therapist intentions, therapist response modes, client reactions, and client behaviors. *Journal of Counseling and Development, 70*, 728–739.

Hill, C. E., Carter, J. A., & O'Farrell, M. K. (1983). A case study of the process and outcome of time-limited counseling. *Journal of Counseling Psychology, 30*, 3–18.

Hill, C. E., Corbett, M. M., Kanitz, B., Rios, P., Lightsey, R., & Gomez, M. (1992). Client behavior in counseling and therapy sessions: Development of a pantheoretical measure. *Journal of Counseling Psychology, 39*, 539–549.

Hill, C. E., & Gormally, J. (1977). The effects of reflections, restatements, probes, and nonverbal behavior on client affect. *Journal of Counseling Psychology, 24*, 92–97.

Hill, C. E., & Gronsky, B. (1984). Research: Why and how? In J. M. Whitely, N. Kagan, L. W. Harmon, B. R. Fretz, & F. Tanney (Eds.) *The coming decade in counseling psychology* (pp. 149– 159). Schenectady, NY: Character Research Press.

Hill, C. E., Helms, J., Spiegel, S. B., & Tichenor, V. (1988). Development of a system for categorizing client reactions to therapist interventions. *Journal of Counseling Psychology, 35*, 27–36.

Hill, C. E., Helms, J., Tichenor, V., Spiegel, S. B., O'Grady, K. E., & Perry, E. S. (1988). The effects of therapist response modes in brief psychotherapy. *Journal of Counseling Psychology, 35*, 222–233.

Hill, C. E., & O'Grady, K. E. (1985). List of therapist intentions illustrated in a case study and with therapists of varying theoretical orientations. *Journal of Counseling Psychology, 32*, 3–22.

Hill, C. E., O'Grady, K. E., Balenger, V., Busse, W., Falk, D., Hill, M., Rios,

P., & Taffe, R. (in press). A methodological examination of videotape-assisted reviews in brief therapy: Helpfulness ratings, therapist intentions, client reactions, mood, and session evaluation. *Journal of Counseling Psychology*.

Hill, C. E., Thames, T. B., & Rardin, D. (1979). A comparison of Rogers, Perls, and Ellis on the Hill Counselor Verbal Response Category System. *Journal of Counseling Psychology, 26*, 198–203.

Hill, C. E., Thompson, B. J., Cogar, M. M., & Denman, D. W. III. (1993). Beneath the surface of long-term therapy: Client and therapist report of their own and each other's covert processes. *Journal of Counseling Psychology, 40*, 278–288.

Hill, C. E., Thompson, B. J., & Corbett, M. M. (1992). The impact of therapist ability to perceive displayed and hidden client reactions on immediate outcome in first sessions of brief therapy. *Psychotherapy Research, 2*, 143–155.

Hoffman, M. A., & Spencer, G. P. (1977). Effect of interviewer self-disclosure and interview–subject sex pairing on perceived and actual subject behavior. *Journal of Counseling Psychology, 24*, 383–390.

Hoshmand, L. L. S. T. (1989). Alternate research paradigms: A review and teaching proposal. *The Counseling Psychologist, 17*, 3–79.

Ivey, A. E., & Authier, J. (1978). *Microcounseling: Innovations in interviewing, counseling, psychotherapy, and psychoeducation*. Springfield, IL: Charles C Thomas.

Kagan, N. (1975). *Interpersonal process recall: A method of influencing human interaction*. (Available from N. Kagan, Educational Psychology Department, University of Houston, University Park, Houston, TX 77004)

Kanfer, F. H., & Marston, A. R. (1964). Characteristics of interactional behavior in a psychotherapy analogue. *Journal of Consulting Psychology, 28*, 456–467.

Kerlinger, F. N. (1973). *Foundations of behavioral research* (2nd ed.). New York: Holt, Rinehart & Winston.

Kiesler, D. J. (1966). Basic methodological issues implicit in psychotherapy process research. *American Journal of Psychotherapy, 20*, 135–155.

Klein, M. H., Mathieu, P. L., Gendlin, E. T., & Kiesler, D. J. (1970). *The Experiencing Scale: A research and training manual* (2 vols.). Madison: Bureau of Audio Visual Instruction, University of Wisconsin.

Klein, M. H., Mathieu-Coughlan, P., & Kiesler, D. J. (1986). The Experiencing Scales. In L. S. Greenberg & W. M. Pinsof (Eds.), *The psychotherapeutic process: A research handbook* (pp. 21–72). New York: Guilford Press.

Lambert, M. J., & Hill, C. E. (1994). Assessing psychotherapy outcomes and processes. In A. E. Bergin & S. L. Garfield (Eds.), *Handbook of psychotherapy and behavior change* (4th ed., pp. 72–113). New York: Wiley.

Mahrer, A. R. (1988). Discovery-oriented psychotherapy research. *American Psychologist, 43,* 694–702.

Martin, J. (1984). The cognitive mediational paradigm for research on counseling. *Journal of Counseling Psychology, 31,* 558–571.

Martin, J., Martin, W., Meyer, M., & Slemon, A. (1986). An empirical test of the cognitive mediational paradigm for research on counseling. *Journal of Counseling Psychology, 33,* 115–123.

Orlinsky, D. E., & Howard, K. I. (1975). *Varieties of psychotherapeutic experience.* New York: Teachers College Press.

Regan, A. M., & Hill, C. E. (1992). An investigation of what clients and counselors do not say in brief therapy. *Journal of Counseling Psychology, 39,* 168–174.

Rennie, D. (in press). Clients' deference in psychotherapy. *Journal of Counseling Psychology.*

Russell, R. L., & Trull, T. J. (1986). Sequential analyses of language variables in psychotherapy process research. *Journal of Consulting and Clinical Psychology, 54,* 16–21.

Snyder, W. U. (1945). An investigation of the nature of nondirective psychotherapy. *Journal of General Psychology, 33,* 193–223.

Spiegel, S. B., & Hill, C. E. (1989). Guidelines for research on therapist interpretation: Toward greater methodological rigor and relevance to practice. *Journal of Counseling Psychology, 36,* 121–129.

Stiles, W. B. (1979). Verbal response modes and psychotherapeutic technique. *Psychiatry, 42,* 49–62.

Stockwell, S. R., & Dye, A. (1980). Effects of counselor touch on counseling outcome. *Journal of Counseling Psychology, 27,* 443–446.

Strong, S. R., Wambach, C. A., Lopez, F. G., & Cooper, R. K. (1979). Motivational and equipping functions of interpretation in counseling. *Journal of Counseling Psychology, 26,* 98–107.

Tepper, D. T., & Haase, R. F. (1978). Verbal and nonverbal communication of facilitative conditions. *Journal of Counseling Psychology, 25,* 35–44.

Thompson, B. J., & Hill, C. E. (1991). Therapist perceptions of client reactions. *Journal of Counseling and Development, 69,* 261–265.

Tichenor, V., & Hill, C. E. (1989). A comparison of six measures of working alliance. *Psychotherapy, 26,* 195–199.

CHAPTER 6

Critically Reading Psychotherapy Process Research
A Brief Enactment

ROBERT L. RUSSELL

Much of the impetus for empirical psychotherapy research came from widespread dissatisfaction with the scientific status of the type of knowledge secured in collections of psychodynamic and other case studies, and from the attempt to establish the superior efficacy of alternative treatments based on competing models, especially that of the client-centered model (Russell, 1984). There are obvious problems with the uncontrolled case study in terms of the reliability and validity of the results obtained therefrom, when considered from the methodological point of view of the experimental sciences (e.g., Kazdin, 1981); from the same perspective, there appear to be obvious problems in the specification of researchable hypotheses that are derived from psychoanalytic theory (e.g., Grunbaum, 1979; Meehl, 1978). Complicating this situation is the fact that meticulous studies of the discourse comprising the "talking cure" have seldom been developed in terms of an explicit link to a single theoretical perspective and its metascientific framework (Russell & Staszewski, 1988).

Although there are arguments that attempt to secure the rationality of psychoanalytic studies by relating it to a hermeneutically oriented metascience (e.g., Habermas, 1968; Ricoeur, 1981), scientific status is typically accorded only those empirical studies of psychoanalysis and other forms of psychotherapy that have been conducted according to an experimental methodology and an empiricist metascientific framework, even when aspects of patient–therapist discourse are studied. Such investigations have been shown to be seriously flawed, both conceptually and methodologically (Russell, 1986), but they continue to be conducted and to gain acceptance by their seeming adherence to the methods of science.

Interestingly, as the chapters of this volume attest, there is currently a growing concern that the wholesale advocacy and use of experimental and classical empiricist methodologies may be inadequate to secure a knowledge base sufficient to understand psychotherapeutic practices and outcomes. Not only are the traditional designs (e.g., the randomized, double-blind, clinical trial), statistical analyses (process–outcome correlations), and experimental control (analogue studies) found to be deficient, but the very language in terms of which therapeutic phenomena are denominated has been argued to be unnecessarily restrictive, inappropriate, and/or biasing (see, e.g., Hill, Chapter 5, this volume; Orlinsky, 1989; Stiles & Shapiro, 1989; Russell, 1984, 1987). That these criticisms are not simply sinister or sectarian "interpretations" and may have some validity is indicated by the astonishing fact that those making them have often been among the staunchest supporters of the empiricist paradigm for psychotherapy research. The sobering fact that the implementation of this paradigm has not met with unmitigated success can be dramatized by underscoring a recent finding in one of the most central areas of investigation—namely, the investigation of therapeutic technique. In four major studies of psychotherapy outcome, conducted by some of the very best psychotherapy researchers, only 1.9% of outcome variance could be accounted for by therapist technique (Lambert, 1989).

Such a finding should give us—as researchers and scholars, as therapists and patients—good reason to pause and consider the metascientific, theoretical, and methodological auspices under which psychotherapy research has traditionally been carried out. During this pause, we might well wonder where we currently are, conceptually and methodologically, and how we have arrived here.

WEAKNESSES OF THE EMPIRICIST APPROACH

For example, let us consider the idiom currently recommended and most frequently used to articulate such a fundamental aspect of psychotherapy as its techniques. We are told that the concept of "strength of treatment" is a critical dimension in terms of which optimal therapeutic practices can be defined (Yeaton & Sechrest, 1981). These authors admit that they "really do not know exactly how applicable the concept of strength of treatment may be in relation to interventions by psychologists" (p. 157). This admission may indeed epitomize a lack of explicit warrant for this terminology—a circumstance that most users of this terminology would admit, if pressed by rigorous questioning. But even in the context of this admission, the authors do not analyze or describe the "grounds" of their uncertainty, or consider alternative conceptions that may not be so difficult to assess.

If we engage in a close textual reading of the proponents of this idiom, a set of presuppositions become clear. Thus, from the wording "in relation to interventions by psychologists," it is easy to infer that the authors do know how applicable the concept of strength of treatment is to interventions by practitioners other than psychologists—namely, by physicians administering pharmacological substances to alleviate physical disorders (e.g., infection caused by a foreign substance invading the body, pain caused by the breakdown of tissues, etc.). Yeaton and Sechrest's uncertainty about the generality of the strength-of-treatment concept must stem from a question concerning its analogical extension from the medical context in which it has its roots to the psychotherapeutic context, where it is commonly employed and/or presupposed. Consequently, the applicability of the concept will be unproblematic only insofar as psychotherapeutic treatments are analogous to medical treatments.

Yeaton and Sechrest (1981) tell us that strength of treatment refers to "the a priori likelihood that the treatment could have its intended outcome" (p. 156). A strong treatment is one that contains "large amounts in pure form of those ingredients leading to change" (p. 156). It is important to note that "ingredients" are here talked about as though it makes *a priori* sense to apply the language of "substances" and "individuation" in describing them. Ontologically, this implies that whatever it is that comprises the effective ingredients, such ingredients will be "things" (i.e., substantial substances). In addition, such substances will be amenable to individuation, that is, they will have distinct "borders," or unique signatures captured by some mechanical device. Basically, this means that the ingredients will be definable in terms of ostensive procedures. In the paradigmatic case, a finger will be able to abut the visible, resistant borders of a thing, which can then be duly dubbed, tagged, or labeled, presumably with an identifying word, mark, or other indexing expression free of any and all theoretically derived surpluses of meaning.

The two examples Yeaton and Sechrest give to illustrate their notion of strong treatment concern the use of chemotherapy in the treatment of cancer, and, in analogy to the chemotherapy, the use of electric shock and verbal punishment procedures for the elimination of problem behaviors in the process of psychotherapeutic care. It is illuminating to consider what is implied by analogically coupling these "therapeutic" procedures. First, we might concede that the language of substance and individuation works very well in an attempt to describe the strength of chemotherapy: An active ingredient can be specified in terms of its molecular structure (i.e., we can define what the chemical is) and the quantitative amount of the substance in any given dose can be varied precisely and increased or decreased at will, outside and independent of the context of administration (although even this is an oversimplification, when active ingredients might be better assessed by blood levels, etc.). Moreover, the strength of the dose can indeed be varied independently of its effects—whether these be positive, null, negative, or iatrogenic.

With respect to the verbal punishment procedure, we could, by definition, count any physical parameters of the acoustic noise that the therapist periodically emits as punishment, if it decreases the likelihood of the patient's responses that it follows. Even here, there are some significant disanalogies, since the functional specification of what will count as "punishment" tautologically includes aspects of its so-called effects in its definition, and also, significantly, aspects of the context of administration. Letting these disanalogies pass for the moment, we may find it more instructive to consider the fact that the definitional analogy requires the language of the therapist (to be precise, we should say language per se, since the therapist's idiolectal qualities of sound making should be considered an aspect of the context of administration) to be reduced to, or be considered solely in terms of, its meaningless physical properties (i.e., its length, frequency, stress, etc.). In other words, verbal punishment procedures can be described in terms of the substantial characteristics of noises, and thus can be included in that class of things ostensively defined in terms of "substance" and "individuation" (albeit now the defining finger has to point to readouts from sophisticated noise-analyzing machinery, rather than to thing/objects per se).

Yeaton and Sechrest employ other such examples in their exposition. Morphine is a strong treatment for pain, aspirin a weak one. Weak antibacterial drugs can produce bad effects (growth of resistant strains of bacteria) just as a weak therapy may leave the psychological problem more resistant to change. "Hooked" psychotherapy patients are compared to drug-dependent patients. An optimum treatment is defined as the "weakest that works." And we are reminded that "physicians do not prescribe morphine for tension headaches. Neither do they persist in prescribing escalating doses of penicillin for gonorrhea when faced with an intractable case" (p. 160). What all these analogies seem to foster is a view of psychotherapeutic ingredients—in particular, techniques—as individuated, meaningless substances that can be ostensively defined and varied, outside and independent of the context of administration, by a therapist or any other qualified professional, in terms of measurable quantities.

It is important to realize that the adoption of such a view is being recommended as a future methodological strategy by Yeaton and Sechrest, not as a description of current or past practices. This recommendation is floated as if the field of psychotherapy had not as yet realized and thus capitalized, in its theoretical, investigative, and practical contexts, on the many points of analogy with the physicalist conception of medical treatment. Even a cursory glance at the history of empirical research on therapeutic techniques, however, should convince the most skeptical novitice that the underlying presuppositions identified above have massively informed investigators' research efforts ever since the commencement of empirical studies (see Russell, 1984).

To give one example from the tradition to back this claim, let us consider only two of Bergman's (1951) recommendations for research into therapist techniques, formulated over 40 years ago: (1) "That a defined unit of response within a counseling interview can be treated as a statistical unit rather than as a context-determined particular of a unique whole" (p. 223); and (2) "That such response units can be assigned an equal statistical weight as representing the same qualitative factor as to meaning and relationship to process when derived from several cases which differ in terms of individuals involved, length, and 'success'" (p. 223). With respect to the first assumption, it is hard to see how the therapist's meaning in using a particular utterance could be discerned without the use of contextual information—at a minimum, the immediate sociolinguistic context of the patient–therapist discourse! Treating the therapist's utterance as a statistical unit would seem to entail that the unit be considered in terms of its structural, situationally invariant features such as its grammatical form, or in terms of its situationally invariant semantic meaning—(e.g., "Yeah, what a truly brilliant guy" could not mean in any context "What an intellectual rogue!"). In other words, one would at best be studying the meaning of isolated utterances, rather than the meanings intended by the speaker, since the latter intended meanings are always constrained by—as they define and are embedded in—the discourse situation and all of its protean particularities. Presumably, to identify something as a context-dependent particular of a unique whole is to lip-lock it with the scientific kiss of death, since it would make problematic any numerically expressed equivalences between particulars, and would consequently thwart any attempt to obtain the mathematical rigor associated, *secundum artem,* with the "advanced" sciences. Instead, relationships between particulars would have to be verbally expressed in the language of analogy, interpretation, and/or discursive argumentation—perhaps passable languages for common sense, art, history, politics, and philosophy, but not for the science of psychotherapy.

The second assumption further promotes the idea that the meaning of utterances is univocal and invariant, much like the signs in formal logic (e.g., conjunction and negation), or like those most prized assertions in logic and science that are deemed "true once and for all or false once and for all independently of time [and circumstance]" (Quine, 1941, p. 6). Not only are the meanings of utterances rigidly fixed in terms of an acontextual semantics, but the psychological salience of a given utterance is taken to be equivalent across all of its possible contexts of use. In other words, the hysterically inclined patient given to hyperbole and the suicidal patient later given over to the morgue will have said the same thing with equal psychological salience when each of them uttered to their respective therapists the intentionless and disembodied prediction, "I'll kill myself if I spend another minute alone." Methodological dicta formulated 40 years ago encourage the "thingification" of speech, so that, in the pursuit of science, psychotherapy researchers might come to agree in their pointing to the hypostatized ortho-graphic representation of a stream of sound and in their locating a corresponding entry in a companion universal dictionary for the representation's semantic label.

Bergman (1951) should perhaps be thanked for his explicit-ness, and Yeaton and Sechrest (1981) chastised for their lapse in scholarship. As I have shown elsewhere (Russell, 1984), Bergman's was not a renegade perspective; rather, it represented only one prominent self-reflective ripple on the mounting wave of "method worship" that swept through the field in the 1950s, 1960s, and 1970s, only then truly becoming the tacit knowledge into which every mid-1970s student was methodically inducted via graduate research apprenticeships and other professional activities. That the empiricist presuppositions have gone "underground" and are still there at present is evident in part in Yeaton and Sechrest's erro-neous, implicit claim to novelty in their physicalist (or at least ob-jectivist) treatment of therapist techniques.

INFLUENCE OF THE EMPIRICIST APPROACH IN THE WORK OF ITS CRITICS

However, the extensive and largely unacknowledged influence of these tacit presuppositions is perhaps better gleaned from the work of investigators who would explicitly identify themselves as skeptical of the empiricist tradition and its recommended methods. We would not expect vocal critics of this tradition to argue for the "thingification" of intentions, or the cross-theory equivalence of techniques, when based solely on an empirical determination that there is a significant overlap in the identified classes of utterances. But this is in fact what can be found.

For example, in a recent paper by Elliott et al. (1987), six thera-pist verbal response mode systems were compared with the express purpose of determining "a set of primary modes" that would serve to summarize any therapist's verbal behavior. With this set of pri-mary modes, researchers could be assured of the comparability of their results, presumably because they would all be using identical descriptive systems. What therapists said could then be partitioned and classified in identical ways by researchers working in different labs and studying different "occasions" of therapy, under slightly varying conditions. In other words, this set of primary modes could be identified from a vantage point presumably free of any theory that might distort direct observation.

Note that this goal is virtually stated: The "comparability" of results stemming from different systems of verbal response modes was considered low or virtually impossible because systems of response modes included "the use of different labels for similar categories, . . . different measurement assumptions and rating procedures (e.g., differences in scoring units), and theoretical biases, resulting in overemphasis on certain verbal behaviors and restricted applicability to therapist behaviors of a particular orientation" (p. 218). Each of these apparent flaws, however, can be formulated as a flaw only on the basis of certain presuppositions concerning the preferred relation between theory and observation, and between the role of theories *vis à vis* other theories in the conduct of science. Such presuppositions affect how research is conducted at the most detailed levels of interest—namely, at the levels of discourse segmentation, categorization, and measurement. Although these authors in their roles as therapists are no doubt champions of pluralism in matters of personal meaning and signification (broadly defined), when it comes to studying the activity of therapy, specifically—therapist and patient verbal behavior—they seem to have unwittingly espoused that form of nominalism and realism that has so often gone hand in hand with empiricist conceptions of science and meaning.

Note, however, that the quest for an observational language free from any and all theoretical influence—one whose terms point unambiguously at their material referents, and provide the final adjudicatory bedrock in relation to which frameworks must be comparatively assessed and their competing claims justified—has in fact failed, and in principle *must* fail. One of the many reasons for this failure is that language constructs as it describes, and construction always proceeds from a limited perspective, whether such perspective is rooted in everyday or theoretical languages. Making our research reports easier to understand by having empirical translation rules whereby competing language category systems become reductively identified in a third such system appears reasonable and do-able, only if we have come to believe (1) that such translation is possible; (2) that if possible, it can be accomplished through the application of a third language category system built up from ostensive procedures for word and/or propositional definition; (3) that the third language category system, because of its realist and referential theory of meaning, has somehow escaped the perspectival constraints on language per se; and (4) that the initial programmatic link between the meaning (sense) of the categories in the language category system and the particular researcher's theory of discourse and psychotherapy is largely superfluous or, equivalently, that severance of this link would not result in a significant loss of meaning. Should we be convinced?

Perhaps the most believable assertion is assumption 4, not because severance of this link is in principle immune to significant losses of meaning, but precisely because so few researchers have developed programmatic links between the meaning or sense of the categories in their systems and the larger theories of language, discourse and psychotherapy from which they ought to have been explicitly derived and critically articulated. At best, we seem to get either very paltry or foolishly sensational "theory bites" in an introductory paragraph or two giving the "rationale" for a particular researcher's category system. As should be expected, however, like the media's "sound bites," these loosely connected introductory paragraphs can hardly hope to withstand a sustained critical reading.

Consider an analogy from the "hard" sciences: In the Ptolemaic category system, the celestial object nearest our planet was classified as another planet. In the Copernican category system, the celestial object nearest our planet is classified as a moon. The empirical object to which both refer can be located at the same point along almost any telescopic crosshairs. Cut from their theoretical nets, however, the terms "moon" and "planet" must be seen to be morphemes lacking any discriminating sense, or to gain whatever distinctive sense that they may have from their new relation (possibly, but not necessarily, of identity) in a third theory. What we understand about the moon/planet "object" that we are pointing to is determined in and by reference to the currently operative astronomical/cosmological theory. Such theories were then and are now hardly of the same order as introductory "sound bytes."

When looking at research on therapeutic discourse, we should be asking pointed theoretical questions. What theories help us to understand the meaning of the therapist's or patient's linguistic "objects"? Or, better, what theories need we refer to in order to comprehend the meaning of a given class label, such as "interpreta-tions" or "disclosures"? Currently, we seem to have pitifully few. To review the category systems in the aforementioned collaborative paper (Elliott et al., 1987), it appears that only Stiles's categories are derived from principles (albeit principles that are themselves hardly derived from theory—see Russell, 1986) relating to both discourse in general and psychotherapeutic discourse in particular. For Stiles, for example, a disclosure is identified along three dichotomous di-mensions: as an utterance that concerns the speaker's rather than the other's experience, that is understood in the speaker's rather than the other's frame of reference, and that is focused on the speaker rather than the other (i.e., makes no presumption of the other's experience or frame of reference). For Stiles's colleagues, on the other hand, disclosure is not related to sets of dimensions or to a theory of discourse (or speech acts). The meaning of the term "disclosure" is merely stated in common-sense terms or terms that relate vaguely to the therapy situation (see Essig & Russell, 1988, for an explication of the implicit theory of disclosure underlying each of these systems and the development of an alternative explicit theory).

Descriptively, the authors highlight the overlap of the linguistic objects that would fall under each of the disclosure categories across the six systems, and suggest that they are therefore basically equival-ent. In doing so, the authors seem simply to eliminate the goal of theory development and its relation to observation. Although the category systems may be pointing to largely overlapping sets of objects, the sense of the objects, of their meaning, and of their theoretical significance is given in relation to the theoretical system in which they were developed and defined. That there are so few explicitly theory-driven category systems perhaps attests to the con-tinued influence of inductivism and objectivism in this area of re-search—that is, to the implicit assumption that we can get to theory from inductions from theoretically immaculate observational sen-tences, and that our observational sentences, even when concerning meaning, should serve to fix things through processes of reference (I have more to say on this below). Only assumptions of this kind seem to be able to legitimate "reductive" projects such as that of Elliott et al. (1987).

But what of that much-lauded descriptive language that is thought to be free from all theoretical and pragmatic bias, and that can be trained like a beacon on the things themselves, as is articulated in assumptions 2 and 3? No doubt such a pure descriptive language has had a hold in one form or another on the philosophical and scientific imagination ever since Descartes's mechanistic conception of the universe. Indeed, a search for such a language will be a requisite for science or any kind of knowledge, just so long as we adopt that form of naive realism "that regards the reality of objects as something directly and unequivocally given" (Cassirer, 1946, p. 6), and the goal of science as mirroring the structure of the world in all of its colossal detail. The search for such a language is necessitated, according to Cassirer, because

> all mental processes fail to grasp reality itself, and in order to represent it, to hold it at all, they are driven to the use of symbols. But all symbolism harbors the curse of mediacy; its bound to obscure what it seeks to reveal. . . . All that "denotation" to which the spoken word lays claim is really nothing more than mere suggestion; a "suggestion" which, in face of the concrete variegated and totality of actual experience, must always appear a poor and simple shell. (1946, p. 7)

As Cassirer goes on to explain, this perspective ultimately entails that "not only myth, art, language, but even theoretical knowledge itself becomes a phantasmagoria; for even knowledge can never reproduce the true nature of things as they are, but must frame their essence in 'concepts'" (1946, p. 7). Thus, in order to capture the world as it is outside of our symbolic nets, realist assumptions tend to result in the need to advocate for a language that does not mediate in any way—ironically, for a language that is not a language.

Has this search for an observational language free of all theoretical bias been successful? Many philosophers of science have addressed this question, and many feel the search to be empirically frustrated and theoretically futile. Even early advocates of the search, such as Carl Hempel, have noted the failure of even the most sophisticated attempts to construct such an observational language at the level of individual sentences. In fact, he concluded that

> the cognitive meaning of a statement in an empiricist language is reflected in the totality of its logical relationships to all of the sentences in that language and not to the observation sentences alone. In this sense, the statements of empirical science have a surplus of meaning

over and above what can be expressed in terms of relevant observation sentences. (Hempel, 1959, p. 123)

In other words, even the observational sentences, formulated in a "thing" language, are imbued with theoretical significance that cannot be eliminated.

Moreover, when read closely, even the realist assumptions we so often attribute to all of the early positivists must be carefully gauged. For example, Carnap (1950/1967) is explicit on this point:

> If someone decides to accept the thing language, there is no objection against saying that he has accepted the world of things. But this may not be interpreted as if it meant his acceptance of a belief in the reality of the thing world. . . . To accept the thing world means nothing more than to accept a certain form of language, in other words, to accept rules for forming statements and for testing, accepting, or rejecting them. . . . But the thesis of the reality of the thing world cannot be among these statements, because it cannot be formulated in the thing language or, it seems, in any other theoretical language. (p. 74)

To drive the point home, let us consider finally one of my favorite examples from the writings of Nelson Goodman. In trying to assess the truth of such simple statements as "The sun always moves" and "The sun never moves," he reminds us that they are not complete statements in and of themselves with unique truth values, but rather statements that are "elliptical for some such statements as 'Under frame of reference A, the sun always move' and 'Under frame of reference B, the sun never moves'—statements that may both be true of the same world" (Goodman, 1978, p. 2). Goodman goes on to underline the fact that frames of reference do not belong to, or reside in, that aspect of the world that is described, but rather to "systems of description." To questions about the structure or content of the world, we can answer "how it is only under one or more frames of reference. We are confined to ways of describing whatever is described. Our universe, so to speak, consists of these ways rather than of a world or of worlds" (Goodman, 1978, p. 3).

Returning to the Elliott et al. (1987) study, we might now ask a pointed question of each of the contributors: "Under what system of description or frame of reference, did you choose to call this utterance a 'disclosure,' and this utterance an 'interpretation,' and so on?" As I have indicated, the answers to this question are not at all evident. It is as if the utterances had been named miraculously from a position outside of any frame of reference. But, in fact, the names can gain sense and meaning only by their relations in frames of reference. We cannot tell how or what these utterances are without using of such frames of reference. Implicit in each of the verbal response systems is at least one frame of reference—most likely, that which is imbedded in our everyday common sense and our clinical lore. These frames of reference have remained essentially opaque and wrought with contradiction. Surely, we cannot expect to develop our science without more attention to our theoretical frames of reference.

This last point needs amplification, because the Elliott et al. (1987) paper seems to suggest that it would be an advance if all of the regrettably implicit frames of reference were to converge and "become as one." But here again an early ideal of the positivists (i.e., the unification-of-science program, with its goal of a unified language and reducibility of all branches of science into a unified set of laws) seems to be operating, when the current history and philosophy of science suggest a radical alternative. Progress in science results from the critical clash between not just theories, but other conflicting fragments of culture as well. It does not advance in pursuing the fabled achievement of univocality and uniformity. As Feyerabend (1975) attempts to show,

> the evidence that might refute a theory can often be unearthed only with the help of an incompatible alternative: the advice (which goes back to Newton and which is still very popular today) to use alternatives only when refutations have already discredited the orthodox theory puts the cart before the horse. Also, some of the most important formal properties of a theory are found by contrast, and not by analysis. A scientist who wishes to maximize the empirical content of the view he holds and who wants to understand them as clearly as he possibly can must therefore introduce other views; that is, he must adopt a *pluralistic methodology*. He must compare ideas with other ideas rather than with "experience" and he must try to improve rather than discard the views that have failed in the competition. . . . Knowledge so conceived is not a series of self-consistent theories that converge towards an ideal view; it is not a gradual approach to the truth. It is rather an ever increasing *ocean of mutually incompatible (and perhaps even incommensurable) alternatives*, each single theory, fairy tale, each myth

that is part of the collection forcing the others into greater articulation and all of them contributing, via this process of competition, to the development of consciousness. (pp. 29–30; italics added)

Even if the frameworks in Elliott et al. (1987) had been explicit and had been radically different in theoretical outlook, conflating all of them (especially at the level of experience) would have been at variance with the goal of attaining the recommended critical vantage point afforded by pluralism, and with the newer views of how one obtains growth in scientific knowledge.

If the still powerful sway of empiricism and its constituent trappings had surreptitiously made their way only into the work of Elliott et al. (1987), the development of alternative conceptual and research frameworks to study psychotherapeutic processes might seem to be most imperiled not from within, but from without. However, this is not the case. As indicated above, other examples can be found even among the work of the tradition's critics. For example, one would not expect the advocates of a new "postmodernist" approach for the study of psychotherapeutic discourse to advocate an objectivist view of intentions—that is, to insist that a speaker's intentions are observable. Stiles (1987), however, does just that. If his article is read closely, throwbacks to realism and objectivism are apparent, and perhaps even somewhat sensational. Consider how Stiles handles the question of the ontological and epistemological status of a speaker's intentions. He attempts to persuade us that intended meanings are "on record" in an observable, consensually recognized public space, and presumably that they are readily accessed by conversational participants as well as investigative eavesdroppers. At the same time, arguments are developed to the effect that "unless a speaker is trained in the use of a particular VRM [verbal response mode] coding system, he or she might be unable to correctly classify the literal meaning or the intended meaning of his or her own utterances" (p. 237). The situation might be put like this: As a speaker, I may be ignorant of the "correct" label for my intended meaning in saying whatever I have said, although I am in possession of correct knowledge of the nature of my intended meaning. This situation might be glossed simply as another manifestation of the problem of multiple but redundant terminologies, à la Elliott et al. (1987): The participant dubs the intent of his or her utterance with one everyday term ready at hand in his or her vernacular, and the trained coder dubs it with another term learned through hours of practice. So what? The catch is that both participant and coder are understood to be pointing to the same "observable" record of the utterance's intent, inscribed somehow/somewhere in an ortho-graphic transcription or video. If this gloss is apt, all the problems attending Elliott et al.'s work apply. At worst, we are back to the realist program, with its struggle to hit upon that one language that will shine its immaculate beacon on the way the world truly is, apart from our many competing systems of description. At best, we are in the business, not of recovering the intended meanings inscribed in discourse and present to the participants, but of concocting theories and objectivistic categories that will help us better predict and con-trol, rather than understand, the verbal behavior of conversational partners. (See Russell, 1986, for a more extensive critique.)

It is unnecessary to ask empirical questions (e.g., "Can you show me a piece or a trace of an intention by pointing to a substantial property of the material world or its mechanistically recorded sig-nature on some intention-detecting machine?") to raise questions about the aptness of Stiles's description of intentions as observable. Recalling Goodman's illustration above, we can see that such terms as "intention" "(subjectivity," "intersubjectivity," etc.) belong, not to the "one objective" world, but to systems of description. From this perspective, it can only seem something like a theoretical sleight of hand to try to push the ideality of the system of description into the materiality of whatever it is that is supposed to be described.

We can come at this problem from another angle (see Russell, in press). Terms such as "intention" are best thought of as abstract terms, proffered from a particular point of view, to organize con-crete "observables" in particular ways for particular theoretical pur-poses. In other words, "intention" functions more like a term such as "university" than like one such as "gym.". Although it makes some sense to point to a building as that which is represented or referred to by the term "gym," it hardly would do to point at anything to get at that which is represented or referred to by "university". The latter term, like the term "intention," helps organize and relate the things we might point to, but is surely not clarified by pointing to a concrete entity that is itself among the very things it is meant to organize. Its "reality" is conceptual, and its worth is to be assessed pragmatically (or perhaps aesthetically or politically), by its value in helping us to explain and to understand, in this instance, psychotherapeutic discourse.

AN ALTERNATIVE

A close reading of these particular works of Elliott et al. (1987) and of Stiles (1987) indicates that the authors unwittingly echo some of the very same presuppositions as those identified in the Yeaton and Sechrest (1981) article. It is as if even these critics of tradition are unconsciously bound by it, and, at least in these articles, have not erased its linguistic and conceptual stranglehold. This, of course, is an ever-present susceptibility we should expect to be made painfully manifest by other readers in our critical dialogues. As anyone familiar with the works of Gadamer (1982) and Derrida (1976) knows, traditions have a way of insinuating themselves into the very heart of the work of those who would topple them.

It is precisely because of this universal susceptibility that we must each articulate as best as possible our particular frames of reference and systems of description, and must volunteer to serve as one another's severest critics. It may be instructive to listen to the kind of respectful and playful attitude that can make this work a delight:

> This essay [*Against Method*] is the first part of a book on rationalism that was to be written by Imre Lakatos and myself. I was to attack the rationalist position, Imre was to restate and to defend it, making mincemeat of me in the process. Taken together, the two parts were supposed to give an account of our long debate concerning the matters that had started in 1964, had continued, in letters, lectures, telephone calls, papers, almost to the last day of Imre's life and had become a natural part of my daily routine. The origin explains the style of the essay: it is a long and rather personal letter to Imre and every wicked phrase it contains was written in anticipation of an even more wicked reply from the recipient. . . . (Feyerabend, 1975, n.p.)

Critical perspectivism cannot flourish or even survive without dialogical partners whose exchange of readings is informed by an agreement to disagree, knowing that knowledge increases through the bittersweet clash of ideas.

In this brief chapter, then, I have attempted to give close public readings of particular works of those whose reasoning I respect. Not only is the enterprise of some intrinsic interest, but it has been my hope to engage in the type of critical reading that I deem too scarce, especially in a field in increasing transition. My impression, at least as concerns the investigation of psychotherapeutic discourse, is that the momentum and impetus in the field have been aimed at a productivity defined by the rate of empirical studies produced by a particular lab. The reasons for this are various and tied to social as well as institutional values (see Wachtel, 1980, for a discussion). The explicitness or soundness or depth or simplicity of the theory that propels the programmatic research is seldom run through the gauntlet of critical peer review. We get "theory bites," followed by gobs of method and data that seem to be uncritically consumed, if read at all. This should change.

Reading comes into play in a second context. Perspectivism entails knowledge of multiple perspectives. These are waiting to be had in our and many other disciplines that hold the potential to be crucially relevant to the goal of understanding therapeutic discourse. Such scholarship is not inimical to achieving greatness in "hard-boiled" empirical as well as in ethereal theoretical work; witness the erudition of Piaget, Festinger, Freud, Bruner, and others. Our scholarly habits as well as our graduate curriculums may well deserve to be reviewed—not only to see which American Psychological Association and licensure requirements are being met, but to ensure the development and pursuit of scholarly curiosities as a valued and essential ingredient in earning Ph.D.'s.

In conclusion, then, my alternative to the tradition of research on psychotherapeutic discourse is as simple as it is bold: We must read! And in doing so, we must place more value on the public exchange of critical readings of implicit or explicit systems of description than on the data themselves in the work of each of our colleagues. It will serve to enlighten us, as well as to begin to cut the rate of production of forgettable hordes of "data." To the cry "Back to the things [i.e., the psychotherapeutic texts] themselves," I answer, "Back further—not to the things, but to our descriptions that construct whatever we are looking at as things."

REFERENCES

Bergman, D. (1951). Counseling method and client responses. *Journal of Consulting Psychology, 15*, 216–224.

Carnap, R. (1967). Empiricism, semantics, and ontology. In R. Rorty (Ed.), *The linguistic turn* (pp. 72–84). Chicago: University of Chicago Press. (Original work published 1950)

Cassirer, E. (1946). *Language and myth*. New York: Dover.

Derrida, J. (1976). *Of grammatology*. Baltimore: Johns Hopkins University Press.

Elliott, R., Hill, C., Stiles, W., Friedlander, L., Mahrer, A., & Margison, F. (1987). Primary therapist response modes: Comparison of six rating systems. *Journal of Consulting and Clinical Psychology, 55*, 218–223.

Essig, T., & Russell, R. (1988). Analyzing subjectivity in theraputic discourse. *Psychotherapy: Theory, Research, Practice, and Training, 27*, 271–281.

Feyerabend, P. (1975). *Against method*. London: Verso.

Gadamer, H.-G. (1982). *Truth and method*. New York: Crossroads.

Goodman, N. (1978). *Ways of worldmaking*. Indianapolis: Hackett.

Grunbaum, A. (1979). Epistemological liabilities of the clinical appraisal of psychoanalytic theory. *Psychoanalysis and Contemporary Society, 2*, 451–526.

Habermas, J. (1968). *Knowledge and human interests*. Boston: Beacon Press.

Hempel, C. (1959). The empiricist criterion of meaning. In A. Yoder (Ed.), *Logical positivism* (pp. 108–129). New York: Free Press.

Kazdin, A. (1981). Drawing valid inferences from case studies. *Journal of Consulting and Clinical Psychology, 49*, 183–192.

Lambert, M. (1989). The individual therapist's contribution to psychotherapy process and outcome. *Clinical Psychology Review, 9*, 469–485.

Meehl, P. (1978). Theoretical risks and tabular asterisks: Sir Karl, Sir Ronald, and the slow progress of soft psychology. *Journal of Consulting and Clinical Psychology, 46*, 806–834.

Orlinsky, D. (1989). Researchers' images of psychotherapy: Their origins and influence on research. *Clinical Psychology Review, 9*, 413–441.

Quine, W. V. O. (1941). *Elementary logic*. Cambridge, MA: Harvard University Press.

Ricoeur, P. (1981). *Hermeneutics and the human sciences* (J. B. Thompson, Ed. and Trans.). Cambridge, England: Cambridge University Press.

Russell, R. L.(in press). Anthropomorphism in mother–infant interaction: Cultural necessity or scientific acumen? In R. W. Mitchell & N. S. Thompson (Eds.), *Anthropomorphism, anecdotes, and animals: The emperor's new clothes?* Lincoln: University of Nebraska Press.

Russell, R. L. (1986). Verbal response modes as species of speech acts? *Explorations in Knowledge*, *3*, 14–24.

Russell, R. L. (1984). *Empirical investigations of psychotherapeutic techniques: A critique of and prospects for language analyses.* Ann Arbor: University Microfilms International.

Russell, R. L. (1987). Psychotherapeutic discourse: Future directions and the critical pluralist attitude. In R. L. Russell (Ed.), *Language in psychotherapy* (pp. 341–351). New York: Plenum.

Russell, R. L., & Staszewski, C. (1988). The unit problem: Some systematic distinctions and critical dilemmas for psychotherapy process research. *Psychotherapy: Theory, Research, Practice, and Training*, *25*, 191–200.

Stiles, W. B. (1987). Some intentions are observable. *Journal of Counseling Psychology*, *34*, 236–239.

Stiles, W. B. & Shapiro, D. A. (1989). Abuse of the drug metaphor in psychotherapy process–outcome research. *Clinical Psychology Review*, *9*, 521–543.

Wachtel, P. L. (1980). Investigation and its discontents. *American Psychologist*, *35*, 399–408.

Yeaton, W., & Sechrest, L. (1981). Critical dimensions in the choice and maintenance of successful treatments: Strength, integrity, and effectiveness. *Journal of Consulting and Clinical Psychology*, *49*, 156–167.

CHAPTER 7

Tradition and Change in Psychotherapy Research
Notes on the Fourth Generation

DAVID E. ORLINSKY
ROBERT L. RUSSELL

A field of scientific research can be viewed intellectually, sociologically, and historically.[1] Intellectually, a field is characterized by its research questions, the observational methods used to answer them, the body of facts accumulated by those methods, and the theories used to interpret and explain those facts. Alternatively, in sociological terms, a scientific field consists of the investigators who at any given time work to solve or reformulate the field's recognized intellectual problems, the journals and other media they use to communicate, the societies in which they assemble, and the standards to which they hold themselves as members of an intellectual community. Finally, from a historical perspective, a scientific field can be defined in terms of its evolving traditions of intellectual activity, whose directions and redirections are determined by successive generations of researchers.

In this chapter, we use this threefold perspective to present a thumbnail sketch of psychotherapy research as a scientific field. Our immediate aim is to provide readers with a sense of the context in which the preceding chapters in this volume have been written, and to highlight some of the common concerns represented in the work of these contributors. In doing so, we hope to lay a groundwork for the more ambitious long-term goal of constructing an adequate intellectual and cultural history of psychotherapy research as a field of inquiry.

One convenient way to construct a historical outline of the field is to list a series of "landmark" volumes (as shown in Table 7.1). This should at least stir the personal memories of veterans and provide newcomers with a valuable bibliographic resource. However, any list of book-length publications introduces distortions that must be taken into account. Because scientific research is published mainly in journals, one major distortion is the introduction of a time lag— occasionally a decade or more[2]—between the time when studies were originally carried out and first presented at conferences and in journals, and their publication in books. Since publication in book format is not as strongly prescribed in scientific as in clinical or scholarly fields, another distortion to be aware of is the omission or underrepresentation of certain active and influential researchers (e.g., Jack Butler, Maurice Lorr, Morris Parloff).

A further problem is the inevitable incompleteness of any particular list.[3] Most prominent by their absence from our list are titles representing research in the behavioral therapies.[4] This omission reflects a regrettable but persistent splitting of the field into separate, though partly overlapping, research communities. Psychotherapy researchers, for the most part, have been adherents of psychodynamic, interpersonal, experiential, cognitive, or eclectic models of clinical practice. Behavioral researchers, on the other hand, have been exponents of treatments based mainly on classical conditioning, operant conditioning, or social learning models (though also including behaviorally oriented cognitive therapists). Unfortunately, full and free communication between these two research communities has been prevented by striking differences in theoretical language, contrasting preferences in research methods, divergent styles of clinical work, and strident debates often marred by intemperate rhetoric. As a result, psychotherapy researchers and behavioral researchers still tend to read and publish in different journals, and to meet at different conferences.[5]

Another feature of our list that will inevitably introduce some distortions is the periodic structure that we have imposed on its chronology. Following a pioneering period, which we describe below as Phase I (c. 1927–1954), we distinguish three further periods in the development of psychotherapy research as a scientific field: Phase II (c. 1955–1969), Phase III (c. 1970–1983), and Phase IV (c. 1984–present). This scheme oversimplifies matters and should be

TABLE 7.1. Some Landmark Volumes in Psychotherapy Research

Authors/editors	Title
	Phase I (c. 1943–1954)[a]

Project reports	
Rogers & Dymond (1954)	*Psychotherapy and personality change*
Anthologies	
Wolff & Precker (1952)	*Success in psychotherapy*
Mowrer (1953)	*Psychotherapy: Theory and research*

	Phase II (c. 1955–1969)

Project reports	
Apfelbaum (1958)	*Dimensions of transference in psychotherapy*
Holt & Luborsky (1958)	*Personality patterns of psychiatrists*
Lennard & Bernstein (1960)	*The anatomy of psychotherapy*
Pittenger, Hockett, & Danehy (1960)	*The first five minutes: A sample of microscopic interview analysis*
Strupp (1960)	*Psychotherapists in action*
Gottschalk (1961)	*A comparative linguistic analysis of two psychotherapeutic interviews*
Snyder (1961)	*The psychotherapy relationship*
Goldstein (1962)	*Patient–therapist expectancies in psychotherapy*
Heine (1962)	*The student physician as psychotherapist*
Snyder (1963)	*Dependency in psychotherapy*
English (1965)	*Strategy and structure in psychotherapy: Three research studies of the Whitaker–Malone multiple therapy*
Stieper & Wiener (1965)	*Dimensions of psychotherapy*
Volsky, Magoon, Norman, & Hoyt (1965)	*The outcomes of counseling and psychotherapy*
Strupp, Fox, & Lessler (1966)	*Patients view their psychotherapy*
Paul (1966)	*Insight versus desensitization in psychotherapy*
Rogers, Gendlin, Kiesler, & Truax (1967)	*The therapeutic relationship and its impact*
Truax & Carkhuff (1967)	*Toward effective counseling and psychotherapy*
Kadushin (1969)	*Why people go to psychiatrists*
Surveys and handbooks	
Reznikoff & Toomey (1959)	*Evaluation of changes associated with psychiatric treatment*
Frank (1961)	*Persuasion and healing: A comparative study of psychotherapy*
Goldstein, Heller, & Sechrest (1966)	*Psychotherapy and the psychology of behavior change*
Lesse (1968)	*An evaluation of the results of the psychotherapies*

(continued)

TABLE 7.1. (continued)

Authors/editors	Title
Surveys and handbooks	
Rubinstein & Parloff (1962)	*Research in psychotherapy* (Vol 1: 1 1958 APA conference)
Strupp & Luborsky (1962)	*Research in psychotherapy* (Vol. II: 2 1961 APA conference)
Shlien, Hunt, Matarazzo, & Savage (1968)	*Research in psychotherapy* (Vol. III: 3 1966 APA conference)
Gottschalk & Auerbach (1966)	*Methods of research in psychotherapy*
Stollak, Guerney, & Rothberg (1966)	*Psychotherapy research: Selected readings*

Phase III (c. 1970–1983)

Project reports	
DiLoreto (1971)	*Comparative psychotherapy: An experimental analysis*
Lerner (1971)	*Therapy in the ghetto*
Henry, Sims, & Spray (1971)	*The fifth profession*
Henry, Sims, & Spray (1973)	*Public and private lives of psychotherapists*
Lieberman, Yalom, & Miles (1973)	*Encounter groups: First facts*
Scheflen (1973)	*Communicational structure: Analysis of a psychotherapy transaction*
Horwitz (1974)	*Clinical prediction in psychotherapy*
Sloane, Staples, Cristol, Yorkston, & Whipple (1975)	*Psychotherapy versus behavior therapy*
Orlinsky & Howard (1975)	*Varieties of psychotherapeutic experience*
Malan (1976)	*Toward the validation of dynamic psychotherapy*
Labov & Fanshel (1977)	*Therapeutic discourse: Psychotherapy as conversation*
Frank, Hoehn-Saric, Imber, Liberman, & Stone (1978)	*Effective ingredients of successful psychotherapy*
Smith, Glass, & Miller (1980)	*The benefits of psychotherapy*
Gelso & Johnson (1983)	*Explorations in time-limited counseling and psychotherapy*
Surveys and handbooks	
Meltzoff & Kornreich (1970)	*Research in psychotherapy*
Bergin & Garfield (1971)	*Handbook of psychotherapy and behavior change (1st ed.)*
Bergin & Strupp (1972)	*Changing frontiers in the science of psychotherapy*
Kiesler (1973)	*The process of psychotherapy: Empirical foundations and systems of analysis*
Strupp (1973)	*Psychotherapy: Clinical, research, and theoretical issues*

TABLE 7.1. (continued)

Authors/editors	Title
Surveys and handbooks (cont.)	
Bordin (1974)	*Research strategies in psychotherapy*
Waskow & Parloff (1975)	*Psychotherapy change measures*
Spitzer & Klein (1976)	*Evaluation of psychological therapies*
Gurman & Razin (1977)	*Effective psychotherapy: A handbook of research*
Strupp, Hadley, & Gomes-Schwartz (1977)	*Psychotherapy for better or worse: The problem of negative effects*
Garfield & Bergin (1978)	*Handbook of psychotherapy and behavior change (2nd ed.)*
Lambert (1979)	*The effects of psychotherapy*
Karasu (1982)	*Psychotherapy research: Methodological and efficacy issues*
Lambert, Christensen, & DeJulio (1983)	*The assessment of psychotherapy outcome*
Anthologies	
Wexler & Rice (1974)	*Innovations in client-centered therapy*
Claghorn (1976)	*Successful psychotherapy*
Harvey & Parks (1982)	*Psychotherapy research and behavior change*

Phase IV (c. 1984–present)

Project reports	
Rice & Greenberg (1984)	*Patterns of change: Intensive analysis of psychotherapy process*
Wallerstein (1986)	*Forty-two lives in treatment: A study of psychoanalysis and psychotherapy*
Luborsky, Crits-Christoph, Mintz, & Auerbach (1988)	*Who will benefit from psychotherapy? Predicting therapeutic outcomes*
Hill (1989)	*Therapist techniques and client outcomes: Eight cases of brief psychotherapy*
Luborsky & Crits-Christoph (1990)	*Understanding transference: The CCRT method*
Skovholt & Rønnestad (1992)	*The evolving professional self: Stages and themes in therapist and counselor development*
Surveys and handbooks	
Williams & Spitzer (1984)	*Psychotherapy research: Where are we and where should we go?*
Garfield & Bergin (1986)	*Handbook of psychotherapy and behavior change (3rd ed.)*
Greenberg & Pinsof (1986)	*The psychotherapeutic process: A research handbook*
Russell (1987)	*Language in psychotherapy*
Beutler & Clarkin (1990)	*Systematic treatment selection*
Beutler & Crago (1991)	*Psychotherapy research: An international review of programmatic research*

(continued)

TABLE 7.1. (continued)

Authors/editors	Title
Surveys and handbooks (cont.)	
Miller, Luborsky, Barber, & Docherty (1993)	*Psychodynamic treatment research: A handbook for clinical practice*
Bergin & Garfield (1994)	*Handbook of psychotherapy and behavior change* (4th ed.)
Talley, Butler, & Strupp (1994)	*Research findings and clinical practice: Bridging the chasm*
Bongar & Beutler (in press)	*Foundations of psychotherapy: Theory, research, and practice*
Horvath & Greenberg (in press)	*The working alliance: Theory and research*
Anthologies	
Hersen, Michelson, & Bellack (1984)	*Issues in psychotherapy research*
Huber (1987)	*Progress in psychotherapy research*
Dahl, Kächele, & Thomä (1988)	*Psychoanalytic process research strategies*
Lietaer, Rombauts, & Van Balen (1990)	*Client-centered and experiential psychotherapy in the nineties*
Toukmanian & Rennie (1992)	*Psychotherapy process research: Paradigmatic and narrative approaches*
Aveline & Shapiro (in press)	*Research foundations for psychotherapy*
Russell (present volume)	*Reassessing Psychotherapy Research*

[a]As noted in the text, Phase I covers the period c. 1927–1954, but no book-length reports of research undertaken before 1943 were published.

understood merely as a heuristic device, to be improved by future scholarship. Its main virtue for the present is that it permits us to approach our limited goal of suggesting how the work described by the contributions to this volume can be understood in terms of its intellectual, sociological, and historical context.

PHASE I (c. 1927–1954): ESTABLISHING A ROLE FOR SCIENTIFIC RESEARCH

The field as we know it today can be traced to several points of origin. Bergin (1971) noted that the earliest statistical tabulations of therapeutic outcomes were published in the late 1920s (Fenichel, 1930, cited in Bergin, 1971; Huddleson, 1927; Matz, 1929). Outcome research of an elementary sort continued to appear at a slow but steady rate (one or two studies per year) through the early 1940s, then stopped during the war years, and did not fully resume[6] until the 1950s, after the terms of debate had been decisively reformulated by Eysenck's (1952) critical challenge. None of the investigators involved in those very early studies continued to be active in later years.

The roots of process research can be dated to the first phonographic recordings of counseling sessions in the early 1940s (Bernard, 1943; Porter, 1943; Rogers, 1942; Snyder, 1945).[7] Investigators inspired by Carl Rogers in the early 1940s at Ohio State University, and after 1945 at the University of Chicago, had accumulated enough research by the late 1940s to be featured together in a special issue of the *Journal of Consulting Psychology* (Carr, 1949; Haigh, 1949; Hoffman, 1949; Seeman, 1949; Sheerer, 1949; Stock, 1949).[8] In the autumn of 1949, Rogers and his coworkers at the University of Chicago Counseling Center organized one of the first major long-term programs of process and outcome research in the field (Gordon, Grummon, Rogers, & Seeman, 1954).

The other program, founded virtually simultaneously (or soon afterward[9]), was the Psychotherapy Research Unit established by Jerome Frank and his coworkers at the Johns Hopkins Medical School (Stone, 1978), following work on an earlier project on group psychotherapy sponsored by the U.S. Veterans Administration (Powdermaker & Frank, 1953). By this time, pioneers like Bordin, Luborsky, and Snyder—who helped create the field of psychotherapy research through their individual efforts and as founders of influential research groups—were already engaged in investigations (Bordin, 1948; Cattell & Luborsky, 1950; Snyder, 1953).[10]

Very shortly, the first wave of pioneering research reached a crest with the publication of the first book-length report of research on psychotherapy (Rogers & Dymond, 1954) and with two substantial anthologies of papers (Mowrer, 1953; Wolff & Precker, 1952). Together with Eysenck's (1952) critical review and early rejoinders to it (e.g., Luborsky, 1954; Rosenzweig, 1954), these works signaled the end of the initial historical phase in which the main concern of researchers was to demonstrate the feasibility and necessity of applying scientific methods to the study of psychotherapy.

The principal achievement of Phase I was to demonstrate how the complex personal phenomena of psychotherapy could be brought out of the private consulting room into the purview of scientific study without disrupting these phenomena beyond recognition. Privacy might be compromised to some degree, but not confidentiality. Similarly, an investigator could try to put numbers to such delicate butterflies as feelings, perceptions, and thoughts, without tearing their wings—agreeing, as Rogers and his colleagues did, "that Thorndike's dictum is essentially correct—that 'anything that exists, exists in some quantity that can be measured'" (Gordon et al., 1954, p. 13).

In a positive thrust, the generation of pioneers who produced Phase I demonstrated that sound recordings of therapy sessions could be the means of making psychotherapeutic phenomena accessible in scientific investigation, and psychometric scaling in the tradition of Thurstone, linked to new model of statistical analysis (e.g., Stephenson, 1953), could be a means of quantifying these phenomena. At the same time, Eysenck's (1952) negative thrust raised critical questions about the clinical value and scientific legitimacy of psychotherapy—questions that were formulated in terms of research evidence and could only be answered in terms of research evidence. However, Eysenck's critique only brought to clear awareness a search for scientific legitimacy that was inherent in the theoretical traditions of modern psychotherapies, which view themselves as applications of already developed or newly discovered sciences of the mind. This theoretical allegiance to the ideal of science had been manifested by those early researchers who, in the 1930s and 1940s, had sought to document the effects of treatment.

PHASE II (c. 1955–1969): SEARCHING FOR SCIENTIFIC RIGOR

Modern studies of therapeutic process and outcome thus were launched more or less concurrently in the years around 1950. Having taken root firmly at midcentury, psychotherapy research grew vigorously in the years from about 1955 through 1969. This second phase of work reflected the extension of earlier efforts by younger workers among the pioneers (e.g., Bordin, Butler, Fiedler, Frank, Luborsky, Rogers, Snyder, Strupp), and the recruitment of a new generation of colleagues who joined established research teams and started new ones (e.g., Bergin, Garfield, Gendlin, Goldstein, Imber,

Kiesler, Lorr, Parloff, Rice, Shlien, Truax). Together with their contemporaries, these investigators constituted a second generation of psychotherapy researchers.

The central task of Phase II in the evolution of psychotherapy research was fulfilling the promise of the preceding phase by building what the second generation believed would be a rigorously scientific field of study. In process research, this took the form of developing objective methods for measuring the events of recorded therapy sessions. In outcome research, it took the form of meeting Eysenck's challenge—that is, establishing the fact that "psychotherapy works" by demonstrating its effectiveness in controlled experiments.

The second generation of researchers undertook this task largely in accordance with the philosophy of science prevailing in American psychology during the 1950s—logical positivism.[11] Radical positivists affirmed that physically measurable dimensions of publicly observable events alone could be made the objects of scientific study, and this doctrine was interpreted by psychologists to mean that in order to be objective, their research had to focus on the overt behaviors of individuals. Thus, the preferred data for psychotherapy research became measures of overtly observable (and mechanically recordable) patient and therapist behaviors during therapy sessions. The subjective states of the participants and their perceptions of the meanings of events either were regarded as objectively unverifiable or were suspected of self-serving bias, and were avoided unless they could be directly linked to externally observed behaviors. Only consensually validated perceptions by "external" or nonparticipant observers were viewed as scientifically trustworthy. This view of scientific work was reinforced by a general commitment to nomothetic group designs (especially controlled experimentation) and to the associated Fisherian statistical methodology (mainly t tests and analysis of variance, Pearson correlations, and their nonparametric parallels).

In process studies, reliance on audio recordings encouraged researchers to focus on aspects of patient and therapist behavior that could be readily quantified (e.g., type–token ratios and the use of self-referential terms in verbal behavior), and, since recordings could be replayed at will, to examine these in microscopic detail (e.g., using sentences, "thought units," or very brief chronological periods as rating units). Recordings of therapy sessions quickly accumulated, each containing hundreds of content units, and researchers soon found themselves possessed of more raw material than they could analyze. The transcription and rating of each session entailed prodigious amounts of labor.[12] In order to cope with this situation, strategies of time sampling were typically developed (e.g., 5 minutes randomly selected from the first, middle, and final thirds of sessions drawn randomly from the first, middle, and final thirds of treatment), and the measurements based on these samples of patient or therapist behavior were typically averaged together (often for whole groups of patients or therapists) in the hope of forming a reliable quantitative estimate for the specified aspect of therapeutic process. Nevertheless, only a relatively small number of cases could be accumulated even by major research programs, and the resulting process indices were unfortunately often far removed from clinical experience and from the theoretical constructs that inspired them.

Although Phase II was marked by a great proliferation of process studies (see Table 7.1), it is probably fair to say that process research during the 1960s was largely dominated by the intensive efforts of client-centered researchers to provide objective evidence of the validity of Rogers's (1957) elegant theoretical formulation concerning the necessary and sufficient conditions of therapeutic personality change. Paradoxically, although Rogers's theory emphasized the client's experience of the "facilitative conditions" (therapist empathy, warmth, and self-congruence), positivist methodological biases led most researchers[13] to use objectified, nonparticipant-observational measures of therapist behavior (Truax & Mitchell, 1971; but see also Mitchell, Bozarth, & Krauft, 1977). Nevertheless, the net result of this peculiarly flawed research was to document the singular importance of relationship factors, especially in client-centered therapy, although this line of work on the Rogerian conditions virtually ceased by the mid-1970s.

Outcome studies were harnessed from the outset to pre–post experimental designs, in which the patient's personality and psychopathology were evaluated once at intake[14] and once at the end of treatment, with a follow-up assessment (if possible) made after some time had passed. Although there have been many variants on this design (see, e.g., Kazdin, 1992), the basic logic required that treated groups be compared in the degree of change from pretreatment to posttreatment levels[15] on the variables selected for assessment with control groups, which were presumably equivalent in all relevant respects. These assessments were usually quite elaborate, frequently involving lengthy interviews and batteries of psychological tests. Practicality, if nothing else, encouraged the assumption that two or three such evaluations per subject were sufficient to define the basic features of a person's mental status and to provide adequate evidence of an eventual change in status.

From today's perspective, it seems clear that no single experiment by itself could ever provide the rigorous demonstration of treatment effectiveness that was sought in response to Eysenck's challenge and in the rush to create a positivistically respectable science. It also seems possible to question whether the ideals of objectivity and experimental control that guided the quest for rigor were not wrongly conceived by the second generation.

PHASE III (c. 1970–1983): EXPANSION, DIFFERENTIATION, AND ORGANIZATION

The second period of development was marked by a steady expansion of the psychotherapy research community. Even by the late 1950s, there were enough people working in the new field to create a need for communication beyond what is normally possible in a journal format. In recognition of this, conferences were organized in 1958, 1961, and 1966 by the American Psychological Association, with support from the National Institute of Mental Health (NIMH), at which leaders in the field were invited to engage in extended discussion of basic research issues (Rubinstein & Parloff, 1962; Strupp & Luborsky, 1962; Shlien, Hunt, Matarazzo, & Savage, 1968). Shortly thereafter, responding to limitations of the "invitational" format, researchers themselves created an open interdisciplinary organization called the Society for Psychotherapy Research (SPR), in order to meet their own needs for scientific and collegial communication on a regular basis (Orlinsky, 1993).

These organizational developments were parallelled, on the intellectual side, by the appearance of books surveying the achievements of the first two phases—for example, Meltzoff and Kornreich's (1970) comprehensive synopsis of research findings, and the first edition of Bergin and Garfield's (1971) *Handbook of Psychotherapy and Behavior Change*. Absorption in meeting demands for increased methodological rigor probably contributed to a trend among researchers to view process and outcome research as separate specialties, although this dichotomization was often remarked on with some dismay. Kiesler (1973) provided an influential review and collation of observational methods in process research. Waskow and Parloff (1975) organized a panel of experts for the NIMH to provide a similar handbook on psychotherapy outcome measures. These signalled the coalescence of a research mainstream committed to a program of objective, quantitative—and, where possible, experimental—studies that characterized Phase III of research on psychotherapy. The course of development during this third phase primarily involved expansion and refinement within the methodological mainstream in process and outcome research, although a significant subcurrent of phenomenologically oriented work on process that started in the mid-1960s also began to gain recognition (e.g., Barrett-Lennard, 1986; Orlinsky & Howard, 1975, 1986).

In the experimental mainstream, comparative outcome studies such as that reported by Sloane, Staples, Cristol, Yorkston, and Whipple (1975) were widely heralded as state-of-the-art, and by the end of the decade plans were already being laid at the NIHM for a much more ambitious controlled clinical trial to compare psychosocial treatments of depression (Elkin, Parloff, Hadley, & Autry, 1986). This trial entailed a strenuous effort to specify, control, and differentiate the treatments actually delivered to patients in various experimental conditions, through the development of formal treatment manuals and the evaluation of process to ensure treatment integrity.

Major achievements of this period were summarized in the second and third editions of the *Handbook of Psychotherapy and Behavior Change* (Garfield & Bergin, 1978, 1986). Even more noteworthy, perhaps, was the marshaling of experimental evidence by the new statistical technique of meta-analysis to provide a convincing positive answer to Eysenck's question about treatment effectiveness (Smith, Glass, & Miller, 1980; see also Shapiro & Shapiro, 1982; Lipsey & Wilson, 1993). Having affirmed in a general way that "psychotherapy works," this pivotal work ushered in a new period for outcome researchers, in which attention came to be focused on the evaluation of components of specific treatments and the comparison of alternative treatments for specific disorders.

After the mid-1970s, new impetus was given to process research by Bordin's (1979)[16] reformulation of the crucial relationship between patient and therapist as a "working alliance," which stimulated the construction of new measurement instruments[17] and their application in a still undiminished spate of studies (Horvath & Greenberg, in press). Together with the sophisticated observational systems developed by Benjamin (1974) and Kiesler (1987) from earlier circumplex models of interpersonal behavior (e.g., Leary, 1957), these gave investigators who were disappointed in the results of Rogerian studies of "facilitative conditions" new conceptual and methodological bases for examining the therapeutic relationship. The next transition in process research was marked by the introduction of a "task-analytic" approach by Rice and Greenberg (1984) and their colleagues, which seriously challenged the established methodological tradition of the mainstream. The advent of meta-analysis and the renewal of process studies defined much of the agenda for the next, most recent stage of development in psychotherapy research.

PHASE IV (c. 1984–PRESENT): CONSOLIDATION, DISSATISFACTION, AND REFORMULATION

Our commentary on developments in the past decade concentrates primarily on the authors collected in the present volume. Although this unfortunately omits many who have also made significant contributions,[18] the authors represented here are all major figures in the fourth generation of psychotherapy researchers.[19] Though leading in rather different directions, their chapters in this book reflect a shared sense of dissatisfaction with the methodological tradition in which they were trained and did their early work. We shall explore the significance of that dissatisfaction and its causes as our contribution to this volume.

One way to do this is to compare their implicit and explicit metascientific "prejudices" with those of the previous generations of researchers. In addition to noting the differing predominant influences to which these researchers have responded, it is useful to try to specify how such influences have seemed to shape differing methodological practices in the conduct of research. As an exemplar of the pioneering first generation of researchers, we will focus again on the program initiated under Carl Rogers, and specifically on his attempts to study the techniques of client-centered therapy. Rogers and his group felt that the techniques of therapy could be studied "objectively" because the use of phonographic recordings of the therapy sessions objectified the external events of therapy. Therapy could thus become "a process based on known and tested principles, with tested techniques for implementing those principles" (Rogers, 1942, p. 434). The research group could now "investigate almost any phase of psychotherapy about which we wish to know, from the subtlest aspect of the counselor–client relationship to measures of behavior change" (Rogers, 1951, p. 13). Previously, Rogers had been focused on explicating client-centered therapeutic practices, linking verbatim examples of counselor–client interchanges to theoretical principles that could provide a terminology for their description and a rationale for their use. Here he proceeded without being bound by the principles of objectivism; but rather, he attempted to give "good reasons" for describing and interpreting the experiential processes of therapy in terms of client-centered theory. As Russell (1984, pp. 26–27) has pointed out,

> It is important to note that in such illustrations there is a conspicuous absence of any concern with the formal methodological problems of reliable unitization, taxonomic classification of techniques, or the requirement of stating operational or analytic definitions of therapists' utterances. [However,] in changing the primary focus from explicating a new therapeutic approach [to clinical practice] to securing its status on a scientific basis, such methodological problems became central. For Rogers and [especially for] his research group, securing the status of client-centered theory and practice on a scientific basis meant [wholeheartedly embracing] "the conviction that Thorndike's dictum is essentially correct—that "anything that exists, exists in some quantity that can be measured" (Gordon, Grummon, Rogers, & Seeman, 1954, p. 13).

From the tasks involved in the narrative and theoretical explication of a new therapeutic practice, Rogers and his group moved to the tasks involved in its scientific study. Like others during the 1940s and 1950s, the research group was guided by empiricism and objectivism in its attempts to investigate therapy scientifically. The group's first tasks were identified as constructing appropriate experimental contexts and tests and their associated objective measurements, now couched in terms of scaling techniques and tests of statistical significance, as we have noted above.

This new focus, however, brought with it a subtle but almost complete shift in the research paradigm envisioned by Rogers and his research group. Such a shift can be at least partially attributed to the leveling effect of adopting the prevalent positivist and objectivist metascientific framework, and to the group's focus on methodological questions. At the outset, Rogers had advocated a very specific model of scientific research, his description of which is worth quoting in some detail:

> It appears to the writer that the somewhat critical attitude which is usually held toward anything which may be defined as a "school of thought" grows out of a lack of appreciation of the way in which science grows. In a new field of investigation which is being opened up to objective study, the school of thought is a necessary cultural step. Where objective evidence is limited, it is almost inevitable that markedly different hypotheses will be developed and offered to explain the phenomena which [are] observed. The corollaries and ramifications of any such hypotheses constitute a system which is a school of thought. These schools of thought will not be abolished by wishful thinking. The person who attempts to reconcile them by compromise will find himself left with a superficial eclecticism which does not increase objectivity, and which leads nowhere. Truth is not arrived at by concessions from differing schools of thought. (Rogers, 1951, p. 8)

Consequently, Rogers and his group felt that they could

> test a coherent set of hypotheses growing out of a consistent body of personality theory. We have endeavored to avoid the testing of atomistic hypotheses where proof or disproof has little relation to any larger body of theory. We have, on the contrary, attempted to make sure that each hypothesis we have tested has a significant place in the developing theory of personality in client-centered therapy. . . . It is in this way, we believe, that we avoid piling up a meaningless body of isolated facts and promote instead the genuine advance of science. (Rogers & Dymond, 1954, pp. 6–7)

But, in fact, by 1950 both of the above-described principles had been systematically eroded in the conduct of the group's empirical research on psychotherapeutic techniques (Russell, 1984).

The erosion of these principles can be attributed to the understandable but somewhat self-blinding adoption of the prevailing methodological practices of positivistic empiricism. Thus, for example, the meaning of the use of particular therapeutic techniques in each and every therapy had to be restricted, in order to be amenable to classification in largely nominal category systems. To be used in statistical analyses, such technique categories had to be thought of as independent and mutually exclusive. They had to be assumed to carry the same statistical weight wherever they occurred in the session, and were treated as if they occurred largely at random in the process of treatment. Moreover, the categories themselves were thought to gain in scientific usefulness as they became defined in a more and more universal but possibly clinically irrelevant terminology—one that was, clinically speaking, pantheoretical or atheoretical.

The upshot of all this focus on methodological rigor was that differing therapies came to be compared on a small set of categories whose clinical relevance was unclear. The comparisons were usually made on the frequencies of use of these categories, obviating any real examination of the processes that were the stated target of investigation. Moreover, the results did not feed back into theory development as demanded and as thought by Rogers and his group. How could they? The development of categories of description aimed at theory-free descriptions of objective events devoid of their pluralistic meanings necessarily had little to do in the end with the clinical theories being examined.

The extent of this process can be seen in the work of one of the most research-oriented of Rogers's students. Seeman (1948), after developing his own category system that purported to be free of any theoretical or valuational biases, suggested that other sets of categories simply be generated as "hypotheses in action." Such category systems would then compete until one of them proved more useful in terms of utility. As in the positivistic metascience, where the context of hypothesis discovery and generation was deemed irrelevant, no critical or evaluative attention was thought to be necessary or usefully applied to the "context of discovery" in which a researcher happened to choose this or that set of descriptive categories. The only relevant context to attend to was considered to be that in which the categories could be put to a critical test as to the number of interesting empirical relations in which they came to participate.

Even for the construction of one's basic descriptive categories, the context of verification came to be the primary focus of interest. In such a context, those category systems participating in more interesting empirical relations would survive, and knowledge would be built up through induction and a bottom-up process of generalization. This dovetailed nicely with the empiricism that the early researchers strove to emulate in their investigations.

The crucial cost of such methodologism has been spelled out by Russell:

> The value, the meaning, the cogency, etc. of the system of categories can thus be determined, not in terms of its (i.e., the system's) "sense" vis-a-vis some [clinical] conceptual framework, but [only] in terms of the progress it achieves in its struggle with other systems to produce the type of data through which empirical generalizations and law-like statements can be secured. The [clinical or other] "sense" or "meaning" of the categories, in other words, remains to be determined by the set of empirical relations in which each of them participate. Even the "interpretation" of the meaning of the categories can be viewed to be somewhat adjunctive or superfluous to their "true" empirical meaning, given by the empirical relations in which they participate. Thus, not only is it irrelevant how the categories were selected or generated in the first place (whether by reason or by whim), it is also essentially irrelevant how the categories are to be interpreted, once it is known what their empirical relationships are. (Russell, 1984, pp. 44– 45)

The quest to study the experiential processes of psychotherapy by applying the received model of scientific methodology could be said to have ended in just the state that Rogers had hoped to avoid— namely, with the accumulation of theoretically irrelevant facts of little clinical significance, and with the subtle dissolution of the putative relevance of "schools of thought" in the methodological aspects associated with the empirical enterprise. Every school of thought, every theory, every phenomenon had to be submitted to the same process of objectification, measurement, and test. With this uniformity of methodological practice, so too came the leveling of theoretical differences and the seeming neglect of the special individuality of the phenomena under study.

Or so the early work came to be seen, once the hold of positivism weakened and other philosophies of science came to exert explicit or implicit influence in the field of psychology. If the transition from Rogers's early explicative work to his group's quest for scientific standing can be described as a move from emphasizing the context of discovery to the context of verification (understood in a positivistic sense), then the work of the fourth generation of investigators as illustrated in this volume might be described as an attempt to move back to the context of discovery. However, the move back has occurred in very different metascientific and cultural circumstances. The "unity of science" program of the positivists could hardly exert much pressure today, given the proliferation of philosophies of science and the cultural and scientific embrace of pluralism in its many forms. This provides the impetus to look at the phenomena one wishes to study from multiple, sometimes incommensurable perspectives, without necessarily being bound to reduce the phenomena so as to comport with the principles of one particular metascience. Moreover, as other false dualisms, the dichotomy between the contexts of discovery and verification has been eroded by the new philosophies of scientific practice. This has made the scientific focus on "discovery" as legitimate as the scientific focus on "verification," to use the old terminology. Equally important, methods have been devised or adapted to lend rigor to the qualitative investigation of the processes of therapy. This has at least meant that "discoveries" can be consensually assessed through peer review before being tested quantitatively in positivist paradigms, and, at most, that "verification" can be achieved through narrative, nonquantitative, nonobjectivist methods. Finally, from within the field of psychotherapy research itself, there has seemed to be a consensus that the work of the first three generations has accomplished at least one very admirable task—that of demonstrating that therapy actually achieves significant positive effects over and above control conditions.[20] Consequently, a focus on how such effects are achieved has become a pressing second concern, with a whole set of puzzling methodological and theoretical questions of its own. But the question of process is itself now being addressed in very different scientific and cultural circumstance than the first outcome questions.

For example, the present volume's first chapter, by Shapiro et al., might be read as an attempt to apply the most sophisticated review methodology (i.e., meta-analysis and multiple regression) to ascertain what is known about the relation between process variables and outcomes. Does anything rise above the noise contributed by statistical, construct, internal, and external validity issues? We quote:

"seven dummy variables representing the effects of eight types of therapist intervention exerted no significant independent effect upon [outcome] effect size" (p. 26). The empirical research relating processes to outcomes appears, at least from this perspective, to be bankrupt. Or, alternatively, an area is thrown wide open for renewed and novel investigation, without the constraints of the objectivism and other prejudices associated with the "drug metaphor" and the previous generations' use of positivism as the only guide to methodology.

If Shapiro et al. seek in Chapter 1 to present an empirical demonstration of our lack of knowledge of one aspect of the process–outcome relationship,[21] Chapter 2, by Stiles, Shapiro, and Harper, can be seen as an attempt to discursively deconstruct component conceptual and methodological practices associated with the "drug metaphor." In addition, this second chapter showcases an alternative model whereby process–outcome relationships can be investigated as they take shape across and within sessions. Its reliance on developmentalism and narrativism contrasts sharply with the previous generations' reliance on positivism and measurement as the guiding paradigms. With its new "prejudices," the researcher is thrown into a position that requires the qualitative sifting through the details of the actual processes taking place between therapist and client. It turns back to the phenomena (as mechanically recorded), guided by models of change and understanding very different from that afforded by the drug metaphor. Note, however, that this fine-grained sifting of the phenomena is not offered simply as a method to apply in what used to be dismissed as the context of discovery, to be augmented later by observed process–outcome correlations or demonstrated in an experimental clinical trial. Instead, its method is being offered as a new way to discover verifiable relations between processes and outcomes, defined in very different terms.

Elliott and Anderson, too, sound an expansive note in Chapter 3. Although one might characterize the quest for knowledge about therapeutic processes as becoming more and more sophisticated over the previous three generations in terms of its application of the quantitative paradigms associated with the positivist version of empiricism, these authors note untapped directions for research. Even-handedly, these authors note extremes at almost every crucial decision point for conducting research—extremes that can render quantitative studies embarrassingly simple and qualitative studies embarrassingly complex. However, the authors acknowledge that simplicity has seemed to have had its day, at the cost of losing sight of the complex phenomena that together comprise the process of psychotherapy. Discovering the real complexities is as important as verifying simple regularities.

Greenberg, in Chapter 4, also sounds an alarm: Discover the important phenomena before proceeding to tests of causal relationships. He and his colleagues have been painstakingly rigorous in developing methods of discovery—a critical-event methodology—with no apology that they are thereby doing something other than science, even though they have abandoned a random-sampling approach to the study of the processes of psychotherapy. So too, in Hill's Chapter 5, one can see Hill's attempt to better confront the experiential processes of therapy as it occurs in naturalistic settings and as it appears to those who have been involved in its processes.

Whether it is called a discovery-oriented, exploratory, descriptive, qualitative, narrative, or critical-event approach, we see that each author or group of authors wants to push investigators to face the complexities of the phenomena of therapy from a variety of perspectives. Even Russell, in Chapter 6, asks investigators to critically revel in rather than be put off by pluralism and its seeming cacophony of descriptive, methodological, and theoretical terminologies. Here the call to get back to the phenomena is couched in terms of an invitation to engage in a discursive conflict aimed at assessing differing descriptive frameworks—not as an activity that is somehow extrascientific, but as an activity that is quintessentially scientific.[22]

In summary, then, the present volume of papers summarizes another shift in emphasis between generations of psychotherapy researchers. We have broadly characterized this shift as one from a concentration on the context of verification, understood in positivistic terms, to a renewed concentration—with new methods, models, and theories—on the context of discovery, mostly applied to questions of the relation between process and outcome. To understand this shift, one has to appreciate how the division between discovery and verification is itself considered to be somewhat simplistic: Science as practiced does not so easily cleave into this classical dichotomy.

ACKNOWLEDGMENT

Work on this chapter by the first author [Orlinsky] was partially supported by research grant R-01-MH42901 from the National Institute of Mental Health.

NOTES

1. Our approach is based largely on Thomas Kuhn's (1970) conception of normal science.

2. The most extreme examples of this are probably Frank, Hoehn-Saric, Imber, Liberman, and Stone (1978) and Wallerstein (1986).

3. We apologize to authors of worthy volumes that have been inadvertently overlooked. Also, some volumes not uniquely concerned with psychotherapy research but greatly influential upon it might have been mentioned—for example, Campbell and Stanely (1963), Chassan (1967), Kazdin (1980, 1992), Cohen and Cohen (1983), and Cohen (1988).

4. Research on behavioral treatments began in the 1960s, following their theoretical definition in the 1950s. Landmark volumes for the period 1950–1965, listed by date of publication, would include Dollard and Miller (1950), Skinner (1953), Rotter (1954), Wolpe (1958), Eysenck (1960), Bandura and Walters (1963), Franks (1964), and Krasner and Ullmann (1965).

5. A thorough-going history would have to describe both groups in some detail, but for the present we can deal only with the nonbehavioral segment of the psychotherapy research community. Given the current movement toward eclecticism and integration, we hope that the future will bring an increasing rapprochement between the two segments of the research community.

6. A partial exception to this generalization is the work of Muench (1947).

7. Hill and Corbett (1993) attribute the first research use of recorded counseling interviews to Frank Robinson in 1938 at Ohio State University.

8. See Seeman and Raskin (1953) for a review of early research by Rogers's students and collaborators; and note also the early publications of Hathaway (1948), Raimy (1948), and Fiedler (1950).

9. Stone (1978), acting as historian of the Psychotherapy Research Unit, gives the date as October 1, 1949; Frank (1992), perhaps relying on personal memory, wrote: "In 1951, I was invited to Johns Hopkins ... " (p. 392).

10. Bordin joined the University of Michigan psychology department in 1948 (Strupp & Howard, 1992); Luborsky joined the Menninger Foundation in 1947 (Luborsky, 1992); Snyder organized the research group at Penn State around 1950 (Strupp & Howard, 1992). We apologize for failing to mention (or know) the contributions of other pioneers in the field.

11. The commitment to logical positivism is represented, for example, in the *International Encyclopedia of Unified Science* (Neurath, Carnap, & Morris, 1955) and the reader edited by Feigl and Brodbeck (1953).

12. For example, Gordon et al. (1954) estimated that "nearly seven hundred man-hours [were] invested in gathering the data on . . . one case, without any account of the time needed for analyzing the material thus gathered" (p. 27).

13. The work of Barrett-Lennard (1959, 1986) was an important exception to this trend.

14. Or twice, if a waiting period was used to establish an own-control condition.

15. And from pretreatment to follow-up or posttreatment to follow-up levels.

16. Presented to colleagues at the 1975 annual meeting of the SPR.

17. For examples, see Greenberg and Pinsof (1986).

18. We hope to remedy this omission at a later date.

19. For instance, Greenberg, Shapiro, and Hill each have already been elected to serve as president of the International Society for Psychotherapy Research, and Elliott has served as president of the North American SPR.

20. Orlinsky, Grawe, and Parks (1994) document further research achievements of the first three generations (and the fourth) with respect to process–outcome connections.

21. But see Orlinsky, Grawe, and Parks (1994) for a contrasting view of the field.

22. Orlinsky, while sharing this pluralist vision (Orlinsky, 1989), favors an approach to research that might be described as a postpositivist empiricism embracing appropriate combinations of qualitative and quantitative methodologies.

REFERENCES

Apfelbaum, B. (1958). *Dimensions of transference in psychotherapy.* Berkeley: University of California Press.

Aveline, M., & Shapiro, D. (Eds.). (in press). *Research foundations for psychotherapy.* Chichester, England: Wiley.

Bandura, A., & Walters, R. H. (1963). *Social learning and personality develop-*

ment. New York: Holt, Rinehart & Winston.

Barrett-Lennard, G. T. (1959). Therapeutic personality change as a function of perceived therapist response. *American Psychologist, 14,* 376.

Barrett-Lennard, G. T. (1986). The Relationship Inventory now: Issues and advances in theory, method, and use. In L. S. Greenberg & W. M. Pinsof (Eds.), *The psychotherapeutic process: A research handbook* (pp. 439–476). New York: Guilford Press.

Benjamin, L. S. (1974). Structural Analysis of Social Behavior. *Psychological Review, 81,* 392–425.

Bergin, A. E. (1971). The evaluation of therapeutic outcomes. In A. E. Bergin & S. L. Garfield (Eds.), *Handbook of psychotherapy and behavior change* (1st ed., pp. 217–270). New York: Wiley.

Bergin, A. E., & Garfield, S. L. (Eds.). (1971). *Handbook of psychotherapy and behavior change* (1st ed.). New York: Wiley.

Bergin, A. E., & Garfield, S. L. (Eds.). (1994). *Handbook of psychotherapy and behavior change* (4th ed.). New York: Wiley.

Bergin, A. E., & Strupp, H. H. (1972). *Changing frontiers in the science of psychotherapy.* Chicago: Aldine–Atherton.

Bernard, J. (1943). Studies in the phonographic recordings of verbal material: I. The use of phonographic recordings in counseling practice and research. II. A transcribing device. *Journal of Consulting Psychology, 6,* 105–113, 149–153.

Beutler, L. E., & Clarkin, J. F. (1990). *Systematic treatment selection.* New York: Brunner/Mazel.

Beutler, L. E., & Crago, M. (Eds.). (1991). *Psychotherapy research: An international review of programmatic research.* Washington, DC: American Psychological Association.

Bongar, B., & Beutler, L. E. (Eds.). (1994). *Foundations of psychotherapy: Theory, research, and practice.* New York: Oxford University Press.

Bordin, E. S. (1948). Dimensions in the counseling process. *Journal of Clinical Psychology, 4,* 240–244.

Bordin, E. S. (1974). *Research strategies in psychotherapy.* New York: Wiley–Interscience.

Bordin, E. S. (1979). The generalizability of the psychoanalytic concept of the working alliance. *Psychotherapy: Theory, Research, and Practice, 16,* 252–260.

Campbell, D. T., & Stanley, J. C. (1963). *Experimental and quasi-experimental designs for research.* Chicago: Rand McNally.

Carr, A. C. (1949). An evaluation of nine nondirective psychotherapy cases by means of the Rorschach. *Journal of Consulting Psychology, 13,* 196–205.

Cattell, R. B., & Luborsky, L. B. (1950). P-technique demonstrated as a new clinical method for determining personality and symptom structure.

Journal of General Psychology, 42, 3–24.

Claghorn, J. L. (Ed.). (1976). *Successful psychotherapy.* New York: Brunner/Mazel.

Chassan, J. B. (1967). *Research designs in clinical psychology and psychiatry.* New York: Appleton-Century-Crofts.

Cohen, J. (1988). *Statistical power analysis for the behavioral sciences.* Hillsdale, NJ: Erlbaum.

Cohen, J., & Cohen, P. (1983). *Applied multiple regression/correlation for the behavioral sciences.* Hillsdale, NJ: Erlbaum.

Dahl, H., Kächele, H., & Thomä, H. (Eds.). (1988). *Psychoanalytic process research strategies.* Berlin: Springer-Verlag.

DiLoreto, A. O. (1971). *Comparative psychotherapy: An experimental analysis.* Chicago: Aldine-Atherton.

Dollard, J., & Miller, N. E. (1950). *Personality and psychotherapy.* New York: McGraw-Hill.

Elkin, I. E., Parloff, M. B., Hadley, S. W., & Autry, J. H. (1985). NIMH Treatment of Depression Collaborative Research Program: Background and research plan. *Archives of General Psychiatry, 42,* 305–316.

English, O. S. (Ed.). (1965). *Strategy and structure in psychotherapy: Three research studies of the Whitaker–Malone multiple therapy.* Philadelphia: Eastern Pennsylvania Psychiatric Institute.

Eysenck, H. J. (1952). The effects of psychotherapy: An evaluation. *Journal of Consulting Psychology, 16,* 319–324.

Eysenck, H. J. (Ed.). (1960). *Behavior therapy and the neuroses.* Elmsford, NY: Pergamon Press.

Feigl, H., & Brodbeck, M. (Eds.). (1953). *Readings in the philosophy of science.* New York: Appleton-Century-Crofts.

Fiedler, F. (1950). A comparison of therapeutic relationships in psychoanalytic, nondirective and Adlerian therapy. *Journal of Consulting Psychology, 14,* 426–445.

Frank, J. D. (1961). *Persuasion and healing: A comparative study of psychotherapy.* New York: Schocken Books.

Frank, J. D. (1992). The Johns Hopkins Psychotherapy Research Project. In D. K. Freedheim (Ed.), *History of psychotherapy: A century of change* (pp. 392–396). Washington, DC: American Psychological Association.

Frank, J. D., Hoehn-Saric, R., Imber, S. D., Liberman, B. L., & Stone, A. R. (1978). *Effective ingredients of successful psychotherapy.* New York: Brunner/Mazel.

Franks, C. M. (Ed.). (1964). *Conditioning techniques in clinical practice and research.* New York: Springer.

Garfield, S. L., & Bergin, A. E. (Eds.). (1978). *Handbook of psychotherapy and behavior change* (2nd ed.). New York: Wiley.

Garfield, S. L., & Bergin, A. E. (Eds.). (1986). *Handbook of psychotherapy and behavior change* (3rd ed.). New York: Wiley.

Gelso, C. J., & Johnson, D. H. (1983). *Explorations in time-limited counseling and psychotherapy*. New York: Teachers College, Columbia University.

Goldstein, A. P. (1962). *Patient–therapist expectancies in psychotherapy*. Elmsford, NY: Pergamon Press.

Goldstein, A. P., Heller, K., & Sechrest, L. B. (1966). *Psychotherapy and the psychology of behavior change*. New York: Wiley.

Gordon, T., Grummon, D. L., Rogers, C. R., & Seeman, J. (1954). Developing a program of research in psychotherapy. In C. R. Rogers & R. F. Dymond (Eds.), *Psychotherapy and personality change* (pp. 12–34). Chicago: University of Chicago Press.

Gottschalk, L. A. (Ed.). (1961). *A comparative linguistic analysis of two psychotherapeutic interviews*. New York: International Universities Press.

Gottschalk, L. A., & Auerbach, A. H. (Eds.). (1966). *Methods of research in psychotherapy*. New York: Appleton-Century-Crofts.

Greenberg, L. S., & Pinsof, W. M. (Eds.). (1986). *The psychotherapeutic process: A research handbook*. New York: Guilford Press.

Gurman, A. S., & Razin, A. M. (Eds.). (1977). *Effective psychotherapy: A handbook of research*. Oxford: Pergamon Press.

Haigh, G. V. (1949). Defensive behavior in client-centered therapy. *Journal of Consulting Psychology, 13*, 181–189.

Harvey, J. H., & Parks, M. M. (Eds.). (1982). *Psychotherapy research and behavior change*. Washington, DC: American Psychology.

Hathaway, S. R. (1948). Some considerations relative to nondirective counseling as therapy. *Journal of Clinical Psychology, 4*, 226–231.

Heine, R. W. (Ed.). (1962). *The student physician as psychotherapist*. Chicago: University of Chicago Press.

Henry, W. E., Sims, J. H., & Spray, S. L. (1971). *The fifth profession*. San Francisco: Jossey-Bass.

Henry, W. E., Sims, J. H., & Spray, S. L. (1973). *Public and private lives of psychotherapists*. San Francisco: Jossey-Bass.

Hersen, M., Michelson, L., & Bellack, A. S. (Eds.). (1984). *Issues in psychotherapy research*. New York: Plenum Press.

Hill, C. E. (1989). *Therapist techniques and client outcomes: Eight cases of brief psychotherapy*. Newbury Park, CA: Sage.

Hill, C. E., & Corbett, M. M. (1993). A perspective on the history of process and outcome research in counseling psychology. *Journal of Counseling Psychology, 40*, 3–24.

Hoffman, A. E. (1949). A study of reported behavior changes in counseling. *Journal of Consulting Psychology, 13*, 190–195.

Holt, R. R., & Luborsky, L. (1958). *Personality patterns of psychiatrists*. New York: Basic Books.

Horvath, A. O., & Greenberg, L. S. (Eds.). (in press). *The working alliance:*

Theory and research. New York: Wiley.

Horwitz, L. (1974). *Clinical prediction in psychotherapy*. New York: Jason Aronson.

Huber, W. (Ed.). (1987). *Progress in psychotherapy research*. Louvain-la-Neuve, Belgium: Presses Universitaires de Louvain.

Huddleson, J. H. (1927). Psychotherapy in two hundred cases of psychoneurosis. *Military Surgeon, 60,* 161–170.

Kadushin, C. (1969). *Why people go to psychiatrists*. New York: Atherton.

Karasu, T. B. (Ed.). (1982). *Psychotherapy research: Methodological and efficacy issues*. Washington, DC: American Psychiatric Press.

Kazdin, A. E. (1980). *Research design in clinical psychology*. New York: Harper & Row.

Kazdin, A. E. (1992). *Research design in clinical psychology* (2nd ed.). Boston: Allyn & Bacon.

Kiesler, D. J. (Ed.). (1973). *The process of psychotherapy: Empirical foundations and systems of analysis*. Chicago: Aldine.

Kiesler, D. J. (1987). *Check list of psychotherapy transactions—revised (CLOPT-R) and Check list of interpersonal transactions—revised (CLOIT-R)*. Richmond: Virginia Commonwealth University Press.

Krasner, L., & Ullmann, L. P. (1965). *Research in behavior modification*. New York: Holt, Rinehart & Winston.

Kuhn, T. (1970). *The structure of scientific revolutions* (2nd ed.). Chicago: University of Chicago Press.

Labov, W., & Fanshel, D. (1977). *Therapeutic discourse: Psychotherapy as conversation*. New York: Academic Press.

Lambert, M. J. (1979). *The effects of psychotherapy*. Montreal: Eden Press.

Lambert, M. J., Christensen, E. R., & DeJulio, S. S. (1983). *The assessment of psychotherapy outcome*. New York: Wiley.

Leary, T. (1957). *Interpersonal diagnosis of personality: A functional theory and methodologogy for personality evaluation*. New York: Ronald Press.

Lennard, H. L., & Bernstein, A. (1960). *The anatomy of psychotherapy*. New York: Columbia University Press.

Lerner, B. (1971). *Therapy in the ghetto*. Baltimore: Johns Hopkins University Press.

Lesse, S. (Ed.). (1968). *An evaluation of the results of the psychotherapies*.

Lieberman, M. A., Yalom, I. D., & Miles, M. B. (1973). *Encounter groups: First facts*. New York: Basic Books.

Lietaer, G., Rombauts, J., & Van Balen, R. (Eds.). (1990). *Client-centered and experiential psychotherapy in the nineties*. Louvain-la-Neuve, Belgium: Presses Universitaires de Louvain.

Lipsey, M. W., & Wilson, W. B. (1993). The efficacy of psychological, educational, and behavioral treatment. *American Psychologist, 48,* 1181–1209.

Luborsky, L. (1954). A note on Eysenck's article, "The effects of psychotherapy: An evaluation." *British Journal of Psychology, 45,* 129–131.

Luborsky, L. (1992). The Penn Research Project. In D. K. Freedheim (Ed.). *History of psychotherapy: A century of change* (pp. 396–401). Washington, DC: American Psychological Association.

Luborsky, L., & Crits-Christoph, P. (1990). *Understanding transference: The CCRT method.* New York: Basic Books.

Luborsky, L., Crits-Christoph, P., Mintz, J., & Auerbach, A. (1988). *Who will benefit from psychotherapy? Predicting therapeutic outcomes.* New York: Basic Books.

Malan, D. H. (1976). *Toward the validation of dynamic psychotherapy.* New York: Plenum Press.

Matz, P. B. (1929). Outcome of hospital treatment of ex-service patients with nervous and mental disease in the U.S. *U.S. Veterans Bureau Medical Bulletin, 5,* 829–842.

Meltzoff, J., & Kornreich, M. (1970). *Research in psychotherapy.* New York: Atherton.

Miller, N., Luborsky, L., Barber, J., & Docherty, J. (Eds.). (in press). *Psychodynamic treatment research: A handbook for clinical practice.* New York: Basic Books.

Mitchell, K. M., Bozarth, J. D., & Krauft, C. D. (1977). A re-appraisal of the therapeutic effectiveness of accurate empathy, nonpossessive warmth and genuineness. In A. S. Gurman & A. M. Razin (Eds.), *Effective psychotherapy: A handbook of research* (pp. 482–502). Oxford: Pergamon Press.

Mowrer, O. H. (Ed.). (1953). *Psychotherapy: Theory and research.* New York: Ronald Press.

Muench, G. A. (1947). An evaluation of nondirective psychotherapy by means of the Rorschach and other tests. *Applied Psychology Monographs,* No. 13.

Neurath, O., Carnap, R., & Morris, C. W. (Eds.). (1955). *International encyclopedia of unified science* (Vol. 1, Parts 1 & 2). Chicago: University of Chicago Press.

Orlinsky, D. E. (1989). Researchers' images of psychotherapy: Their origins and influence on research. *Clinical Psychology Review, 9,* 413–441.

Orlinsky, D. E. (1993, March 23). *The graying and greening of SPR: A personal memoir on forming the Society for Psychotherapy Research.* Paper presented at the 10th annual conference of the UK Chapter of the Society for Psychotherapy Research, Ravenscar, North Yorkshire, England.

Orlinsky, D. E., Grawe, K., & Parks, B. K. (1994). Process and outcome in psychotherapy—*Noch einmal.* In A. E. Bergin & S. L. Garfield (Eds.), *Handbook of psychotherapy and behavior change* (4th ed., pp. 270–376). New York: Wiley.

Orlinsky, D. E., & Howard, K. I. (1975). *Varieties of psychotherapeutic experience*. New York: Teachers College Press.

Orlinsky, D. E., & Howard, K. I. (1986). The psychological interior of psychotherapy: Explorations with the Therapy Session Reports. In L. S. Greenberg & W. M. Pinsof (Eds.), *The psychotherapeutic process: A research handbook* (pp. 477–501). New York: Guilford Press.

Paul, G. L. (1966). *Insight versus desensitization in psychotherapy*. Stanford, CA: Stanford University Press.

Pittenger, R. E., Hockett, C. F., & Danehy, J. J. (1960). *The first five minutes: A sample of microscopic interview analysis*. Ithaca, NY: Paul Martineau.

Porter, E. H., Jr. (1943). The development and evaluation of a measure of counseling interview procedure. *Educational and Psychological Measurement, 3*, 105–126, 215–238.

Powdermaker, F. B., & Frank, J. D. (1953). *Group psychotherapy*. Cambridge, MA, Harvard University Press.

Raimy, V. C. (1948). Self-reference in counseling interviews. *Journal of Consulting Psychology, 12*, 153–163.

Reznikoff, M., & Toomey, L. C. (Eds.). (1959). *Evaluation of changes associated with psychiatric treatment*. Springfield, IL: Charles C. Thomas.

Rice, L. N., & Greenberg, L. S. (Eds.). (1984). *Patterns of change: Intensive analysis of psychotherapy process*. New York: Guilford Press.

Rogers, C. R. (1942). The use of electrically recorded interviews in improving psychotherapeutic techniques. *American Journal of Orthopsychiatry, 12*, 429–434.

Rogers, C. R. (1951). *Client-centered therapy: Its current practice, implications, and theory*. Boston: Houghton Mifflin.

Rogers, C. R. (1957). The necessary and sufficient conditions of therapeutic personality change. *Journal of Counseling Psychology, 22*, 95–103.

Rogers, C. R., & Dymond, R. F. (Eds.). (1954). *Psychotherapy and personality change*. Chicago: University of Chicago Press.

Rogers, C. R., Gendlin, E. T., Kiesler, D., & Truax, C. B. (Eds.). (1967). *The therapeutic relationship and its impact*. Madison: University of Wisconsin Press.

Rosenzweig, S. (1954). A transvaluation of psychotherapy—a reply to Hans Eysenck. *Journal of Abnormal and Social Psychology, 49*, 298–304.

Rotter, J. B. (1954). *Social learning and clinical psychology*. Englewood Cliffs, NJ: Prentice-Hall.

Rubinstein, E. A., & Parloff, M. B. (Eds.). (1962). *Research in psychotherapy* (Vol. 1). Washington, DC: American Psychological Association.

Russell, R. L. (1984). *Empirical investigations of psychotherapeutic techniques: A critique of and prospects for language analyses*. Ann Arbor, MI: University Microfilms International.

Russell, R. L. (1987). *Language in psychotherapy*. New York: Plenum Press.

Scheflen, A. E. (1973). *Communicational structure: Analysis of a psychotherapy transaction.* Bloomington, IN: Indiana University Press.

Seeman, J. (1948). A study of preliminary interview methods in correctional counseling. *Journal of Consulting Psychology, 12,* 321–330.

Seeman, J. (1949). A study of the process of nondirective therapy. *Journal of Consulting Psychology, 13,* 157–168.

Seeman, J., & Raskin, N. J. (1953). Research perspectives in client-centered therapy. In O. H. Mowrer (Ed.), *Psychotherapy: Theory and research* (pp. 205–234). New York: Ronald Press.

Shapiro, D. A., & Shapiro, D. (1982). Meta-analysis of comparative therapy outcome studies: A replication and refinement. *Psychological Bulletin, 92,* 581–604.

Sheerer, E. T. (1949). An analysis of the relationship between acceptance of and respect for self and acceptance of and respect for others in ten counseling cases. *Journal of Consulting Psychology, 13,* 169–175.

Shlien, J. M., Hunt, H. F., Matarazzo, J. D., & Savage, C. (Eds.). (1968). *Research in psychotherapy* (Vol. 3). Washington, DC: American Psychological Association.

Skinner, B. F. (1953). *Science and human behavior.* New York: Macmillan.

Skovholt, T. M., & Rønnestad, M. H. (1992). *The evolving professional self: Stages and themes in therapist and counselor development.* Chichester, England: Wiley.

Sloane, R. B., Staples, F. R., Cristol, A. H., Yorkston, N. J., & Whipple, K. (1975). *Psychotherapy versus behavior therapy.* Cambridge, MA: Harvard University Press.

Smith, M. L., Glass, E. V., & Miller, T. I. (1980). *The benefits of psychotherapy.* Baltimore: Johns Hopkins University Press.

Snyder, W. U. (1945). An investigation of the nature of nondirective psychotherapy. *Journal of General Psychology, 33,* 193–223.

Snyder, W. U. (Ed.). (1953). *Group report of a program of research in psychotherapy.* State College, PA: Pennsylvania State University.

Snyder, W. U. (1961). *The psychotherapy relationship.* New York: Macmillan.

Snyder, W. U. (1963). *Dependency in psychotherapy.* New York: Macmillan.

Spitzer, R. L., & Klein, D. F. (Eds.). (1976). *Evaluation of psychological therapies: Psychotherapies, behavior therapies, drug therapies, and interactions.* Baltimore, MD: Johns Hopkins University Press.

Stephenson, W. (1953). *The study of behavior: Q-technique and its methodology.* Chicago: University of Chicago Press.

Stieper, D. R., & Wiener, D. N. (1965). *Dimensions of psychotherapy.* Chicago: Aldine.

Stock, D. (1949). An investigation into the inter-relations between the self-concept and feelings directed toward other personas and groups. *Journal of Consulting Psychology, 13,* 176–180.

Stollak, G. E., Guerney, B. G., & Rothberg, M. (Eds.). (1966). *Psychotherapy research: Selected readings.* Chicago: Rand McNally.

Stone, A. R. (1978). The interdisciplinary research team: A case study. In J. D. Frank, R. Hoehn-Saric, S. D. Imber, B. L. Liberman, & A. R. Stone, *Effective ingredients of successful psychotherapy* (pp. 155–170). New York: Brunner/Mazel.

Strupp, H. H. (1960). *Psychotherapists in action.* New York: Grune & Stratton.

Strupp, H. H. (1973). *Psychotherapy: Clinical, research, and theoretical issues.* New York: Grune & Stratton.

Strupp, H. H., Fox, R. E., & Lessler, K. (1966). *Patients view their psychotherapy.* Baltimore: Johns Hopkins University Press.

Strupp, H. H., Hadley, S. W., & Gomes-Schwartz, B. (1977). *Psychotherapy for better or worse: The problem of negative effects.* New York: Jason Aronson.

Strupp, H. H., & Howard, K. I. (1992). A brief history of psychotherapy research. In D. K. Freedheim (Ed.), *History of psychotherapy: A century of change* (pp. 309–334). Washington, DC: American Psychological Association.

Strupp, H. H., & Luborsky, L. (Eds.). (1962). *Research in psychotherapy* (Vol. 2). Washington, DC: American Psychological Association.

Talley, F., Butler, S., & Strupp, H. H. (Eds.). (1994). *Research findings and clinical practice: Bridging the chasm.* New York: Basic Books.

Toukmanian, S. G., & Rennie, D. L. (Eds.) (1992). *Psychotherapy process research: Paradigmatic and narrative approaches.* Newbury Park, CA: Sage.

Truax, C. B., & Carkhuff, R. R. (1967). *Toward effective counseling and psychotherapy.* Chicago: Aldine.

Truax, C. B., & Mitchell, K. M. (1971). Research on certain therapist interpersonal skills in relation to process and outcome. In A. E. Bergin & S. L. Garfield (Eds.), *Handbook of psychotherapy and behavior change* (1st ed.) (pp. 299–344) New York: Wiley.

Volsky, T., Jr., Magoon, T. M., Norman, W. T., & Hoyt, D. P. (1965). *The outcomes of counseling and psychotherapy.* Minneapolis: University of Minnesota Press.

Wallerstein, R. S. (1986). *Forty-two lives in treatment: A study of psychoanalysis and psychotherapy.* New York: Guilford Press.

Waskow, I. E., & Parloff, M. B. (Eds.). (1975). *Psychotherapy change measures.* Rockville, MD: National Institute of Mental Health.

Wexler, D. A., & Rice, L. N. (Eds.). (1974). *Innovations in client-centered therapy.* New York: Wiley.

Williams, J. B. W., & Spitzer, R. L. (1984). *Psychotherapy research: Where are we and where should we go?* New York: Guilford Press.

Wolpe, J. (1958). *Psychotherapy by reciprocal inhibition.* Stanford, CA: Stanford University Press.

Wolff, W., & Precker, J. A. (Eds.). (1952). *Success in psychotherapy.* New York: Grune & Stratton.

Index